W9-ADO-644

Non-Native Educators
in English Language Teaching

Non-Native Educators
in English Language Teaching

Edited by

George Braine
The Chinese University of Hong Kong

1999 LAWRENCE ERLBAUM ASSOCIATES, PUBLISHERS
Mahwah, New Jersey   London

Lawrence Erlbaum Associates, Inc., Publishers
10 Industrial Avenue
Mahwah, NJ 07430

Cover design by Kathryn Houghtaling Lacey

Library of Congress Cataloging-in-Publication Data

Non–native educators in English language teaching /
edited by George Braine.
  p.   cm.
Includes bibliographical references and index.

ISBN 0-8058-3204-1 (cloth : alk. paper) — ISBN
0-8058-3205-X (pbk. : alk. paper).

1. English language—study and teaching—Foreign
speakers. 2. English teachers—Training of—Foreign
countries. 3. Language transfer (Language learning)
I. Braine, George.

PE1128.A2N64   1999
428'.007—dc21   98-50643
                                          CIP

Books published by Lawrence Erlbaum Associates are
printed on acid-free paper, and their bindings are chosen
for strength and durability.

Printed in the United States of America
10 9 8 7 6 5 4 3 2 1

To my co-authors
For their courage and perseverance

Contents

Preface

At the 1995 Teachers of English to Speakers of Other language (TESOL) Convention held in Long Beach, I attended a stimulating colloquium titled "Research Writing, Genre, and Socialization" which examined the role of socialization in non-native speakers' (NNSs) understanding and use of various writing genres (Belcher et al., 1995). Listening to the presentations, I wondered how NNS scholar-writers' perspectives on similar topics would be received. Would their personal histories and first-hand experiences be of interest to a TESOL audience?

I therefore invited a few colleagues to join me in a colloquium at the 1996 TESOL Convention. So, on a freezing Friday morning in Chicago, Suresh Canagarajah, Ulla Connor, Kamal Sridhar, Jacinta Thomas, Devi Chitrapu, and I presented "In Their Own Voices: Non-native Speaker Professionals in TESOL" (Braine et al., 1996). The highly charged, mainly personal narratives of the speakers generated much interest. Most encouraging was the enthusiasm of the NNSs in the audience; some claimed that they finally had a voice. The origin of this book can be traced to the interest generated in NNS issues at the Chicago colloquium. In fact, the colloquium has since spawned five other colloquia at subsequent TESOL conventions and inspired the formation of a TESOL Caucus for non-native educators.

The place of native and non-native speakers in the role of English teachers has probably been an issue ever since English was taught internationally. Although English as a Second Language (ESL) and English as a Foreign language (EFL) literature is awash with, in fact dependent on, the scrutiny of non-native learners, interest in non-native academics and teachers is a fairly recent phenomenon. The Belcher et al. (1995) colloquium is one example of this interest. Until recently, the voices of non-native speakers raising their own concerns have been even rarer. Except for a few prominent names such as Braj Kachru and Claire Kramsch, these voices have been submerged in the multitude of presentations and publications.

Non-Native Educators in English Language Teaching is a response to this notable vacuum in the English Language Teaching (ELT) literature, providing a forum for language educators from diverse geographical origins and language backgrounds. All the authors are non-native speakers of English, all except one have received part of their higher education in North America, and all except two chapters are at least partially contextualized in North America. In addition to presenting autobiographical narratives, these authors argue sociopolitical concerns and discuss implications for teacher education, all relating to the theme of non-native educators in ELT.

Some contributors are long-established professionals; others more recent initiates to the field. Their life stories, from origins in distant countries to becoming professionals in North America and Europe, would be unique and intriguing. But, I resisted the temptation to limit the book to personal narratives and invited the authors to explore other issues and concerns that relate to non-native educators. Experienced first hand by the authors, these issues and concerns have implications for a wider audience. Hence, every chapter, whatever the theme, bears the mark of the authors' personal experiences as a non-native speaker.

Due to the unique nature of its contributors and contents, the book should make an impact on applied linguistics in general and on ELT in particular. It is meant for non-native speakers who aspire to enter the profession, graduate students in TESOL programs, teacher educators, and all those who are interested in the role of non-native speaker educators in ELT.

In Part I of the book, Who We Are, the first four chapters draw on the authors' personal experiences to explore the issues of credibility, journey from the Periphery to the Center, and development as established writers in English—two literacy autobiographies. The fifth chapter takes a non-autobiographical stance, examining the effects of written English on the social and cultural identities of two non-native learners.

Part II, Sociopolitical Concerns, moves the focus from personal to a broader perspective. The sixth chapter examines the native speaker fallacy from its linguistic, pedagogical, and political perspectives. The next chapters explore how non-native speaker status, when added to sexism and racism, discriminates immigrant women teachers in Canada, and the entrenched policies and practices among native speaker educators in one of TESOL's largest international affiliates.

In Part III, Implications for Teacher Education, the first chapters examine the self-perceptions of non-native graduate students in TESOL programs, consider the need to modify the curriculum of TESOL programs in view of the enrollment of many NNS students, and describe the impact of non-native educators on ESL learners as seen from the educators' viewpoint. The next chapter moves the discussion away from North America to Hungary, with the argument that effective English teachers need to be near-native speakers of the language. In the final chapter, an experienced teacher-educator argues that teacher preparation programs in North America, the United Kingdom, and Australia do not prepare NNS (international) teacher trainees adequately.

Acknowledgments

I wish to thank all those who helped to make this book a reality, especially Ruth Spack, who laid the foundation for the book by collecting transcripts from the 1996 colloquium; Naomi Silverman and Lori Hawver at Lawrence Erlbaum for their support; Jun Liu for liaisoning from the United States; and Diane Belcher for her consistent support of non-native speaker professionals. I owe a special thanks to Cheung Suk Yee for her suggestions and patient and meticulous editorial assistance. Finally, I thank my coauthors whose contributions made this book possible.

George Braine

References

Belcher, D., Pearson Casanave, C., Dudley-Evans, T., Johns, A., Prior, P., Samraj, B., & Shaw, P. (1995, March). *Research writing, genre, and socialization.* Colloquium presented at the annual meeting of the Teachers of English to Speakers of Other Languages, Long Beach, CA.

Braine, G., Canagarajah, S., Connor, U., Sridhar, K., Thomas, J., & Chitrapu, D. (1996, March). *In their own voices: Nonnative speaker professionals in TESOL.* Colloquium presented at the annual meeting of the Teachers of English to Speakers of Other Languages, Chicago.

Introduction

George Braine

In a delightful article in *The New Yorker*, the Indian-born doctor Abraham Verghese recalls an incident that occurred soon after his arrival in the United States. Emboldened by his medical abilities and high scores in the required examinations, Verghese is confident of obtaining an internship at a "Plymouth Rock" hospital affiliated to a prestigious medical school. However, a more experienced compatriot warns him that these hospitals "have never taken a foreign medical graduate" and advises Verghese "not even to bother with that kind of place." Instead, he is told to apply to more humble "Ellis Island" hospitals, those situated in inner cities and rural areas, which U.S. doctors avoid. "We are" Verghese's compatriot continues, "like a transplanted organ—lifesaving and desperately needed, but rejected because we are foreign tissue" (1997).

The foreign medical graduate anecdote is an apt analogy for this book, because it too deals mainly with foreign-born professionals who have moved to North America to advance their education and careers. However, unlike foreign medical graduates, non-native educators are not considered vital or lifesaving; instead, they are often regarded as unnecessary by-products of the MA and Ph.D. programs in applied linguistics and TESOL in North America. Although many foreign medical graduates eventually get internships filling positions that U.S. graduates refuse to accept, NNS English teachers are less fortunate in finding employment. Nevertheless, the prospect of unemployment, of being denied to practice what they have been trained to do, is only one of the problems that these educators face. Almost from their arrival, many of them discover that their credentials are questioned, their accents are misunderstood, and that they are marginalized in the profession.

Non-Native Educators in English Language Teaching is best defined in terms of what it does not set out to do. For the most part, it does not deal with English teachers from Periphery or non-English speaking (EFL) countries. A majority of English speakers can be considered non-natives and a proportionate number of NNSs would be teaching English in all parts of the world. They and their situations are unique to each country, depending on their first language backgrounds, level of education and training, teaching methods, aspirations and career prospects, and the status of English in those countries. However, such a broad topic would be clearly beyond the scope of this book.

Nor is this book is about the dominance of English in Periphery countries, often to the detriment of local languages. Phillipson dealt adequately with this topic in his thought-provoking *Linguistic Imperialism* (1992). In fact, non-native English teachers may have no opposition to the power and spread of English. Indeed, the English language has been their passport to better educational and career prospects and the gateway to career, economic, and social betterment.

Non-Native Educators in English Language Teaching deals only in passing with the Native Speaker (NS) versus NNS debate. It makes no attempt to define these two categories of English users; Davies, in *The Native Speaker in Applied Linguistics* (1991), covered this topic comprehensively, discussing the psycholinguistic, linguistic, and sociolinguistic aspects of the issue.

The Native Speaker in Language Pedagogy

A non-native speaker of a language is defined against a native speaker of that language. However, the notion of the native speaker, and all the linguistic, social, and economic connotations that accompany it, are troublesome and open to controversy. As Phillipson (1992) pointed out, the origins of a number of fallacies regarding English language teaching can be traced to the Commonwealth Conference on the Teaching of English as a Second Language, held at Makarere, Uganda, in 1961. The Makarere Conference bestowed legitimacy to many of the beliefs of a profession that had little theoretical foundation or pedagogical methods.

According to Phillipson, one of the key tenets of the conference was that "the ideal teacher of English is a native speaker" (1992, p. 185). According to the Makarere tenet, native speakers of a language have a better command of fluent, idiomatically correct language forms, are more knowledgeable about the cultural connotations of a language, and are the final arbiters of "the acceptability of any given samples of the language" (quoted in Phillipson, p. 194). Undoubtedly, this tenet has had a lasting effect on the teaching of English in both EFL and ESL contexts.

Phillipson called this the *native speaker fallacy* and pointed out a number of weaknesses and contradictions of the Makarere tenet. For instance, the features attributed to native speakers of a language, earlier, can be instilled through teacher training. Further, insights into the language learning process, the correct forms and appropriate use of language, and the ability to analyze and explain the language are within the reach of non-native teachers as well. In addition, the very fact that non-native speakers of a language have undergone the process of learning a language makes them better qualified to teach the language than those who are born to it (1992, pp. 194–199). Phillipson attributed the native speaker fallacy to the period when language teaching was synonymous with the teaching of culture, and said that the fallacy predates tape recorders and other equipment that can effectively replicate native speakers in the classroom.

Kramsch (1997) also questioned the idealization of the native speaker and attributed it to the importance placed on spoken communicative competence in foreign language pedagogy since the 1960s. She argued that NSs do not speak the idealized, standardized version of their language: their speech is influenced by geography, occupation, age, and social status of the speakers. She questioned why students of a foreign language, who have multilingual perspectives on the target language, its literature, and culture, should emulate the idealized [non-existent] native speaker. She further argued that grammatical intuition, linguistic acceptability, and the ability to communicate fluently with full competence does not make one a native speaker of a language. According to Kramsch, native speakership is neither a privilege of birth nor of education, but "acceptance by the group that created the distinction between native and nonnative speakers" (p. 363).

In language pedagogy, the linguistic authority of the native speaker has been further bolstered by Chomsky's notion of the terms *native speaker* and *competence* (1965). However, as defined by Chomsky, a native speaker of a language is an "ideal speaker-listener, in a completely homogeneous speech community, who knows its language perfectly" (p. 3). At best, such a speaker is an abstraction, with no resemblance to a living human being. For Chomsky, competence has to do with intuitive knowledge of what is grammatical and ungrammatical in a language. But, as Paikeday in *The Native Speaker Is Dead* (1985) pointed out, the native speaker as the final authority on the "grammaticality and acceptability of language . . . represents an ideal, a convenient fiction, or a shibboleth rather than a reality like Dick or Jane" (quoted in Kramsch, 1997).

Examining the question of standards in the teaching of English, Widdowson (1994) argued that native speakers have "no say . . . no right to intervene or pass judgment" on how English develops internationally (p. 385). Noting that the insistence on the use of authentic, naturally occurring English for instructional purposes privileges native speaker teachers, making them "custodians and arbiters not only of proper English but of proper pedagogy as well" (p. 387), Widdowson stated that when the emphasis is moved from the contexts of use to contexts of learning, the advantage that native speaker teachers have disappears. In essence, the native speaker teacher is better aware of the appropriate contexts of language use, not the contexts of language learning.

Employment Concerns

In the case of non-native teachers operating in ESL contexts, no issue is more troubling than that of discrimination in employment. This issue is rarely mentioned in the popular literature in ELT, which however does express a deep concern with other sociopolitical causes. *TESOL Matters,* a bimonthly publication distributed to every member of the TESOL organization, usually includes a number of articles and opinion pieces on sociopolitical causes. In the February/March 1998 issue, for instance, the leading article described the TESOL Board's endorsement of an affiliate's opposition to the Unz Initiative in California, which limits structured English immersion for California children to one year. Another article was based on immigration legislation and undocumented (illegal) residents in the U.S. A third item, titled "Sociopolitical Concerns at TESOL '98," mentioned the impact of United States immigration laws on foreign-born students, AIDS education, and linguistic imperialism among the issues to be discussed at the upcoming 1998 TESOL Convention. Despite such strident championing of politically correct issues and opposition to all forms of discrimination, a significant number of native speakers in ELT do not support the employment of NNSs to teach English in ESL contexts.

Especially at the Master's degree level, where most ELT jobs are restricted to intensive English programs, few NNSs have succeeded in breaking the unwritten rule "No non-native speakers need apply." Despite the TESOL organization's explicit opposition to hiring practices that discriminate against NNSs (see Appendix A), many intensive program administrators do not hire NNSs. In fact, some administrators have openly stated so at professional conferences and job interviews.

The most frequent excuse for this discrimination is that ESL students prefer to be taught by native speakers. In fact, some newly arrived ESL students naively subscribe to the native speaker fallacy, the belief stemming mainly from their experience with incompetent, barely proficient English teachers in their own countries. However, as they become better acquainted with qualified, competent, non-native teachers, students offer clamor to be in their classes, knowing that the non-native teachers better understand their language problems.

Perhaps the main reason is never explicitly stated but nevertheless apparent. A fairly recent phenomenon in Western academia is the increasing presence of foreigners, as teachers, researchers, and scholars, in almost every discipline, including ELT. Although this is only to be expected—there are at least four NNSs to every native speaker of English—it is naturally resented when scarce jobs are threatened. Many administrators and teachers appear to view ELT as the last domain of the native speaker, to be defended at any cost. This attitude is highly ironic, considering the profession's strident championing of multiculturalism, diversity, and other sociopolitical causes, often on behalf of ESL students and immigrants. Although ESL students are praised and admired for the multiculturalism and diversity they bring into language classes, non-native English teachers, who can also contribute their rich multicultural, multilingual experiences, are often barred from the same classes.

The Search for an Identity

Davies (1991) stated that the notion of the native speaker arose out of the need for such a phenomenon in applied linguistics, and began his volume, *The Native Speaker in Applied Linguistics*, with the claim that no proper definition of a native speaker exists. In fact, a similar claim could be made for NNSs, too.

About a year ago, I began a movement to form a caucus for non-native educators within the TESOL organization. Because the term "non-native speaker" did not appeal to some prospective members of the caucus (one said that to call ourselves non-native speakers was akin to using the slave-owner's language), I solicited a more appropriate term. The variety of terms suggested, listed here, indicates the struggle for self-definition and the identity crisis that prevails among non-native professionals:

- second language speaking professionals
- English teachers speaking other languages
- non-native speakers of English in TESOL
- non-native professionals in TESOL
- non-native teachers of English
- non-native English speaking professionals
- second language teaching professionals
- non-native English teachers

A more detailed response was as follows:

By using the title *non-native speakers*, you are "backgrounding" and hence providing acceptance and legitimacy to the very distinction, the effects of which you are combating. To acquiesce to the use of the term *NNS* in the absence of any but an ethnopolitical definition of NS is tantamount to accepting the basis for a differential consideration. Hence, the caucus will look self-contradictory and self-defeating. So substitute a less ideologically loaded term like second language speaker.

Understandably, this lack of an identity could lead to low self-confidence and to an acute sense of one's marginalized, unstable status in the ELT profession. This is clearly seen in the following message that I received from a non-native teacher who is also an accomplished author:

All this self-doubt may have to do with what I experienced recently. Last semester, a professor whom I consider a good friend observed my class for my promotion. He gave high praise to my teaching and the warm rapport he observed between my students and I, but he also pointed out, almost as a side note, that my English was less than idiomatic. He quickly added, though, that the errors were not at the expense of meaning and students took them in stride. But since he is someone I respect a lot, I believe his observation was honest and as well intended as one could be. But as I tried to imagine what a less friendly observer would say, I had a cold realization that I was living at the mercy and tolerance of others. If others are willing to tolerate my deficiency in the language, and choose to focus on my dedication and other merits, I have a foothold; if not, they have every reason to dismiss me . . . Not that I don't have confidence in my English, for I know I write better than average native speakers . . . and my accent is better than most NNSs, but that does not necessarily qualify me for the teaching of the language I have not completely mastered.

The Empire Strikes Back

As Phillipson (1992) showed, the spread of English played a key role in the continuing expansion of the cultural, economic, and political influence of Britain and the United States in less-developed countries. Especially in government and education, the high status of English perpetuates the dependency of the less developed countries (the Periphery) on the powerful Western countries and interests (the Center)[1]. In the Center and Periphery, the elites are linked by common interests in economic, political, military, social, and cultural matters. Although the majority of the elite in the Periphery are locals, they have been educated in the Center or in the languages of the Center. The Periphery are the consumers of the expertise, methodology, and materials dispensed by the Center.

Phillipson (1992) also described how the export of English to former British colonies, instead of leading to modernization and prosperity, has led to a number of adverse effects on these countries. Learners of English have become less literate in indigenous languages; on the other hand, for those who do not learn English, their economic and social advancement have been impeded. English has little relevance to the lives of ordinary people in these countries.

Overall, about 450,000 international students are enrolled in U.S. colleges and universities. They comprise 5% of the 14 million university student enrollment. Indirectly, their presence is the result of the spread and dominance of English, testimony to the enormous success of selling English worldwide. If international students and the billions of dollars they generate are part of the reward, the presence of non-native English teachers in the United States and other English-speaking countries could be described as an instance of the empire striking back. The selling of English has succeeded to such an extent that it has produced English teachers competent to teach native speakers and in English-speaking contexts.

References

Chomsky, N. (1965). *Aspects of the theory of syntax.* Cambridge, MA: MIT Press.
Davies, A. (1991). *The native speaker in applied linguistics.* Edinburgh, England: Edinburgh University Press.

---

[1] See Galtung (1980).

Galtung, J. (1980). *The true worlds: A transnational perspective.* New York: The Free Press.

Kramsch, C. (1997). The privilege of the nonnative speaker. *PMLA, 112,* 359–369.

Phillipson, R. (1992). *Linguistic imperialism.* Oxford, England: Oxford University Press.

Verghese, A (1997, June 23 & 30). The cowpath to America. *The New Yorker,* 70–88.

Widdowson, H. (1994). The ownership of English. *TESOL Quarterly, 28,* 377–389.

Appendix A

A TESOL Statement on Nonnative Speakers of English and Hiring Practices

Whereas TESOL is an international association concerned with the teaching of English to speakers of other languages and composed of professionals who are both active and nonnative speakers of English, and

Whereas employment decisions in this profession which are based solely upon the criterion that an individual is or is not a native speaker of English discriminate against well qualified individuals, especially when they are made in the absence of any defensible criteria, and

Whereas such decisions, not based on sound criteria, must therefore be in contradiction to sound linguistic research and pedagogical practice,

Therefore be it resolved that the Executive Board and the Officers of TESOL shall make every effort to prevent such discrimination in the employment support structures operated by TESOL and its own practices, and

Therefore be it further resolved that the Executive Board of TESOL shall instruct the committee on Professional Standards (and such other TESOL bodies as the Board sees fit to involve) to work towards the creation and publication of minimal language proficiency standards that may be applied to all ESOL teachers without reference to the nativeness of their English.

This resolution is moved by the Sociopolitical Concerns Committee, having been drafted by the Employment Issues Sub-committee and endorsed by the committee of the whole.

The Sociopolitical Concerns Committee urges that, should this resolution be duly passed, the Executive Board establish a deadline by which the actions herein mandated are to be implemented.

October 1991

PART ONE

Who We Are

The NS-NNS dichotomy can be a highly personal issue for non-native teachers of English. Hence, every chapter in this book displays the personal touch of the author(s), albeit more explicitly in Part I than in others.

In the opening chapter, Jacinta Thomas explores the fundamental issue of credibility that confronts NNS professionals in ESL contexts. She examines the challenges to credibility in various contexts and perspectives—in hiring practices, from professional organizations, from students, and during graduate studies. She then explores the effects of these challenges to credibility by delving into her personal experiences and by frequently citing the experiences of her colleagues as well. Thomas claims that NNS teachers have to work twice as hard as their NS colleagues, proving themselves as effective users of the language before being accepted as professionals. This thoughtful and poignant narrative provides an insight to the struggles that many NNS teachers face in their professional development and provides a fitting opening to the volume.

By most accounts, there are at least four NNS to every NS of English. As the British Empire dwindles to a few obscure specks on the world map, the ownership of English is being shared with the former colonists and the brash newcomers to the field—the Americans. Although the flow of English language teaching expertise has been from the Center countries—where the dominant groups are NSs of English—to the Periphery, scholars from the Periphery have more recently begun to establish themselves in Center countries. In the second chapter, arguing that some NS professionals from the Center appear to be unaware of the backgrounds of their NNS colleagues from the Periphery, George Braine recounts his journey as a teacher at a village school in Sri Lanka to the Center, as a graduate student in the United States, as a teacher at international universities in the United States and in Asia, and as the coeditor of the *Asian Journal of English Language Teaching*. Braine recalls his acquisition of academic literacy and also describes how he first became aware of his non-nativeness. Drawing on his experiences and that of others, Braine describes how the challenges for NNS Periphery scholars continue even when they leave the Center, because the need to publish internationally continues in some parts of the Periphery. As he reflects upon his journey, Braine presents some scenes from the past as four vignettes, which help him to illustrate his reflections.

A literacy biography is an account of significant factors and events that have contributed to one's development as a reader and writer. In chapter 3, Ulla Connor traces her development as an established writer in English, beginning with concurrent Master's theses in English language and literature at the University of Helsinki in her native Finland and in English literature at the University of Florida. Recalling that she first wrote in English in the voice of her mentor, Connor describes how she began to master the orderly, coherent writing of research during her doctoral studies at the University of Wisconsin and gradually began to acquire her own voice and confidence as a writer in English. She also recounts the advantages of collaborative writing, noting that her co-authors also acted as mentors. At the conclusion of the chapter, Connor describes how, when attempting to write later in Finnish, she discovered that she had become a "completely Americanized" writer. She also offers a number of suggestions to other ESL writers. Connor's literacy autobiography typifies the journey of many NNS professionals in ELT in Center countries.

With the thawing of relations between the United States and China in the 1970s, Chinese graduate students and scholars began to trickle into the United States. The trickle later became a flood, and in the late 1990s, the largest number of international students in the United States is from China. How would a Chinese scholar who spent her teens as a Red Guard, thereby missing high school, survive the thrust into U.S. graduate school? In chapter 4, Xiao-ming Li, the author of *"Good Writing" in Cross-Cultural Context* (1996), describes her initiation into academic discourse under the tutelage of Donald Murray at the University of New Hampshire. Weaving in and out of her deeply instilled Chinese experiences, Li delightfully recalls her bewilderment at U.S. idioms, which in turn led to her first publication, in *The Boston Globe*. Li concludes with a description of how *"Good Writing"* almost destroyed her career and how the writing community rallied to her support. Li's chapter is a literacy autobiography recalled with clarity and the poignancy of an accomplished writer.

In the final chapter of Part One, Claire Kramsch and Eva Lam examine the role textuality plays in the native-nonnative relationship and the effect written language has on the development of a learner's social and cultural identity. Citing the experiences of two NNSs of English, Kramsch and Lam argue that, unlike everyday conversations, texts can be reproduced, reread, cited, and annotated by every user. It is therefore important that language teachers themselves cultivate both an insider's and an outsider's attitude toward English. Kramsch and Lam further argue that such a position implies a tension between the standardized, native norms of the English language and the ability of the non-native writer/reader to see through these norms and to test their limits. Rather than being used primarily for socializing non-natives into the ways of the natives, the written language can offer the opportunity to express human thoughts and feelings that NNSs have experienced particularly acutely.

References

Li, X. (1987, February 1). Trying to make sense out of nonsense. *The Boston Sunday Globe*, p. A26.

Li, X. (1996). *"Good writing" in cross cultural context*. Albany, New York: State University of New York Press.

CHAPTER 1

Voices from the Periphery:
Non-Native Teachers and Issues of Credibility

Jacinta Thomas
College of Lake County

It is the first day of class and I am nervous. This is going to be the first time that I teach a class of "native speakers of American English." My recently acquired Ph.D. and my almost 7 years of teaching give me little confidence as I enter the classroom 10 minutes early to make sure that I have everything that I need for class, including a working overhead projector and chalk. A few minutes later, a young woman sticks her head in, stares at me in confusion, walks outside to check the room number, comes in again and asks: "Is this an English class?"

Experiences such as this are not really isolated incidents. It is one example of the type of challenges that many non-native teachers of American English are forced to face both from within and outside the profession. Like Okawa (1995), I have felt that "my initial credibility as a teacher (or lack thereof—was related to my race" (p. 1), and I would like to add to my language and accent as well. NNSs are not merely "strangers in academia," a term used by Zamel (1995) to describe English as a Second or Other Language (ESOL) students and teachers in a university setting; we are sometimes strangers on the periphery. Although we may not always have to respond openly, "Yes, this IS an ENGLISH class and I AM the teacher," we often find ourselves in situations where we have to establish our credibility as teachers of ESOL before we can proceed to be taken seriously as professionals. In the words of a colleague of mine, "I sometimes feel that I have to do twice as well to be accepted."

From outside the TESOL profession, there is sometimes a little confusion and often amusement about us foreigners with our accents. A 95-year-old neighbor of mine, a dear sweet old lady, recently introduced me to her daughter as a college teacher and quickly added "Guess what she teaches?" "What?" her daughter asked. "English. Imagine someone coming from India to teach English here," replied my neighbor with a slight chuckle.

This notion that one only has to be a "native speaker" of English to be able to teach it is one that I encounter as coordinator of an Academic English program in a community college. I receive telephone calls from people who want to teach in my program. When I ask them for their qualifications (we require at least a master's degree), I sometimes hear answers that range from "I am a native speaker of English, and I speak English well" to "I am sensitive to the needs of people from different cultures." Although these are desirable qualities in teachers I hire, by themselves they are insufficient. Notions that they are sufficient undermine the training and knowledge necessary to be a good ESOL teacher. In fact, they are part of a much larger picture of false assumptions that challenge the credibility of NNSs of English.

Challenges to Credibility: Hiring Practices

The challenges that NNSs face, unfortunately, are not always merely uninformed or innocuous. Walelign's (1986) "Non-Native Speakers Need Not Apply" documented some of the prejudice that NNSs face in the hiring process abroad. This "birthright mentality" (p. 40) gives in to the fallacy that anyone who speaks a certain variety of English as the native language can teach it. More important, it is part of a "double standard" that ignores the routine hiring in many foreign language departments throughout Europe and America of NNSs to teach non-European languages (p. 41).

The uniform blanket exclusion of NNSs as potential teachers of English is nothing short of discrimination. Although stories of unintelligible foreign teaching assistants abound, the fact remains that there are good teachers and "not-so-good" teachers, and there are "not-so-good" teachers among the ranks of NSs of English as well. To say that "Non-Native Speakers Need Not Apply" is exclusionary, and any policy that blindly bars certain groups should be suspect.

It is very disturbing that even some professionals involved in TESOL believe that being a NS of English is a necessary condition to teach English (see Braine, Chap. 2, and Kamhi-Stein, Chap. 10, this volume). At the 1995 TESOL Convention, I attended an early morning discussion on Intensive English programs. The topic for discussion was recruitment. One person commented: "One thing that we do when we recruit, is that we tell students that they will only be taught by NSs. After all these students don't come so far to be taught by someone who doesn't speak English." An obvious implication of such a statement is that anyone who is not a NS of English cannot speak the language; beyond this, such a statement begs the question of who a "native speaker" is and whether NS of various international varieties of English, such as Indian English, Singapore English, Nigerian English, or Englishes that Kachru (1985) characterized as belonging to the outer circle are to be counted as "native speakers," and therefore eligible to teach English. The modification of the requirement of being a "native speaker" to having "near native proficiency" adds further confusion to this issue.

It is my suspicion that the professional who boasted that her program only hired "native speakers of English" would not hire NS of international varieties of English merely because they do not fit the profile of the "native speaker." I say this because I have been frequently complimented on my good English even after I tell people I am a NS of Indian/Singapore English. Such compliments stem from the fallacy that there is only one kind of English, the right kind—the kind spoken by people belonging to the "inner circle" (Kachru, 1985). Furthermore, it undermines the competence of both NSs and those who have "near native proficiency" in international varieties of English.

Challenges to Credibility: Organizational Invisibility

The challenges that NNSs face are not limited to discriminatory hiring practices. At times, our place within the TESOL organization is not clearly defined. Although the membership of TESOL is diverse, our presence is sometimes ignored. Our invisibility as professionals is nowhere more evident than in a statement made by Denise Murray, a former President of TESOL, in a chapter discussing diversity in ESOL classrooms. She said: "In many cases, our student's life experiences have been so different from ours, their teachers, that we cannot assume that they bring the same background knowledge to the classroom as white, middle class children" (1996, p. 436). What Murray appears to assume in this statement is that all ESOL teachers can in fact identify with the background of "white, middle class children" because they are from white, middle class backgrounds themselves.

Perhaps this is just a single statement that may appear to be taken out of context. Yet it is just a part of a much larger picture of, perhaps, unconscious exclusion. Although our academic journals are supposed to represent the TESOL profession on the whole, they seem to be dominated by the voices of only some. As professionals, NNSs may be seen on the covers of our publications, but are they heard? To what degree are their real voices represented in our major journals? At one level, as Canagarajah (1996) suggested, the "nondiscursive" requirements of academic journals, such as the requirement of stamps, envelopes, multiple copies or a soft copy, serve to exclude the voices of scholars from the Third World. At another level, the Western rhetorical style of most "international" journals is "sometimes ethnocentrically considered the universal academic discourse" (Canagarajah, 1996, p. 436). In order to be published in those journals, NNSs often need to adhere to the standards set by their NS peers. As an international body, to what extent will TESOL tolerate different accents in writing or different varieties of English used in its international journals? Do we, or are we willing, to accommodate a pluralistic rhetoric in our journals? Although we are willing to publish the works of our ESOL students in their original voices, are we willing to do the same with our professionals?

At a TESOL Convention presentation in 1995, a panel of prominent writing specialists argued that ESOL writing teachers need to challenge prescriptive rules. A young woman stepped up to the microphone during the question session and said "You talk about challenging rules, and that is good if they don't have validity. But it is easier for you to do that: you are four white women. People will listen to you. Will they listen to me, an Asian with an accent?" There was no response to this question, only a period of rather uncomfortable silence.

Challenges to Credibility: From Students

The challenges that NNSs face stem not only from professionals in the field or from the organization as a whole but also from their non-native students (see Braine, Chap. 2, this volume, for a similar experience). This trickle-down effect is inevitable. We usually learn to value what we see valued and to undermine what we see undermined.

I remember one of the best writing classes I have taught. It was an intermediate writing class during which I got to know my students really well, and we often spent time talking as a class or after class. On one occasion, a topic arose related to race, language, and assumptions. One of my students said, "You know when I saw you enter the class on the first day, I was disappointed. I had spent a lot of money to come to the United States and I was hoping to get a NS to teach the class. When I first saw you, I felt certain that I wouldn't like your class." I recently had the opportunity to talk to some former students of mine, including a couple who themselves aspire to be ESOL teachers, about their impressions of a

NNS teaching them English. Several repeated that they felt a little disappointed when they first saw me, "a foreigner" with a different accent, as they put it (see Amin, 1997, for a discussion of the issue of race and linguistic identity of the non-native ESOL teacher). Although these students said that their initial reaction to me changed after I began to teach, I wonder about those students who perhaps may have never given me a second chance only because I was not a NS of American English.

Challenges to Credibility: As a Student

My struggles with credibility did not just begin when I became a teacher. I found myself and my abilities challenged when I was an aspiring teacher, a doctoral student in an applied linguistics program. Some students appear to share a perception of a separate grading system for foreign students—a "foreign-student A, B or C" given on compassionate grounds to these students. Such an idea suggests that NNS students are not as capable as their NS counterparts and are awarded grades that take into account their "handicap." Beyond that, it suggests that English is indeed a handicap for NNSs and undermines the accomplishments of NNSs.

Effects of Challenges

For NNSs, the effects of these challenges to their credibility can sometimes be unnerving if not debilitating. Broyard (1950) claimed that one of the dangers of stereotypes is that they can make those who are pigeonholed believe in these depictions and unconsciously try to maintain them. Similarly, I have found that experiences that challenge my credibility make me apologetic, nervous about my ability to succeed, and sometimes even lead to a kind of paranoia born of experience. Several months ago, I had the opportunity to talk to a NNS like me, a Chinese woman with a Ph.D.; inevitably, we talked about some of the challenges we face as NNSs. "You know," said my colleague "I always feel that I have to perform, or to show people that I am just as good as they are. I have NS colleagues, most of them without Ph.D.s, who somehow see me as not just different but as inferior. It's not that they say anything, but I sense it. And then I find myself stammering and stuttering and making grammatical mistakes as I talk to them. When this happens, I feel that they are criticizing me, wondering how I could possibly teach the language."

I completely understand what my colleague describes because I find myself often reacting in the same way. A few months ago, I had student evaluations from the previous semester returned to me. The evaluations were generally good with remarks such as "She is a very good teacher," "I like her encouragement, correction and advise," "She has a very good style to teach; I liked how she encouraged us to learn more and more," "I liked everything about this course, especially my teacher because she teach [sic] carefully, and her topics were interesting." In the middle of this evaluation package, I came upon one evaluation that responded positively to the question, "What did you like about the course, the instructor and the instructional style?" The response was: "She was very kind, so I can learn English comfortably." However, the response to the question "What did you dislike?" was rather different. It read: "We need native speaker teacher. It will be better."

As I read that comment, I felt my heart sink. All the positive comments I had received were suddenly less important; they did not seem to matter. Although I had received negative comments before, this comment hurt, especially because it was directed at who I was, not at my teaching abilities as evidenced by his or her positive remarks about my teaching. I am well aware of prejudice and yet this one remark suddenly left me feeling unsure of my abilities (see Kamhi-Stein, Chap. 10, this volume, for a similar experience).

This lack of confidence is one of the unfortunate results of these challenges to credibility. The same type of uncertainty follows me as I encounter some of my NS colleagues and as I enter every class. It is my baggage. It is not unlike the insecurity experienced by many U.S. academics of color who "carry the colony wherever [they] go" (Villanueva, 1993, p. xiv).

I do not know how to interpret the nonacknowledgement that I receive from some colleagues. Are they having a bad day, or are they unfriendly, or do they see me as a nonperson because of my race and my accent? What should I think when a student tells me that he is only interested in taking a reading and pronunciation class (which just happen to be taught by a NS) and not a writing class (which happens to be taught by me)? Sometimes I find myself doubting my own abilities, wondering if I really am good enough.

This lack of confidence, this uncertainty about one's abilities, is damaging because it sometimes stands in the way of NNSs being all that they possibly can be and of realizing their full potential. As a first semester graduate student in an American university, I sat silently in all my classes the entire semester. Although there was a cultural explanation for my silence, I now realize that there was a psychological one too; I did not feel I was as capable as my U.S. counterparts. At the end of that semester, one of my U.S. professors who had just read my final paper called me aside and told me that I was "hiding my light under a bushel." His statement was a shock to me because I had not realized I had a "light" to begin with; hence, I sat silent despite my prior academic and professional successes. I had begun to believe the stereotypes of me as a student and a professional.

Facing Challenges

Although NNSs may be challenged at several levels including challenges arising from the TESOL profession itself, this is not to suggest that TESOL has completely ignored their scholarship. In addition, the profession has made a conscious effort to see that the leadership of this organization does include minorities through its Minority Leadership Training Program.

However, perhaps there is a need to do more. We live in a time of intolerance, particularly in the United States where we have movements such as the English Only movement; a time when anti-immigrant movements have lead to measures such as Proposition 187 and welfare reform that negatively impact on immigrants. We live in a time when linguistic differences are ridiculed, sometimes even by elected officials. Not too long ago, a prominent Republican senator mimicked on public radio the nonexistent "Japanese accent" of an equally prominent Japanese-American judge. Although the senator halfheartedly apologized for his action, he continues to play an important role in U.S. politics, questioning, among other things, politicians' "ethics."

These are hard times for our students, and yet, do we tackle these issues, especially in our teacher training programs that have many NNSs enrolled? Do we indeed talk about things such as credibility as we train our teachers? Do we tell our students that even if they do make it, "tokenism, not competence is assumed" (Villanueva, 1993, p. 120). Do we ask our NS students to look critically at this issue? Or do we help NNSs to face the challenges that they will encounter because of linguistic and cultural differences?

As NNSs struggle for credibility in TESOL, it is important that we as a profession acknowledge the unique contribution that NNSs bring to the profession. Dean's (1989) article "Multicultural Classrooms, Monocultural Teachers" highlighted a problem that is at the heart of much composition teaching. I would like to suggest a slight twist to this title, "Multilingual Classrooms, Monolingual Teachers," to underscore a problem that underlies much ESOL teaching. This is not to suggest that all NSs of English are monolingual, but as learners of American English as a second language, NNSs bring to the classroom a unique perspective: we not only recognize but have experienced how high the stakes are when an individual struggles to acquire, not just any language, but a language of immense power. Having been there, we can not only empathize with our students' struggles but also share our stories as well.

On the first day of class, I have an exercise in which I ask students to write in their journals about why they want to learn English and to talk about a time that they were misunderstood. Students share their stories; sometimes there is laughter, sometimes silence, and sometimes tears. I tell them my stories too. I tell them of my own shame, hurt, and anger when I have not been understood. I also tell them of some of the things that worked for me as I struggled with linguistic and cultural marginality and the need for acceptance. Something happens on that first day that creates a bond among us. One student wrote in her journal: "I am happy. You are like us. You understand my feelings about English."

NNSs not only empathize with their students but they make another very vital contribution to the field, although rarely acknowledged. They bring something unique to the ESOL profession. They are role models; they are success stories; they are real images of what students can aspire to be. Instead of being the exception, NNSs need to be the rule, found in every rank and level of ESOL teaching.

If our profession is truly to be a pedagogy of possibility, we need to show our students by example that they can be all that they aspire to be. As Okawa (1995) suggested, "an obvious contradiction exists between claims that literacy can be universally liberating and the reality that proves non-minority teachers remain in control of that power" (p. 4). To acknowledge the presence of what Edge (1996) called the "cross-cultural paradoxes" in our profession is just the first step. It is time that our profession goes beyond just "respecting differences" as suggested by Edge; we need to value diversity and to acknowledge the presence of the NNS professional, as an important, vital, and very credible force in the TESOL profession. It is time to go beyond lip service. It is time to clean house and to truly value diversity.

References

Amin, N. (1997). Race and identity of the non-native ESL teacher. *TESOL Quarterly, 31,* 580–583.

Broyard, A. (1950). Portrait of the inauthentic negro. *Commentary, 10*, 56–64.

Canagarajah, A. S. (1996). "Nondiscursive" requirements in academic publishing, material resources of periphery scholars, and the politics of knowledge production. *Written Communication, 13*, 435–472.

Dean, T. (1989). Multicultural classrooms, monocultural teachers. *College Composition and Communication, 40*, 23–37.

Edge, J. (1996). Cross-cultural paradoxes in a profession of values. *TESOL Quarterly, 30*, 9—30.

Kachru, B. B. (1985). Standards, codification and sociolinguistic realism: The English language in the outer circle. In R. Quirk & H. G. Widdowson (Eds.), *English in the world: Teaching and learning the language and literature* (pp. 11—30). Cambridge, England: Cambridge University Press.

Murray, D. (1996). The tapestry of diversity in our classrooms. In K. M. Bailey & D. Nunan (Eds.), *Voices from the language classroom* (pp. 434—448). New York: Cambridge University Press.

Okawa, G. (1995). *Expanding perspectives of teacher knowledge: A descriptive study of autobiographical narratives of writing teachers of color.* Unpublished doctoral dissertation, Indiana University of Pennsylvania, Indiana.

Villanueva, V. Jr. (1993). *Bootstraps: From an American academic of color.* Urbana, IL: National Council of Teachers of English.

Walelign, A. (1986). Non-native speakers need not apply. *English Teaching Forum, 24(2)*, 40—41.

Zamel, V. (1995). Strangers in academia. *College Composition and Communication, 46*, 506—521.

CHAPTER 2

From the Periphery to the Center: One Teacher's Journey

George Braine
The Chinese University of Hong Kong

At casual meetings, colleagues in the ESL profession have occasionally asked me for my "real" name. Others, with decades of ESL teaching experience and exposure to NNSs from diverse language backgrounds, have told me that they could not understand my accent. I have also been told that my skin color and accent do not match my name and asked to explain the historical and genealogical causes for this mismatch.

Despite the growing presence of NNS scholars and teachers from Third World countries in U.S. higher education, a lack of sensitivity and of tolerance from those in the mainstream of our profession is still not uncommon. This is difficult to fathom because many NS teachers of English have had the opportunity to travel and work in the Third World. During the past three decades, the Peace Corps alone has sent thousands of U.S. volunteers to teach English abroad. Many of these novice teachers have remained in the profession, earning higher degrees and attaining influential roles as academics, administrators, and office bearers of professional organizations.

Some professionals in the Center[1] also appear to be unaware of the academic, economic, and technological disadvantages that most third world teachers face in their countries, and which often become barriers to their advancement when entering the profession in the Center. Facilities such as TV, video, computers, professional journals, workshops and conferences, e-mail, and the Internet, which are readily available and often taken for granted in Center countries, are still beyond the reach of most Periphery teachers. As a result, the research or publications records of these individuals, a crucial factor in the job market, may not be as substantial or impressive as of those born in Center countries.

---

[1] See Galtung (1980) for definitions of Periphery and Centre (Center).

As the contents of this volume indicate, a significant number of NNS professionals in ELT have begun to earn higher degrees and enter the profession in the U.S. and other Center countries. This is only to be expected because, worldwide, there are at least four NNSs to every native speaker of English. However, except for the accounts of Shen (1989), Liu (1994), and a handful of others, few noteworthy contributions have been published of teachers' journeys from the Periphery to the Center. This chapter is an attempt to expand this record by recounting my journey, beginning as a teacher at a village school in the Periphery, to the Center, as a graduate student in the United States, as a teacher at international universities in the United States and in Asia, and as the editor of an international journal in ELT. My experience may not be typical of Periphery teachers, but it does illustrate the difficult and sometimes traumatic path that we must traverse in order to enter the academia in Center countries.

In this account, I not only recall my career in the past 30 years but also reflect on my acquisition of academic literacy. This account is not entirely autobiographical; based on my experience and those of others, I form generalizations that apply to other Periphery teachers and scholars. As I reflect upon my career, some scenes from the past are presented as four vignettes, helping me to illustrate my reflections.

Beginnings

First Vignette: *It is January 1972. I travel in a crowded overnight train and then by bus, which is full of plantation laborers and subsistence farmers. The driver drops me off, pointing to a few specks on a far-off hill, indicating Kendagolla Secondary School. Carrying my bag, I trudge up the narrow, rock-strewn path, asking for directions from villagers who peer curiously through doorways. Nearly an hour later, I reach the school and enter the headmaster's office followed by a group of curious students. I inform the headmaster that I am the new English teacher. He is cynical: "What English for these children?" he asks.*

Fresh from a 2-year stint at teachers college, full of enthusiasm for my career, my first job was at a remote village more than a day's journey from Colombo, the capital of Sri Lanka. Although set amid lush tea plantations in the central hill region of the country, poverty and neglect were everywhere. The local population consisted of subsistence farmers or laborers. Despite the cold and the more than 5-mile daily walk for some students, none could afford shoes. I was the first trained teacher of English in the school's 40-year history.

As the only English teacher, I taught Grades 4 through 10, at least six 50-minute classes per day. The smallest class had 35 students. All had textbooks provided free by the government, but I had no visual aids or English newspapers or magazines. Few students had access to radios, which most households could not afford. Many students attended school without a proper breakfast, most only with a cup of tea. I saw the thin, famished faces all around me, and almost every day, a few students in my classes would faint from weakness. Two years later, as I left to take a job at a university, I wondered if my headmaster's cynicism was justified. English was the colonial legacy of the British and had little relevance to the lives of my students. It was a language as remote from their lives as Britain or the United States.

Academia

If I thought that obtaining a coveted job as a university English instructor was an escape from the neglect and isolation of a village school teacher, I was soon to realize that university English teachers were equally low in the social and economic ladder. Most English instructors, like myself, did not have degrees; instead, we had taken training courses at teachers' colleges. Instructors, because of our "doubtful" academic qualifications and the non credit service courses we taught, were at the bottom of the academic ranks, tolerated at the faculty club and academic gatherings more to swell numbers than for our intellectual contributions. The already lowly status of the instructors and their sense of neglect and alienation were exacerbated by the corrugated-iron classrooms where English classes were held.

Scholarship and intellectual advancement were at a standstill. No ELT journals were published locally, and seminars and workshops were few and often unaffordable; during my 8 years at the university, I attended just one in-service course. On a monthly salary that was a pittance by Western standards, no instructor could afford to subscribe to international ELT journals. Even university libraries, restricted to a budget less than that of a rural public library in the United States, would spend their meager allocations on journals in science, medicine, and engineering, areas that were considered more important than ELT. The British Council and the U.S. Information Agency, located in two cities, did carry the more popular reference books, but journals publishing current research were unavailable. As for technology, computers, overhead projectors, and video equipment were nonexistent; an unscarred blackboard was a privilege.

At the university where I taught in the 1970s, all students were required to enroll in the non-credit English classes, which emphasized grammar and reading. Because the ability to speak English was a requirement for social mobility and for getting scarce jobs, many students also enrolled in the numerous cram shops that dotted the university neighborhood, offering "spoken" English. Because teachers at these cram shops taught the more useful skills, the students often held them in higher esteem.

Literacy Autobiography

The Sri Lanka I grew up in was a tolerant, multilingual society. The British, the last colonial rulers after the Portuguese and the Dutch, had departed in 1948 leaving a highly literate population. Until opportunistic politicians began to stir up communal and religious disharmony in the mid-1950s, Ceylon, as it was called then, experienced relative racial harmony and a steady growth in economy, education, and health care.

My genealogy, which reflects the legacy of colonial rule, is an interesting Sinhalese and British mix spiced with Methodist, Episcopalian, and Roman Catholic backgrounds. Because my mother speaks only Sinhala, I grew up in a household that rarely used English. In the mid-1950s, the cartoon page of the Sunday newspaper ("Blondie" and "Bringing Up Father" were my favorite strips), which my father deciphered and translated for his children, and U.S. and British pop music played during the request programs on Radio Ceylon were my main exposures to English. At school, where I studied in the Sinhala medium, English was limited to 1 hour a day, taught through grammar translation and pattern practice. Writing in English classes meant dictation exercises and answering reading comprehension questions. The textbooks used in English lessons were based on the British curriculum: we read about Mr. and Mrs. Brown and their children's lives and the English weather, so unreal in tropical Sri Lanka. My father's occupation as a plantation manager compelled us to live in rural areas away from the cities and their libraries. I read voraciously in Sinhala: newspapers, magazines, and novels, the latter a relatively new genre in Sinhala literature.

Perhaps the most significant event in my acquisition of English literacy occurred at the age of 13, when I was enrolled at a private school run by the Baptist Missionary Society. The school had a rich tradition as a liberal-humanist institution and has produced many of Sri Lanka's best-known sportsmen, politicians, businessmen, and plantation owner-managers. Although the sudden switch to the English medium was a challenge, the move to a city with access to the British Council and U.S. Information Agency libraries, was a boon. I began to haunt these libraries, often at the expense of my schoolwork. I also became addicted to the *Reader's Digest*, devouring every past issue I could get hold of. In retrospect, that may have been bad enough, but the attractive propaganda material distributed by the U.S. Information Agency under the guise of newsmagazines also became part of my staple reading material.

At my new school, the student population was diverse, consisting of Sinhalese, Tamils, Muslims, and Burghers (descendants of European settlers, such as myself), a true reflection of Sri Lanka's ethnic mix. A sprinkling of foreign students, mainly from the Maldives, was also present. English was the lingua franca. Although my classification as a Burgher enabled me to enroll in English medium classes, I was embarrassed because I could barely speak the language. However, within a few months, I had acquired a basic fluency in spoken English, which in turn allowed me access to the English-speaking students of the school. For the first time, oral discourse began to influence my writing in English. Although the chauvinist political parties in power continued to foster the Sinhala language mainly at the cost of English, the school continued to be an oasis for an English-speaking community of teachers and students, recruiting teachers from Britain, encouraging the study of English literature, promoting sports such as rugby and cricket, and generally living up to the best traditions of British public schools on which it was modeled.

The final two years of my schooling were at a Sinhala-medium government school. The official language policy had decreed that university-entrance classes had to be taught either in Sinhala or Tamil. Textbooks had been hastily translated from English, and official glossaries containing coined technical terms in the sciences, medicine, and social sciences had been published. Our teachers, all of them educated in English, struggled through these unfamiliar texts and synthetic terms. The challenge of the highly competitive university entrance examination was compounded by the struggle with learning science in local languages.

Although I failed the university entrance examination in science, my English proficiency was enough to gain admission to a teachers college. In retrospect, the 2-year, full-time teacher training program has been most appropriate and helpful to my teaching, more than the MA in TESOL and the Ph.D. in Foreign Language Education, which I earned later. Based on the British model but designed for Sri Lanka's needs, the teachers college curriculum was based on first-hand experience in Sri

Lankan classrooms and included extensive supervised teaching practice for the trainees.

Although I entered teachers college as a teenager, it took me 10 more years to enter the university; the obligatory period of service as an English teacher after teachers' college and the responsibilities of raising a family contributed to the delay. A degree in English meant a degree in English literature; the course work included the study of drama from the Medieval ages to the 17th Century, literary criticism, poetry from Chaucer to Keats, fiction from Defoe to George Eliot, and modern literature, some of it in translation from the Spanish, Italian, and French. In a course titled "The English Language," I studied the history and structure of the language. During 4 years of course work, the writing consisted almost entirely of literary criticism. The teacher-centered lectures did little to encourage oral discourse, and the written discourse in English was influenced almost entirely by reading. The "academic" style of writing that I acquired during those years has stayed with me until now, which might explain the difficulty I have in composing a more personal, narrative style of writing.

My first attempt at publication came in the early 1980s. While teaching in Oman, I noted striking differences between Sri Lanka and Oman in the preparation of curricula, textbooks, and in-service training of teachers. With only a mental outline, I composed an opinion piece highlighting the more effective Omani approach. This article was printed in a Sri Lankan daily newspaper and launched my "publishing career." Nearly 20 years after its publication, I marvel at the way in which I had used devices such as a thesis statement, topic sentences, and transitions. Because I did not model the article on any published piece (which later became a habit as I began to publish academic papers based on research), I am at a loss to explain how I acquired the correct approach.

My admission to the MA TESOL program in 1984 and the access to academic libraries it provided transformed my reading habits. Instead of reading fiction, I was now under pressure to complete the required readings of the applied linguistics courses I was enrolled in. Instead of reading popular newsmagazines, I began to read the *ESP Journal* and *TESOL Quarterly*. In a course titled "Curriculum Design in English for Specific Purposes," one assignment was a review of an ESP text. Professor Grace Burkhart, the course instructor, gave us detailed instructions on how a book review could be written and also analyzed and discussed sample book reviews from the *ESP Journal*. This was the first time I had received explicit advice on writing.

Second Vignette: *It is the end of the fall term in 1984. I have seen snow for the first time, and Robert Frost's poem "Stopping by Woods . . .," read and analyzed in a hot and humid Sri Lankan classroom, has more meaning now. I lift stacks of heavy books and arrange them on shelves, envying the young undergraduates relaxing in comfortable chairs, often with their feet on the nearest table. Suddenly, Professor Burkhart rounds the corner and, smiling, walks toward me; she had made a few phone calls to track me down. She shows me the book review I have written as a course assignment and asks if I would like to publish it in the ESP Journal, which she edits. I am flattered and exhilarated. My first academic publication!*

Canagarajah (1996) described the limited material conditions of Third World scholars, as I have earlier in this chapter. But, even when they enter Western academia, these scholars face invisible barriers that hinder their assimilation and productivity. For instance, Third World scholars who enter graduate studies in the United States are handicapped in two ways. First, they miss the mandatory freshmen and upper-division writing courses that NS students find so beneficial when they start graduate school. The teaching of writing is very much an U.S. concept, only now being introduced in other countries. Second, the majority of Master's-level programs have no course work in research methods, research writing, or statistics. Hence, most Third World scholars learn citation styles, research methods, and scholarly writing through modeling and painstaking trial-and-error methods.

My transition from an ESL generalist to a writing specialist began through necessity. In order to continue my doctoral studies at the University of Texas, I accepted a teaching assistantship from the English Department. Somewhat demoralized by my new identity as a NNS, I was startled to learn that I would have to teach a first-year writing course to native speakers. Teach writing? Unaware of current writing pedagogy, even of the process approach, I walked into each class meeting embarrassed and insecure, doubtful if I was even the proverbial one step ahead of my students. But, during that traumatic first semester, I began to apply to my writing the techniques I taught to my students: invention strategies, audience analysis, peer reviews, and conferencing, and discovered writing as a shared, creative, and joyous activity.

A Non-Native Speaker

When I began to teach English, I had met only two NSs of English. The first was a British clergyman who taught religion at the secondary school

I attended, and the second was a British Council sponsored visiting lecturer at the teachers college. At first, I had no inkling of the NS-NNS distinction, placing these teachers on par with my Sri Lankan teachers. I was aware that English teachers from Sri Lanka, India, and Pakistan had been serving in some Arab and African countries since the 1960s. Educational administrators in these newly independent countries may have recognized the advantages of hiring NNS teachers, obviously at a lower cost than NS teachers; although it would be prestigious to employ one's former colonizers, they did not come cheap. However, I was not aware of the disparities in salary and benefits between these NNS teachers and NS teachers until my own teaching stint in the Middle East in the early 1980s. Teachers from Britain, often with mere 3- or 6-month teaching certificates, were paid twice the salary of highly qualified and experienced English teachers from the Indian subcontinent, and enjoyed housing and other benefits unheard of by the latter.

Nevertheless, I experienced the full impact of the term *non-native speaker*, and all the accompanying social, psychological, and economic baggage, only when I arrived in the United States to enroll in a Master's program in TESOL in the mid-1980s. By then, I had 14 years experience teaching English. Needing to supplement my partial scholarship, I applied for a tutor position at the university's language center and was turned down almost instantly. Instead, some NS classmates who had no teaching experience were employed. Although not stated explicitly, the message was clear: NNSs need not apply.

When I later applied for a teaching position at an intensive English program in Philadelphia, the director informed me that most teachers in the program, all NSs, were opposed to my appointment. This opposition from fellow ESL professionals (see Amin, Chap. 7, Kamhi-Stein, Chap. 10, and Thomas, Chap. 1, this volume, for similar experiences) is, in retrospect, highly ironic, considering their strident championing of multiculturalism, diversity, and other sociopolitical causes, often on behalf of ESL students and immigrants. Although ESL students are praised and admired for the multiculturalism and diversity that they bring into language classes, NNS teachers who can also contribute their rich multicultural, multilingual experiences to ELT are often barred from ESL classrooms. Paradoxically, the often reviled mainstream English teachers, literature specialists, and heads of English departments with no awareness of ESL politics, are generous and tolerant of our differences and judge NNSs on their merits during the award of financial aid, hiring, and promotion.

I was soon to learn that prejudice toward NNS teachers came from some ESL students as well. I was assigned to teach two courses, the first

NNS to be given this responsibility in the program. About 2 weeks after classes began, I was informed that two students had complained about my accent and requested transfers to classes taught by native speakers. This rejection was more hurtful than the objections of my colleagues. Some ESL students naively subscribe to the native-speaker fallacy—that the ideal English teacher is a NS. This belief stems mainly from their frustration with incompetent, barely proficient English teachers in their own countries and is especially evident in intensive English programs, in which these newly arrived students enroll. When I later taught at a U.S. university, ESL students flocked to my first year and advanced writing classes, relishing the support of fellow ESL students and a NNS teacher, who they said would better understand their language problems.

The U.S. system of higher education has changed the lives of many Third World academics. The scholarships and teaching and research assistantships have enabled them to experience life in the West, to pursue graduate education, and to obtain world-class degrees from U.S. universities. I read my first research article and first used a computer only in 1984, thanks to an U.S. scholarship. But NNSs have also contributed much to the U.S. system of higher education, bringing their rich teaching experience, multiculturalism, and diversity to language classes.

The playing field will not be level for NNS English teachers. They will have to struggle twice as hard to achieve what often comes as a birthright to their NS counterparts: recognition of their teaching ability and respect for their scholarship. Often, teaching ability alone will not suffice for employment or career advancement. They must grow as professionals, taking active roles and assuming leadership in teacher organizations, initiating research (even on a small scale), sharing their ideas through publications, and learning to network with NNS colleagues. As I did, they will meet courageous administrators who will see beyond their accents and pronunciation, mentors who will promote their careers, and colleagues who will support their research and publication efforts.

Third Vignette: *It is a warm day in May, 1990. The Texas Stadium resounds to the cheers of thousands of graduates and their friends and families who have gathered for the Commencement ceremony. The chief guest is the President of the United States. I contemplate the last three years of my life, in crowded graduate housing, working two and sometimes three part-time jobs, the American dream far from my family's grasp. Was it worth it? In my extended family spread to all corners of the globe, and among the 150 classmates in teachers college in 1970-71, I am the first to earn a doctorate. And this is only a beginning.*

Return to the Periphery

Canagarajah (1996) describes the problems faced by Third World scholars who are often marginalized and excluded from the academic publishing process. The situation applies to English teachers in many Asian, African, and South American countries. As the editor of an ELT journal, I receive manuscripts, often typewritten in flawless English, based on sound research. But many references are so outdated, sometimes by 10 to 15 years, that the manuscripts have little chance of publication.

How can scholars from the Periphery, who may lack the resources or the know-how to publish academically, be supported? The *Asian Journal of English Language Teaching (AJELT)*, which I coedit, does this in a number of ways. First, we encourage our reviewers to act as mentors to promising authors, providing extensive comments on multiple drafts of manuscripts. Second, when we realize that authors do not have the facilities to access recent sources relevant to their research, we provide them the relevant references. Third, we assist authors with their graphics, and to a lesser extent, with advice on their statistical analyses. Finally, knowing that some academic libraries are hard-pressed to afford subscriptions to international journals, we have offered free subscriptions to two academic libraries in every Asian country.

The problems are by no means limited to scholars who return to peripheral countries. Those who return to Hong Kong and Singapore, which have advanced and sophisticated academic institutions that rival those of the West, face another challenge. Universities in these countries expect their teachers to publish in Western journals for career advancement and tenure. However, according to Altbach, a Professor of Higher Education at Boston College, a recent survey found "American and British scholars and scientists to be the least internationally minded. In short, it is quite difficult for researchers in other parts of the world to gain acceptance in the competitive and . . . insular world of Western publications" (1997, p. 10). Academic publishing is dominated by the West, and that most readers of academic journals have little interest in what happens in Asian or African language contexts. So, when scholars from outside the West attempt to publish in Western journals, which already have a high rejection rate, they face the additional obstacle in the form of editors and reviewers who may find the research of little interest to their readership.

One way to overcome this barrier is to establish journals that will gain acceptance in Center countries. These journals should appeal not only to regional contributors, but reciprocally to those in the Center as well. *AJELT* is gradually achieving this. It is very much an Asian journal, published in Hong Kong and supported by an editorial board and reviewers who are based mainly in Asia. But it publishes scholarship relating to teaching English to Asians, and Asians study English all over the world. As a result, about 30% of the submissions are from North America. *AJELT* is also a refereed journal (few journals in Asia are refereed), which makes it even more attractive to quality submissions from all over the world.

Musings

After pouring millions of dollars and pounds on the improvement of teacher training facilities and techniques, it is time to ask if English teachers from the Periphery have better facilities and support in the classroom and more opportunities for career advancement. What is the status of English teaching in these countries? Do scholars from these countries have more acceptance in the ELT field? The answers to these questions are not transparent and vary from context to context. In many Peripheral countries, the standard of English has actually declined. Poor salaries and working conditions have compelled the more qualified and experienced English teachers from these countries to work in more affluent Middle Eastern, East Asian, or African countries. Some teacher trainers in Sri Lanka, for instance, complain that recent English teacher recruits are barely proficient in English and fear that the language could be reduced to a Pidgin in the hands of these teachers. As a result, the overall number of fluent English speakers in the population begins to decline. The shortage of qualified professionals also results in importing teacher trainers through the British Council and U.S. Information Agency, which no doubt leads to an infusion of new ideas and methodologies. However, one must take into consideration the warnings by Phillipson (1992) and Canagarajah (Chap. 6, this volume) of the negative consequences of such relationships.

Scholars from peripheral countries are increasingly visible in mainstream ELT publications. For instance, leading journals in the field, such as *TESOL Quarterly* and *TESOL Journal*, have recently added a number of NNSs to their editorial boards. However, the native speaker domination of professional organizations continues. Although 23% of TESOL members are from outside the United States (and I assume a significant number of members both from within and outside the United

States are NNSs), TESOL's Board of Directors appears to have only two NNS members. The power structure within foreign affiliates of TESOL is also worthy of scrutiny. As Oda (Chap. 8, this volume) notes, although 80% of the members of foreign affiliates are NNSs, native speaker members hold 36% of the decision-making positions in these affiliates.

As NNS scholars gradually receive recognition and assume positions of responsibility and influence in the West, prejudice and discrimination is spreading rapidly in Japan, Korea, Taiwan, and Hong Kong. In these countries, being a native speaker of English is often the main qualification to teach English, and this requirement is explicitly stated in job advertisements. In fact, some exchange students at my University, who have no teaching experience, seize this advantage to advertise their services as tutors, emphasizing their NS status.

Ironically, the discrimination is spreading to NS as well. Some Hong Kong institutions from the kindergarten to the tertiary level insist on teachers with British accents at the expense of those with American or Australian accents. A colleague was asked how she could teach English, because she was from the United States! Another U.S. friend, who was interviewed by telephone for a private tutor position, was turned down because she did not have a British accent. The following announcement for a position in Japan, perhaps the most outrageous I have seen recently, appeared on the Internet:

ENGLISH LANGUAGE INSTRUCTOR.
Full-time, 35 hours/week, 25 contact hours/week, . . . Native British speaker. . . . TEFL or TESOL diploma and university degree required. "Speaker of BRITISH ENGLISH (British, Northern Irish, New Zealand and Australian people only). IF YOU HAVE A NORTH AMERICAN ACCENT YOU ARE NOT ELIGIBLE TO APPLY" (emphasis in the original).

Fourth Vignette: *I stop the car at the turn to Kendagolla Secondary School, but those at the bus stop assure me that the road is driveable all the way to the school. It is December 1995. Twenty-three years after my first visit, I am retracing my beginnings. The rock-strewn path I trudged up is now a bus route. The school is closed for the December vacation. Two buildings have been added, but little else has changed. The drafty old classrooms are forlorn and gloomy. Desks and chairs, crusted with dirt, scarred and broken, are scattered everywhere. My son, a senior at an U.S. university, is silent in disbelief at the poverty and neglect. Memories overwhelm me; it has been a long journey.*

References

Altbach, P. (1997, January 10). Straitjacket scholars. *South China Morning Post*, p. 10.

Canagarajah, A. S. (1996). "Nondiscursive" requirements in academic publishing, material resources of periphery scholars, and the politics of knowledge production. *Written Communication, 13*, 435–472.

Galtung, J. (1980). *The true worlds: A transnational perspective.* New York: The Free Press.

Liu, X. G. (1994). Conversing across cultural boundaries: Rewriting "self." *Journal of Advanced Composition, 14*, 455–462.

Phillipson, R. (1992). *Linguistic imperialism.* Oxford, England: Oxford University Press.

Shen, F. (1989). The classroom and the wider culture. *College Composition and Communication, 40*, 459–466.

CHAPTER 3

Learning to Write Academic Prose in a Second Language: A Literacy Autobiography

Ulla Niemelä Connor
Indiana University at Indianapolis

This chapter was first written for a presentation at a 1996 TESOL session at which George Braine had invited a few non-native English-speaking TESOLers to share their experiences in becoming professionals in the field. During the presentation, for the first time ever I shared a personal story at a professional, public meeting. Meant as a celebration for overcoming anxieties as an ESL writer, the private nature of the talk ironically made it quite an anxiety-laden activity.

In the presentation, I described my development as a writer in English as a second language as a graduate student after moving to the United States. Appendix A charts this progress. I was guided, to a degree, by instructions for writing a literacy autobiography (Appendix B) developed by Steve Fox, a colleague at Indiana University-Purdue University at Indianapolis (IUPUI). These instructions are designed to assist native English-speaking students in the United States in undergraduate and graduate classes in writing literacy autobiographies, recently a popular form of writing in the United States.[1] Instead of focusing on childhood memories about learning to read and write in the first language, however, my recollections dealt with the struggles and triumphs of writing in English as a second language.

Twenty-six years ago, I was a 23-year-old master's level student of English language and literature at the University of Helsinki, Finland, when I received a marvelous opportunity to write a master's thesis on the nature of Milton's adjectives with the guidance of a world-renowned Milton scholar, the Estonian-born linguist Ants Oras. Funded by the International Peace Scholarship of the International Women's Organization, I spent a year with Dr. Oras writing a master's thesis for my degree in Finland while simultaneously completing another master's degree in English literature at the University of Florida.

---

[1] See, for example, *My Name's Not Susie* (1995) by my colleague Sharon Hamilton.

Writing as a Graduate Student

A hardworking and eager student, I found myself completely unprepared for the expectations of graduate study in English in the United States. During the four years of study in Finland toward my bachelor's and master's degrees, I had written only two term papers in English—one on Coleridge's "Kubla Khan," the other on a novel by Willa Cather. The rest of the course work had been tested through short question examinations, many of them in Finnish, the native language of the students. Not only were my writing skills in English academic contexts almost nonexistent, but my spoken language ability in English for classroom and seminar settings was lacking. A reserved, "silent Finn" (Lehtonen & Sajavaara, 1985) unaccustomed to the active participation style of U.S. graduate students, I was poorly prepared to take part in the active social construction of meaning characteristic of many courses in the United States. Most current thinking about the socialization process of novices into new genres and disciplines emphasizes the active participation of these novices in making meaning through verbal and written communication with professors, colleagues, fellow students, and others (Berkenkotter & Huckin, 1993). I studied hard, spending long hours in the library. Unfortunately, this left little time for talk, although it was good preparation for written work. Writing term papers was difficult, but I managed, enlisting my U.S. roommates—a nurse and an education major—to help edit the work.

Despite the difficulties, my master's thesis, "The Use of Adjectives in Milton's Earlier and Later Poetry"—a 70-page stylistic analysis, was finished in a year's time and reads like the sort of stylistic analysis acceptable 20 years ago. The following opening paragraph in the first chapter includes a strong voice of the writer:

> The following pages present a stylistic examination of certain aspects of Milton's use of adjectives in the following of his earlier poems: "L'Allegro," "Il Penseroso," and "Lycidas," and also in twelve books of "Paradise Lost." By means of statistical analysis I attempt to trace the gradual change in the position of adjectives in Milton's poetry. I have tried to utilize my data, avoiding as much as possible a merely mechanical approach. I have tried to cite the forms illustrating each practice in sufficient context to show unmistakably their grammatical functions. I have used Helen Darbishere's careful edition of *The Poetical Works of John Milton* (Connor, 1971, p. 8).

The above sample and the entire thesis suggest a competent and confident writer with more than an adequate command of English. But, it was the voice of my untiring mentor, Dr. Oras, who read and reread all the chapters and offered suggestions throughout the thesis from the initial topic selection to the very last stages of revising. Dr. Oras, an Estonian-born linguist with a perfect command of several languages including Finnish, was himself an immigrant to the United States.

An eminent scholar of linguistics and literature, he was active in the Estonian nationalist movement during World War II and was forced to escape Estonia after the war. On his route to England and eventually to the United States, he and his wife spent some time at the University of Helsinki in the 1940s. Thirty years later in Florida, Dr. Oras seemed pleased to mentor a Finnish graduate student of his former colleague, Dr. Tauno F. Mustanoja.

A linguist, poet, and translator, Dr. Oras was a slightly built man, who continuously smiled while he smoked or fiddled with a pipe. He attracted a small but devoted group of graduate students. His classes were seminars, which he led speaking in his soft voice, often quoting poetry. I attended his seminar each semester that I was in Florida while working on the thesis. I remember first semester discussions after class with him over coffee in the local Krispy Kreme donut shop about Milton's poetry and its analysis. Soon, a topic was found for me to investigate, which dealt with Milton's use of adjectives in his earlier and later poems. After months of counting syllables in all of *Paradise Lost* and four other long poems, I discovered that not only did the adjectives get longer in the later poems but that their preferred position also changed from pre-noun to post-noun. I presumed my finding came as no surprise to Dr. Oras, although he made me feel as if I had discovered a truly unique piece of new knowledge.

The actual writing of the thesis took several months, with Dr. Oras commenting an all drafts. I remember clearly biking to his house just off campus to drop off and pick up chapters, often discussing his comments. I recall that his comments and rewrites dealt with all levels of the text, including content, organization, and mechanics. A strong impression remains of Dr. Oras as a patient and caring reader and teacher.

After finishing the thesis and receiving the master's degrees at the University of Florida and the University of Helsinki, I married a U.S. citizen, a graduate student in economics and a good writer, and accompanied him to Madison, Wisconsin, where he had received a fellowship. There I enrolled in a Ph.D. program in the Department of Comparative Literature, an odd choice for a linguist. Without a mentor— I was just another student with no special recommendation or invitation—I found the graduate work difficult, too difficult, but seldom discussed it with others. Of all the professors in the graduate program, I remember only one, Dr. Fannie LeMoine, who took the time to talk with me about a paper I was writing for her course. I remember her telling me to forget myself and simply concentrate on getting the message across when talking in class. Meant as generous advice, advice that probably was very helpful for many (women students in particular), the advice did little to alleviate my fears as a second language speaker in a class of 30 smart, hard-working U.S. students who were accustomed to expressing their opinions loudly and articulately in class. At the end of the first year, I failed a Ph.D. qualifying examination—an oral examination covering world literature for which no reading list had been provided. Needless to say, the failure was devastating to my academic aspirations. I blamed myself for all that went wrong. I lost 30 pounds in a few months, going down from 115 pounds to 85.

An ESL Teacher in Public Schools

As often in life, problems can turn into opportunities. My failure forced me to explore other avenues, including teaching in schools for the first time in my life. I got a job as an ESL teacher (K-12) in the Madison Public Schools—the most rewarding job I have ever had and a job that allowed me to learn about the educational system as well as teaching ESL. I also taught Swedish. Although I did not write for academic purposes during the three years I taught in the Madison schools, it was my first chance to practice professional writing such as the writing of curriculum guidelines and grant proposals in teams with other ESL teachers in the program. And it steered me into a graduate program more suited to my skills and temperament.

Ph.D. Studies

From 1976 to 1979, a Ph.D. program in Education and English linguistics at the University of Wisconsin taught me new skills in statistics and research design and the orderly, coherent writing of research. An empirical research orientation with a strong educational foundation gave me explicit models of good research and good writing for the first time. I adapted them with zeal. More confident in my general language skills after several years in the United States and married to a supportive native English-speaking husband, also a good academic writer, I learned to write up experimental research. My term paper for Charles Read's second language acquisition class was published in *Language Learning*

(Connor & Read, 1978). The paper dealt with the validity of reading comprehension questions in an ESL proficiency test. After receiving a good grade on the paper, I had asked Professor Read if he would co-author the paper for a publication, a bold move on my part. As I remember, he did most of the rewriting and the paper was published without a single revision. A good start for a publishing career!

Although I did not feel confident as an academic writer, I was getting better. I still relied on native speaker editorial help in all my writing, including a tutor in the Writing Center who helped edit surface errors in my dissertation.

Publishing as a Professor

In 1979, my son Timo was born. The next few years as Assistant Professor of Linguistics at Georgetown University and later at IUPUI gave me tenure and promotion and made me a writer. Deborah Tannen, a colleague at Georgetown, kept telling me how much she enjoyed writing, especially books. It was hard for me to believe anyone could enjoy writing; I thought she was just persuading herself to like writing in order to keep going. Much later I learned that she was right—writing need not be painful; it can be enjoyable. Writing has become rewarding. It helps me think and provides a great sense of accomplishment.

At the time, however, I still lacked confidence in my writing ability and my knowledge of applied linguistics. Like anyone who has ever published, I received many rejections, some of which mentioned my non-nativeness, although I usually asked a native speaker to check my final versions. Working in an interdisciplinary field combining ESL and rhetoric studies caused further problems. Furthermore, I began conducting qualitative research in text analysis and case studies, which required a whole different style of writing from the now familiar reporting of experiments.

In the 1980s when I routinely gave five to six national or international presentations and published three or four articles per year, it became increasingly helpful to work with other authors such as Bob Kaplan, Patricia Carrell, Janice Lauer, and Ann Johns. They became an audience, peer responders, and coauthors. From composition theory, I learned later that all writers need feedback through discussions with others in the field.

These scholars were all supportive collaborators and coauthors. None made me self-conscious about my second language status. In each project, I was an equal partner. Each was helpful in editing my English, if needed, but did not focus on its deficiencies. Naturally, scholars have individual styles of writing and collaboration. Bob Kaplan, an editor of several books and journals, assumed a strong editorial presence and volunteered to proofread our entire edited book in the manner to which he was accustomed. I welcomed that. Equally advantageous to collaboration was the less directive approach of Ann Johns in another edited book project. Patricia Carrell and Janice Lauer, from whom I learned a great deal, were coauthors of research articles. Both were competent researchers and editors, Pat in L2 reading research and Janice in L1 composition and rhetoric. They were strong role models as successful women scholars.

In 1990, as the author of more than 50 published articles and 2 coedited books, as well as many presentations, I embarked on a more substantial project: writing a singly authored research reference book on contrastive rhetoric (Connor, 1996). The publishers wanted a survey book more or less, but as I found out, they also wanted my "own voice" to come through. I had developed a style of reporting, summarizing, and synthesizing contrastive rhetoric research into a readable form; letting my own voice come through was more difficult. Perhaps I was reluctant to criticize others' research. Perhaps the unwillingness to take a strong stand stemmed from my Finnish L1 background and our natural penchant for harmony and consensus.

The process of writing a whole book was liberating, however. I learned to write text more quickly. I also became more concerned about presenting my ideas in the Anglo-American direct manner with specific examples and exact transitions to guide the reader. Even though my own research had dealt with contrastive rhetoric before, I had never become as conscious of my own writing as during the gestation of this book. Perhaps I had never written as a Finn is supposed to write (Mauranen, 1993a). For example, Finns do not state their thesis at the beginning of the writing but prefer to delay the introduction of the purpose. Also, in a manner similar to Japanese writers, as documented by Hinds (1983, 1987, 1990), Finnish writers do not use transitions between paragraphs. In other words, Finnish writers are not very reader-friendly; rather, they let the facts speak for themselves. (See Ventola & Mauranen, 1991; Mauranen, 1993b, for discussion of the characteristics of Finnish academic writing.)

But now I found myself writing, or trying to write, like a U.S. writer: I told the reader at the beginning what I was going to say, repeated the main points throughout the text, and ended up with a summary statement that also gave an evaluation or my own opinion. And I supplied a plethora of transitions.

In the writing of the book, I was helped greatly by Ray Keller, professor emeritus at IUPUI. Not only did his comments improve the manuscript, he was also an enthusiastic reader. Ray was particularly conscious of my nonidiomatic second language errors, and he paid close attention to the ways I had organized the often-intractable material of the book. Confronted with heterogeneous approaches to a particular topic, which I was expected to reduce to coherence, I sometimes tended to write "like a Finn" and let the reader create order. But like my other editors and coauthors, Ray kept me honest.

Writing During a Sabbatical in Finland—End of Journey

This awareness of the different rhetorical patterns between U.S. English and Finnish was reinforced during a sabbatical in Finland where I worked with a number of Finnish researchers on a grant proposal writing project. The six-month project produced a Finnish language manual for writing grant proposals in English. (Connor et al., 1995). After many months of data analysis, the booklet was written basically during the month of May 1995 with the help of two Finnish research assistants.

The process of writing was difficult because of different views about the organization of material. My point was that the book described how U.S. English writing differs from Finnish writing; therefore, it was important to show how to state the main thesis at the beginning, giving examples and providing transitions, and repeating the main points. The Finnish research assistants disagreed. I found the first draft of the text incoherent and made many suggestions such as "we need to state the main point at the beginning of the paragraph;" "we shouldn't jump around with ideas, and leave the most important thing to the end of the book;" "English speakers expect a different order of presentation than Finns." I wrote the following summary comment to the research assistants (translated here from Finnish):

> Perhaps I'm reading this text as an American. It's all fine text, but I find it incoherent in places. I expect the main point at the beginning of the paragraph. I expect a paragraph to contain examples about the main point—no jumping between several points. If others (the researchers in the project) don't object to the current presentation, I must be completely Americanized.

I guess I *was* completely Americanized because no major changes based on my suggestions were included in the final version of the Finnish booklet. In addition, the Finns perceived my oral presentation as well as my writing skills as quite typically those of a United States speaker. Unlike Finns, who take pride in a calm and collected speaking style with measured pauses, monotone voice, and lack of gestures or dramatic body language, I spoke with enthusiasm, smiled a lot, used my hands to make points, and was positive. To Finns, I appeared hyper, out of control, an amusing curiosity. This experience and many others in Finland during my sabbatical last year encouraged me to apply for U.S. citizenship.

Do I feel like a U.S. writer now? Well, would I be trying a literacy autobiography, a newly popular U.S. form, if I didn't? Do I feel comfortable writing in English? I do not worry about having all of my writing edited by native speakers but I am still learning to write better and to enjoy it more. I do more publishing than most of my native English-speaking colleagues at my university. Perhaps that is because I have never been shy to ask others to read my drafts and comment on them.

Do I feel bad about not writing anything except personal letters in Finnish? Not really. Most Finnish applied linguists such as Nils Erik Enkvist or Liisa Lautamatti write most of their scholarship in English in the international environment of the new European Union, as do linguists of other nationalities such as Teun A. van Dijk of the University of Amsterdam.

Advice for Other ESL Writers

My experiences are, in many ways, similar to the experiences of a Finnish male graduate student of economics in his second year of graduate study in the United States (Connor & Mayberry, 1996). Both the economics student of the case study and I had been excellent students at the University of Helsinki, as confirmed by our Test of English as a Foreign Language (TOEFL) scores, grades, and ability to obtain overseas scholarships. Yet, despite our high English language test scores after several years of EFL study in Finland, both of us experienced difficulties in *writing* English. Neither of us had been required to write term papers in English. The writing of term papers for both Timo, the subject of the case study, and me was quite a traumatic experience at the beginning. Both of us survived the system, however, and after continued years of writing in English have begun to excel.

Based on these accounts, I would like to offer the following advice for my fellow ESL learners. Naturally, one must remember that what worked for me may not suit every other learner; for one thing, I decided to stay in the United States and became a citizen. Most international students return to their native countries.

1. Find out the expectations of your audience before starting to write. With regard to term papers, the professor is your best source. Seek out your professors; most professors in the United States consider meeting with students during office hours an important part of teaching duties. Talking over topics with the professor is helpful. Ask the professor to share his or her expectations about the required piece of writing if no explicit written guidelines exist.

2. For me, learning how to write an experimental research report was a liberating experience and served as a useful heuristic. For Timo, Swales (1987) moves for research paper introductions—territory, gap, goals—became a writing strategy. Find strategies that work for you.

3. Be prepared to spend a great deal of time writing and revising. Most likely, one draft will not do. Start early and follow a schedule. Find a comfortable place to write, and write something in English every day.

4. Learn to share your writing with others. The best help comes from mentors, your advisor, or other professors interested in your work. Fellow students are also inclined to spend the time to read and respond to your writing. It is important, however, that you do not consider your readers merely as editors but that you learn to discuss and understand their suggestions and corrections. In this way, you do not merely copy others' comments. Thus, schedule a meeting to go over the suggestions. At most U.S. universities, writing centers are available for help in writing. Many writing centers have tutors with previous ESL experience. The disadvantage, however, with some of the help in the writing centers is that tutors are English majors, often with no particular knowledge in your subject matter.

5. Later on in your career, foster collaborative writing contacts with peers. Very few academics are lucky enough to have peers at their own university with whom to collaborate; most have to seek peers outside their institutions. Today, however, thanks to the many modern technologies, conducting research long distance is relatively easy. Remember that each new collaboration requires a negotiation of roles, which is best done at the beginning of the collaborative work. Issues related to specific tasks and authorship roles are best discussed early on so that later problems can be avoided.

6. Finally, and, most important, remember that writing is always a challenge, whether it is in the first or second language. It requires self-discipline, creativity, and practice. No matter how much one has written, every new writing task is a challenge, especially at the beginning and at the finishing stages. The more one writes, however, the easier the process

gets. You learn what works for you as writer; for example, some writers need a clean desk, quiet place, and so forth, for getting writing done. You also learn how much time and help you need to finish a product. Of course, every new genre brings its own challenges. I remember how I struggled some years ago while trying to get started on a short article for an encyclopedia of linguistics, a new type of writing for me. I ended up contacting David Wilkins, the editor, as well as George Yule, another contributor, to discuss what was required. Finding out more about the level of readers, style of writing, and so forth, is always helpful.

7. Keep presenting your work and keep writing. Do not give up. Find your own road. And remember to enjoy your writing.

References

Berkenkotter, C., & Huckin, T. N. (1993). Rethinking genre from a sociocognitive perspective. *Written Communication, 10,* 475–509.

Connor, U. (1996). *Contrastive rhetoric. Cross-cultural aspects of second-language writing.* New York: Cambridge University Press.

Connor, U. (1971). *The use of adjectives in Milton's earlier and later poetry.* Unpublished master's thesis, University of Florida, Gainesville.

Connor, U., Helle, T., Mauranen, A., Ringbom, H., Tirkkonen-Condit, S., & Yli-Antola, M. (1995). *Tehokkaita Eu-projektiehdotuksia. Ohjeita kirjoittajille* [Strategies in successful proposals for European Union research grants]. Helsinki, Finland: TEKES.

Connor, U., & Mayberry, S. (1996). Learning discipline-specific academic writing: A case study of a Finnish graduate student in the United States. In E. Ventola & A. Mauranen (Eds.), *Academic writing: Intercultural and textual issues* (pp. 231–253). Philadelphia: John Benjamins.

Connor, U., & Read, C. (1978). Passage dependency in reading comprehension questions of English language proficiency tests. *Language Learning, 28,* 149–157.

Hamilton, S. (1995). *My name's not Susie.* Portsmouth, NH: Boynton/Cook.

Hinds, J. (1983). Contrastive rhetoric: Japanese and English. *Text, 3,* 183–195.

Hinds, J. (1987). Reader versus writer responsibility: A new typology. In U. Connor & R. B. Kaplan (Eds.), *Writing across languages: Analysis of L2 text* (pp. 141–152). Reading, MA: Addison-Wesley.

Hinds, J. (1990). Inductive, deductive, quasi-inductive: Expository writing in Japanese, Korean, Chinese, and Thai. In U. Connor & A. M. Johns (Eds.), *Coherence: Research and pedagogical perspectives* (pp. 87–110). Arlington, VA: Teachers of English to Speakers of Other Languages.

Lehtonen, J., & Sajavaara, K. (1985). The silent Finn. In D. Tannen & M. Saville-Troike (Eds.), *Perspectives on silence* (pp. 193–201). Norwood, NJ: Ablex.

Mauranen, A. (1993a). Contrastive ESP rhetoric: Metatext in Finnish-English economics texts. *English for Specific Purposes Journal, 12,* 3–22.

Mauranen, A. (1993b). *Cultural differences in academic rhetoric.* Frankfurt am Main, Germany: Peter Lang.

Swales, J. (1987). Utilizing the literatures in teaching the research paper. *TESOL Quarterly, 21,* 41–68.

Ventola, E., & Mauranen, A. (1991). Non-native writing and native revising of scientific articles. In E. Ventola (Ed.), *Functional and systemic linguistics* (pp. 457–492). Berlin, Germany: Mouton De Gruyter.

Appendix A

Development as a Writer in English

Chronology	Types of Writing	L1 vs. L2 Finnish/English	Voice of a Native Speaker
Grad Student (1970 - 1973) Finland Florida Wisconsin	Academic Letters	English Finnish English	No
ESL Teacher (1973 - 1976)	Professional	NA	Trying
Ph.D. Student (1976 - 1979)	Academic	English	Getting There
Professor (1980 - present) GU IUPUI	Academic Professional	English English	Mostly
Sabbatical in Finland (1994 - 1995)	Academic	English	There

Appendix B

Literacy Autobiography

A literacy autobiography is an account of significant factors and events that have contributed to your development as a reader or writer. In writing this autobiography, you will explore in some depth the origins of some of your attitudes and theories about reading and writing as well as your reading and writing practices. Consider your entire life, including pre-school years, and do not confine yourself to school experiences. Also, feel free to discuss the influence of spoken language in your life, for oral discourse influences written discourse. For example, some writers' styles show the influence of sermons, theater, political speeches, oral storytelling, and family conversation.

The form of this account is up to you. The most difficult task for many people will be deciding what to include and what to omit, and then how to organize and focus the selected materials. Although the assignment asks you to focus on language and literacy experiences, you might have to include certain experiences that do not explicitly relate to literacy but provide a context for those experiences, which do. Of course, any autobiography is selective and written from a certain perspective, but you should try to be inclusive enough so that you literacy autobiography represents as wide a range of influences and experiences as possible.

Following are some areas of your experience to consider. You need not write about all of these areas, and you certainly will not want to follow this order in your paper, but brainstorming or thinking about these topics will help you recover and arrange relevant memories.

- The education and literacy levels and the literate activities of current and preceding generations of your family
- The role that written language has played in your home and in your family's social, cultural, occupational, and religious practices (also consider the role of oral language— storytelling, for example, or family talk)
- The role of written language in play and peer groups (how have reading and writing figured into your relationships with your friends at various stages of your life?)
- The kinds of reading and writing you have done in school and outside of school (including purpose and audience)

- The role of libraries and bookstores, of television and computers, of toys (for example, toy typewriter, printing press)
- Significant people who influenced your reading and writing
- Significant memories of successes and failures with language
- The role of reading and writing in developing your identity

I encourage you to ransack your memories, writing down everything that comes to you. It is often helpful to talk to parents, grandparents, and siblings as well; they may remember things about your early years, and also their literacy practices are valuable information. The more detailed information you gather, the easier the paper will be to write, even though you will not use all the information.

CHAPTER 4

Writing From the Vantage Point of an Outsider/Insider[*]

Xiao-ming Li
Long Island University, Brooklyn Campus

"Who are you? Are you Us or Them?" asked one reviewer of my manuscript *"Good Writing" in Cross-Cultural Context*. Her question referred to my confusing use of pronouns in the manuscript, using *we* when presenting the perspectives of the U.S. participants but referring to the same people as *they* when I was elaborating on their Chinese counterparts' views. Mulling over her question, it dawned on me that I am seen by both societies as an outsider, although I prefer to see myself as an insider to both, at least in the Chinese society. In reality, I am probably on the periphery of both worlds. In response to the reviewer's query, I wrote in the Preface:

> My first instinctive response is that I am both [us and them], for I have been educated in both countries; I have earned my spokeswomanship for both cultures by my extended and firsthand experience. Yet, on second thought, I have to say that may be I am neither. The fact is that I have always been treated as Chinese in America . . . yet when I visited China for this project I was treated as a visitor, too, showered with flawless hospitality and planned tours that were granted only to "foreign guests." This is an unnerving recognition. (Li, 1996, p. xiii)

The reviewer's question highlighted my dubious existence in U.S. academia, and, for that matter, in the world as a whole. As a non-native speaker of English who teaches English in an English speaking environment to ESL and native students alike, my cultural and linguistic identity is questionable, and so is my professional credibility. In the last

---

[*] This chapter is dedicated to Donald Murray and Tom Newkirk, who encouraged me to see myself as a good bilingualist rather than as an incompetent ventriloquist.

ten years or so, I have been struggling to find a place in a world where teaching English is seen by many as the exclusive right of
native speakers. I have found, through the writing of *Good Writing*, that hovering between two worlds is not all bad; it is a unique position, which endows me with "a rare double vision, seeing the duality of reality, the truth and untruth in each culture's claim to universal standards" (Li, 1996, p. xiii). Although our credibility and competence as English educators are put to the test every day and occasionally challenged by colleagues and students (see Braine Chap. 2, and Thomas, Chap. 1, this volume), we are compensated with a larger and richer repertoire of pedagogical, linguistic, and cultural knowledge that only between-the-worlds residents are privy to.

Quest for Authenticity

But that was not what I thought when I first came to the United States 13 years ago. Born in the People's Republic of China, I came to the United States in the summer of 1985 on a government scholarship. My college years were the time when China was going through the "Cultural Revolution"—which should be called the "anti-cultural revolution," considering its nihilistic attitude toward Chinese culture and tradition. It was a time when "doing" revolution was the only legitimate and noble ambition and other intellectual desires had to be pursued only on the sidelines, if not in secrecy. Most of our school time was devoted to reading and discussing Marx's and Mao's works, or criticizing revisionist and bourgeois ideologies around and inside us. Although I was an English major, sources for learning the language were scarce. The only source of native speech was *Linguaphone,* a British audio text, which my classmates and I listened to day after day as it was played on a bulky tape recorder, until we had memorized every minute fluctuation in the pitch and tone of the speakers. I was hungry for more. Late at night, I would turn on my little portable radio, plug in the earphones, and listen to the BBC or the Voice of America, trying to pick up some bits and pieces of "authentic English" through a thicket of interference. Several times I woke up the following morning, frightened to find that I had fallen asleep from exhaustion and forgot to turn off the radio. I had heard too many horror stories, real or fictional, of people being caught listening to "foreign radios" and denounced as counterrevolutionaries.

After 3 years as a professor at one of the largest Chinese universities, at an age when most professors in China could just sit back and watch their seniority grow, I became a master's student of linguistics at the University of New Hampshire. Sitting in the same class with bright young graduate students who had been speaking English since birth, I was not self-conscious of my skin color, although I was the only non-White in almost all my classes. But I was intensely aware of my "faulty" accent and usage of English. No matter how carefully I positioned my tongue when pronouncing those so-called apicoalveolar sounds, the tip of my tongue still naturally fell a little behind the alveolar ridge, producing a sound devoid of the crispiness that distinguishes a native speaker from a foreigner. I used *she* and *he* randomly in my speech, with little relevance to the gender of the referee, although I was fully aware that their difference was psychologically real to native speakers; it was not to me. My ego was effectively deflated when I blundered repeatedly in front of a group of 20-year-olds who uttered every syllable effortlessly with admirable precision. If only I could sound like them!

My knowledge of English idioms was another source of embarrassment. One linguistic professor, whose class I took in my first semester in the United States, liked, for some reasons, to use a stock sentence in illustrating Chomsky's transformational grammar: "The shit hit the fan." Knowing the traditional grammar very well I had little difficulty drawing those syntactic trees, but the meaning of that frequently used example forever eluded me. Finally one day, after I had heard it used at least 10 times, I summoned up enough courage and asked, "What does 'the shit hit the fan' mean? In what circumstances does that happen?" It is still a standing joke that the professor is fond of telling: "Xiao-ming asked me to explain in front of the entire class what 'the shit hit the fan' meant and how shit could hit a fan." Of course the whole class doubled up in laughter and when I later learned the answer I laughed too, with embarrassment.

Quest for the Authority Inside

After a year I was granted a teaching assistantship, which allowed me to continue my education in the United States when the scholarship from the Chinese government ran out. After I had earned a Master's degree in English Language and Linguistics, more fascinated with how the language actually works in real life than in abstract rules, I decided to pursue a Ph.D. in Composition Studies and Literature in the same department. The University of New Hampshire happens to have one of the finest programs in Composition Studies in the country. There I met Don Murray, the legendary "teacher of writers," but that was not what I thought when I first saw him. In a red sweater and with a well-trimmed snow-white beard, six feet tall and over 200 pounds, Murray looked more like a Santa Claus ready to deliver Christmas gifts. Yet gifts he was not to deliver; instead, he insisted that everyone could write and that the gift was there inside if only one were willing to reach for it. But I was not convinced: even if that were true, how could it apply to me, who did not have the "intuitive" knowledge that native speakers alone possess? But Murray, a writer rather than a linguist, did not make that distinction.

In class, we sat in a circle, some on couches and chairs, and some on the floor, in the living room of his house. Murray did not give lectures on writing or analyze model works by established authors; he asked us to write along with him. We would all free-write on a topic for some time, then read it out to the class and give off-the-cuff comments on one another's work. We would continue the project during the week and report on the progress in the next week's class, asking for feedback or help if stuck. It was more like a writers' support group than a class as I knew it. Fluency was never my strong suit when it came to writing in English, so I often opted to pass when it was my turn to read out loud, which Murray and the class sympathetically granted, but I would make up for it by writing more after the class. Murray's only requirement for that class was that the end product should be sent out for publication. Of course, that requirement would not apply to me, I thought. All my life I had written only for teachers (there were no writing classes in Chinese colleges), although I was a very good student and always loved writing.

Murray was then working on an article about his wartime experience for his weekly column, "Over Sixty," at *The Boston Globe.* Other graduate students, some full-fledged creative writers, were working on short stories, chapters of novels, journal articles, or research projects. I never perceived myself as a writer and thus had no project in mind. Murray urged me to write something about which I could write with "authority." (An author is one who is an authority on the subject being written, according to Murray. It is no accident that the Chinese language has no word that means author. *Zuojia*, the word that comes closest to it, literally means maker, aptly translated to writer.) Stroking his well-trimmed beard, Murray said, "I could write about how to trim a beard because I do it every day and am pretty good at it and probably know more about it than most people." Having no beard, never even paying much attention to my hair, I decided the only topic that I probably knew more about than most people, at least everyone in that classroom, was how U.S. idioms sounded to a Chinese ear. I listed all the idioms I had learned in two years and collected more from the class. "The shit hit the fan" was high on the list; also on the list were idioms concerning color, animals, food, and sports.

Writing with Murray, we watched how an idea evolved into paragraphs, and paragraphs grew into a first draft, and how he circled, deleted, rewrote, and moved phrases from one place to another, sometimes scrapping an entire paragraph and then restoring it later, rearranging ideas and trying different sequences. I was reminded of a weaver of bamboo mats I once saw in a free market in Shanghai. The weaver, a man in his middle age with hands dexterous as a woman's, wove and unraveled, rewove and unraveled the bamboo mat again and again until he settled for a pattern strikingly simple yet elegant. They both were craftsmen who produced with infinite attention to the overall effect as well as to each and every detail with a sharp critical eye.

Although Murray's workmanship appeared familiar, the genre in which he wrote could not be neatly placed in any category that I knew. He was not writing an editorial, for the piece was very personal, reminiscing about his days in the trenches, but it was not just autobiographical either, because it contemplated the moral and psychological fallout from a "war to end all wars." English has a name for what he writes: *essay*, which is often translated into *zawen* in Chinese. But translation is a poor cultural medium here. If an apple is ever compared to an orange, it is here. An essay, as I soon learned, concentrates on a subject of personal interest, the tone of which is often pondering, exploratory, and philosophical, as well as tentative and introspective. The essay writer abstains from adorning the writing "quaintly" or keeping a "more solemn march," according to Montaigne (1958, p. xxiii), who is widely seen as the forefather of the genre.

On the other hand, what distinguishes *zawen* is less its style or tone than its length and subject matter: the prefix, *za*, literally means miscellaneous. A *zawen* is usually short and topical. The traditional *zawen* takes the stance of an objective observer dispensing nuggets of wisdom and commentary on topics of national interest, its style much more adorned with literary and historical allusions and direct quotations from Confucius and Mencius. At the beginning of the century, *zawen* was adopted by Lu Hsun, one of the founders of Chinese modern literature, as his principal genre of writing. Since then, *zawen* has become to Lu's ardent readers, who ranged from the late Mao Tse-tung to student demonstrators in the 1980s, a literary dagger, short and sharp. Lu Hsun's *zawen*, used as an incisive weapon for lampooning the ruling class and social ills, is anything but personal or introspective.

Writing and Publishing as an Insider/Outsider

Murray's writing bears obvious Montaignesque stamps, distinctively different from Lu Hsun's *zawen*. Its language is conversational and plain yet highly polished. The essay is sprinkled with delightful turns of phrase, fresh metaphors, and sharp perceptions of seemingly mundane subjects. His unblinking gaze at the hard truth of life is mixed with a touching sensitivity. I liked that unpretentious and witty style but I did not want to go fully Montaigne or Murray for I was not entirely comfortable with sharing my personal life in public. Therefore I tempered the traditional writer's stance of an objective observer with a highly subjective and personal perspective. My tone was more playful than serious, more tentative than assertive. Here is the opening paragraph of the article:

> I started to learn English when I was 14, and taught in a distinguished Chinese university before I came to the United States. But when I got here, I discovered a new language. The words were familiar, but the meaning was far beyond my reach. People here speak a language different from the English I was taught. It is a hilarious, odd, even senseless language. (Li, 1987, p. A26)

The article, which I would not call either an essay or a *zawen*, was not introspective like an essay and was certainly not linear. It meandered around an implicit assumption that language is a window on culture. Discussing one U.S. idiom and then another, comparing their denotations and connotations with those of their Chinese counterparts, I explored the shaping force of tradition on language, and in turn, language on the user's perception. Of course, being Chinese, I could not help but allude to history:

> Yellow is a color in Chinese that either goes up to the heavens or down to the gutter, for it is associated with both nobility and pornography. The origin of the former is clear. Yellow used to be the color worn only by emperors and monks who were "the sons of Heaven." Speculation about the origin of the latter meaning is that yellow is the color that cannot be seen from a distance. People who sell pornography are criminals in China, and they prefer to conduct their business in obscurity. Yellow is, to my surprise, the color of cowardice in English. The connection is said to have originated during the French Revolution when traitors' doors were painted yellow. (Li, 1987, p. A26)

I also tried to imagine what some Chinese idioms would mean to American listeners. Here is my description of a white elephant: "A white elephant to the Chinese is a lovely and propitious creature. One of China's famous brands of battery is called 'White Elephant.' I believe this brand would not sell in an American market, for here a 'white elephant sale,' as I found, sells odd and useless things." (Li, 1987, p. A26) An U.S. friend recently told me more about white elephants than I knew when writing that article. Long ago, an Indian prince had a white elephant; being white, it was sacred. He could not use it for labor, nor could he kill it, and it cost a fortune to feed. With great fanfare, he "honored" another wealthy man by giving it to him, forcing him to spend great resources on this sacred and useless animal. Who could have imagined that a desperate nobleman could change a language forever!

As I handed in the paper at the end of the class, I was hoping that Murray would correct my writing, but he did nothing. The paper came back bare of any teacherly remarks, only his suggestion that I send it to *The Boston Globe*. That was not what I expected. I expected him to splash the paper with red ink, removing all signs of my foreign accent. I went to Murray's office and insisted on him doing that, even insinuating that he would be seen as a delinquent professor if he did not correct my errors, which I knew were plentiful. But Murray was equally adamant that he should not. What makes the piece interesting, he insisted, is your unique accent, a different perspective, and a different style and voice. And he asked why I should want to sound like an U.S. writer. He pointed out the best writers do not sound like others; they sound like no one but themselves. Actually some of the best English writers are the ones who write with an accent, he said, and he named his Yugoslavia-born poet colleague Charles Simic, another Pulitzer Prize-winning professor in the department. (Murray won the prize at a much younger age.) Unconvinced, I continued to pester Murray to go over my paper again and correct the errors. Finally, he changed a few articles and punctuation marks, but would do no more.

Although I did not get what I wanted, the idea of *voice* stayed with me. I did not quite understand its full implications at that time and have since read much criticism about it as a mythical and unscientific term, but it meant a lot to me then. Writing took on a new meaning for me. Even when I was writing in my native Chinese (as a Red Guard in the Cultural Revolution, I produced volumes of big character-posters, and when I was working on the state farm later, I was the designated writer of the production team to propagate "good deeds"), writing always resembled ventriloquism to me. To write well, I first perused the official editorial line by line to get the latest ideas and exact phrasing and then faithfully used them in my own writing. After all, the guiding principle for the country was to "unify our thinking under Mao Tse-tung Thought and the Party Central Committee." The thinking was already done for us; all we had to do was emulate. One consequence, I joked with my friends years later, was that the Chinese language was reduced to about 500 words and one red book.

Now, writing in the United States, I have to "push and knock" for words, to use a Chinese idiom, to give fitting forms to the amorphous, elusive "felt sense" that is mine alone. It is a confrontation with my inner self, mediated through words. Words, however, can often block my direct contact with my own body and mind. When I am not vigilant, clichés and jargon take over my writing; repeating the heard and familiar, after all, demands little thinking and is especially easy after years of copying the "Party line." It is particularly tempting to use fashionable jargon that gives one the illusory satisfaction of feeling sophisticated and "in." To honor one's own voice is both liberating and challenging. Each writing becomes an exploration of the world and self, and a constant wrestling with words to go beyond the ready and given. Yet the process is complicated by the fact that I am still a language learner and imitation is part of learning a new language. I have to deal with the conflicting urges within me, between seeing myself as a writer and a language learner, to write both creatively and idiomatically, and to listen to both my own voice and the tenor and tone of the new language I am learning. It is like trying to create one's own music before one has mastered all the notes. (Incidentally, ancient Chinese music was composed with five notes instead of seven.) But being a non-native speaker, I have learned, does give me the license to march to a different drum, to some extent. Actually readers usually expect my writing to be a little "off."

With Murray's repeated encouragement, I sent the article to *The Boston Globe* after the class ended. Beyond my wildest dreams, the article was published in the Feb. 1, 1987 edition of *The Boston Sunday Globe* under the title "Trying to Make Sense out of Nonsense." A few days later, I received a letter from Murray who was on vacation in Florida. Also enclosed in the envelope was a copy of that day's *Boston Globe*, which also carried his "Over Sixty" column. The letter opened with the following: "What a nice surprise to find us in the same paper. I would not have bought it down here for $2.50 if I hadn't been in it. What a bonus to meet you on A26. I hope that you are pleased." He continued, "Now that you have published in English, you can do whatever you want, articles, short stories, poems, non-fiction book, novels, plays. I can hardly wait to see what comes next." I was more than pleased. I was overwhelmed with a sense of exhilaration, as if finding a place I could claim as home in a foreign land.

Challenges and Rewards

I wish I could write a Cinderella story here in which Murray's magic wand turned me into a confident and competent writer, but the fact of the matter is that Murray had to wait for almost 10 years for my next publication. Despite my initial success, I was still embarrassed by my accent in speech and writing and was still unsure whether I could claim the title of an author. Fortunately, my dissertation adviser, Thomas Newkirk, was another professor at the University of New Hampshire who saw my status of outsider as a source of authority rather than an indication of incompetence.

When deciding on my dissertation topic, my first choice was to analyze the grammatical errors in ESL students' writing. I figured that my master's degree in linguistics and my years of error-producing and error-combating history made me very qualified to produce a handbook of some sort for ESL writing instructors. In retrospect, I perceived myself as a native informant, providing the kind of information that anthropologists would usually collect on field trips. Tom was not pleased with my choice, still less with my type casting myself as a native informant. A most congenial and amiable person, Tom was quite serious when he said to me, "How many people can move back and forth between two cultures, two languages so freely as you? You have the responsibility and a unique opportunity to introduce the Chinese experience and Chinese perspective to American educators to help expand our horizons. It is a job only you can do." Tom helped me to see something that I had overlooked in my determined and unsuccessful pursuit of perfect English: the United States has always been an aggregation of differences, a convergence of streams from all directions. As a new member of this rich and dynamic culture, I have an obligation to help expand the mainstream when immersing myself in it. I decided to focus on comparing the culturally bonded perspectives on "good writing" rather than merely compiling data.

With the help of Joseph Tobin, an anthropologist and an author of the highly acclaimed book, *Preschool in Three Cultures: Japan, China, and the United States,* I designed a "multivocal" ethnographic project for my dissertation (Tobin, Wu, & Davidson, 1989). The project involved asking 4 "key" teachers and about sixty writing teachers from China and the United States to give their comments not only on a common set of student papers but on the comments on student papers by other teachers. The participating teachers, therefore, were not just informants providing raw data for the researcher but also cultural interpolators and interpreters. The project created a multiperspective, dialogical encounter between two worlds, with me as the linguistic conduit and mediator.

To interview the key Chinese teachers, I went back to China, where I was born and grew up, but it looked strangely foreign when I first returned home. It was there that my dual identity as both insider and outsider became clear to me. Seeing so many Chinese in one place, a scene I had not witnessed for half a decade, I had the eerie feeling that I was not one of them; I was a crowd watcher who could recognize some familiar faces in the crowd but stood away from them. During my interviews, the Chinese teachers' comments sometimes jolted me back to my years in middle school, when I was reading teachers' comments on my compositions. (Because of the Cultural Revolution, I missed high school and went directly to the university as a so-called "worker-peasant-soldier" student.) The emphasis on convention, organization, poetic images, historical allusions, and moral correctness were all criteria for good writing that I was once schooled in. Yet having studied in the United States for half a decade and become versed in the process approach that Don Murray and others championed, I was aware of another set of criteria: originality, individuality, spontaneity, honesty, rationalism, and the aversion to sentimentality and didacticism. So when I was interviewing the Chinese key teachers, I raised questions about their views as my American self begged to differ. When I was interviewing the U.S. key teachers, likewise, I asked them to clarify ideas that a Chinese teacher would find puzzling. Fluent and proficient in both languages, I also understood that though some concepts could be translated into the other language, they often carried quite different meanings in the two languages. This was especially true of such basic epithets as "meaningful," "healthy," "beautiful," and "honest." Hence, I asked the interviewees to define and elaborate when they used those terms. Writing the dissertation offered me an opportunity to reexamine the underlying assumptions of some of the writing theories and practices in both countries, which I had accepted without much questioning. With the project, I began to see that the U.S. teachers' constant demand for more specifics was just as peculiar as the Chinese teachers' unfailing delight in nature-related images. They were both reasonable and arbitrary.

Professor Newkirk recommended the dissertation to the State University of New York (SUNY) Press when it was completed, and after some revision, it was published as part of the SUNY Series titled "Literacy, Culture, and Learning Theory and Practice." But before I had time to celebrate what should have been the pinnacle of my career, the book created a crisis that almost destroyed it.

By then I had been an assistant professor of English at Long Island University, Brooklyn campus, for 4 years. According to the union contract at the school, I faced a fourth-year review, and if successful, I would be granted promotion to associate professor. The department chair and a senior professor on the department review committee each observed my class. The chair wrote a very positive review of my teaching, but the senior professor, although she acknowledged the high attendance and obvious enthusiasm of the students in the class discussion, pointed out that I made some grammatical errors in my speech, sometimes omitting articles and misusing tenses. The bigger blow came when the committee, in its letter to the dean, wrote that the book was "not a scholarly publication, but rather an impressionistic, unscientific account that relies heavily on anecdotes and concluding nothing." I could not accept that verdict, for I knew that an ethnography should never be measured by positivist standards. Furthermore, I had spent 2 years doing fieldwork on a subject never researched before, engaging in vigorous data collection, screening, and analysis. The book may not be the most sophisticated and cutting-edge document, but it was a solid scholarly publication published by a university press. (I resisted using postmodern jargon in the writing, but I did incorporate some postmodern perspectives in designing the methodology.) I protested, but deep down, I felt like an impostor exposed in public after years of hiding and pretending. Maybe I should not have claimed to be an author: whatever I know about the subject, as a non-native speaker, I could not claim authority over the language.

At this juncture, the writing community rallied to my support. Professor Patricia Bizzell from Holy Cross College, Professor Nancy Lay from City College, CUNY, and my old mentor, Professor Emeritus Don Murray, sent in their letters of support, highly commending the book. Then the news came that the book was nominated and was a close second for the W. Ross Winterowd Award, a prestigious award within the profession. Based on the outside reviewers' positive assessment of the book, the Faculty Review Committee and the dean recommended me for promotion despite the negative decision of the department. In its letter of recommendation, the Faculty Review Committee wrote, "Committee members find her book to be a serious and original study that opens up the category of 'good writing' through her systematic, ethnographic research." A year later, *College English* published an enthusiastic review of the book. The reviewer, Professor Suzie Jacobs, zeroed in on my bilingualism as one of the most important factors in the book's success:

The interviews are fascinating. Not only does Li speak to all four teachers in their home territories (describing each of these places), but, given her language skill and cultural knowledge, she is able to ask the Chinese teachers questions that I believe American teachers would have asked had they been there. Likewise, she speaks to the American teachers from a Chinese perspective. (1997, p. 467–468)

The review ends with the remark, "Informed by Li's sensitivity to both cultures, this book is a gift to a community of teachers seeking cultural distance on the practice of teaching writing" (1997, p. 468).

My reaction to all these went beyond gratitude: I understand that my colleagues at Long Island University and around the country, including those I knew personally, did not think they were doing me a personal favor but were making a principled stand from their genuine belief in cultural plurality. Together they gave a strong signal of affirmation not only to me but also to all non-native speakers dedicated to English education. Coming from a different world, we bring with us a gift to our adoptive country and the country values our contribution.

As I was working on this chapter, which I had put off repeatedly, unable to wave away the shadow of self-doubt that still follows me these days, I received a letter bearing the personal signature of the president of Long Island University. The letter informs me: "At its meeting on May 5, 1998, the Board of Trustees approved a recommendation of its Academic Affairs Committee for awarding you appointment with tenure at the rank of Associate Professor in Long Island University, effective September 1, 1998." There is, after all, a place for a non-native-born English professor, a permanent place for me now. Looking back, I recognize how incredibly fortunate I have been to meet people like Don Murray and Tom Newkirk, who saw my otherness as an asset rather than a liability. But given the broad-based support I received from editors and reviewers at various institutions, I believe Murray and Newkirk, rather than being exceptions, represent the quintessential Americanism, the all embracing Whitmanesque democracy.

I would also be less than honest not to acknowledge that for an English professor not to be able to speak English impeccably is a serious impediment, much like a musician who has no ear for harmony. But John Cage's story tells me that is no reason for giving up. In his book, *Silence* (1967), Cage recalls the time when he first decided to dedicate his life to music:

After I had been studying with him for two years, Schoenberg said, "In order to write music, you must have a feeling for harmony." I explained to him that I had no feeling for harmony. He then said that I would always encounter an obstacle, that I would be as though I came to a wall through which I could not pass. I said, "In that case I will devote my life to beating my head against that wall." (p. 261)

I have always kept that story in my nearest desk drawer and read it every time my head was reeling from a bad collision. After beating his head against the wall for years, Cage emerged as a leading modern musician, credited with "emancipating contemporary American culture from the shackles of European domination . . . Even more to the point, the directional trend of influence has been reversed whereby Cage's ideas have made an irrevocable impact on European avant-garde art" (Tan, 1989, p. 34). It is interesting to note that he did that by dipping his musical bucket into the crosscurrents of the West and the East. Few of us ever dreamed of becoming a second Cage, but Cage's career offers an inspirational lesson: one who knocks his head against the wall all the time is more likely to stamp out a new trail to get around that wall. We can all try that.

References

Cage, J. (1967). *Silence: Lectures and Writings.* Middletown, CT: Wesleyan University Press.

Jacobs, S. (1997). Reflections on pedagogical study [Review of the book *"Good Writing" in Cross Cultural Context*]. *College English, 59,* 461–469.

Li, X. (1987, February 1). Trying to make sense out of nonsense. *The Boston Sunday Globe,* p. A26.

Li, X. (1996). *"Good writing" in cross-cultural context.* Albany: State University of New York Press.

Montaigne, M. De. (1958). *Essays* (J. M. Cohen, Trans.). Hammondsworth, England: Penguin Books. (Original work published 1580)

Tan, M. (1989). 'Taking a nap, I pound the rice': Eastern influences on John Cage. In R. Fleming & W. Duckworth (Eds.), *John Cage at seventy-five* (pp. 34-57). Lewisburg, PA: Bucknell University Press.

Tobin, J., Wu, D., & Davidson, D. (1989). *Preschool in three cultures: Japan, China, and the United States.* New Haven, CT: Yale University Press.

CHAPTER 5

Textual Identities:
The Importance of Being Non-Native

Claire Kramsch and Wan Shun Eva Lam
University of California-Berkeley

The controversy surrounding the respective privileges of native speakers and non-native speakers (see, for example, Kramsch, 1997) becomes moot when we deal with written language. For no one could argue that people are "born" into reading and writing; what Walter Ong has called "the technologizing of the word" (Ong, 1982) is foreign to both native and non-native speakers. Both have to be schooled into literacy and into certain types of academic literacy in order to use language in its written form. For both, the marks on the page have an opacity, a surplus of meaning that blurs the transparency of the spoken word, even if many adults have acquired the illusion that these paper traces are the exact replica of the way people speak. What distinguishes natives from non-natives is the degree of "foreignness" that the language displays when it is represented in writing, in print, or in electronic form.

What's in a Foreign Text?

Consider the following text. In his Preface to *The Order of Things*, Foucault describes a passage in Borges that shattered, as he read it, "all the familiar landmarks of his thought."

> [A] "certain Chinese encyclopaedia" in which it is written that "animals are divided into: (1) belonging to the Emperor, (b) embalmed, (c) tame, (d) sucking pigs, (e) sirens, (f) fabulous, (g) stray dogs, (h) included in the present classification, (i) frenzied, (j) innumerable, (k) drawn with a very fine camel-hair brush, (l) *et cetera*, (m) having just broken the water pitcher, (n) that from a long way off look like flies." (Foucault, 1970, p. xv)

Foucault commented:

> In the wonderment of this taxonomy, the thing we apprehend in
> one great leap, the thing that, by means of the fable, is
> demonstrated as the exotic charm of another system of thought,
> is the limitation of our own, the stark impossibility of thinking
> *that* (p. xv).

Now not every encounter with a foreign language text elicits the kind of
laughter that seized Foucault upon reading Borges' Chinese text. But this
example might help us reflect on the healthy defamiliarization that non-
native readers experience in the presence of foreign texts. The passage
above is written in standard English and is clear enough from an
informational perspective. We can look up "sucking pigs" and "sirens"
in the dictionary, and even gather background knowledge about Chinese
emperors and Chinese embalming practices. But it still will not make this
text less opaque to us. The passage is obviously about more than just the
different animals, practices, and customs of a foreign society; it offers
more than different names for its indigenous animals and things. What
the text describes is a foreign way of ordering, classifying, and
organizing the world through language. Puzzling are not the facts that
are translatable, even though rather awkwardly, into English, but the
logic of their representation on the printed page. The juxtaposition of
stray dogs and sucking pigs, of the real, the fabulous, and the pictorial, is
all the more incongruous to our way of thinking as it attempts to follow
the logical, literate, order of our Western alphabet (a) through (n). It is as
if the Borges text attempted to squeeze the logic of another people's
words, written in a distant time and place, into the logic of our own—
lighting a spark of poetic imagination together with the sudden
realization that the world may not necessarily be the way we see it. Texts
written in a foreign language may put our native world into question.

Written texts are repositories of other texts written for other
purposes and other readerships. Borges quoted this "Chinese
encyclopaedia" in Spanish to entertain his Argentinean readers, but
Foucault requoted it in French to illustrate for his French compatriots the
problematic relationship of words to things. It is once again quoted here,
this time in English, to illustrate the important role that non-nativeness
might play in the teaching of textual competence in English. Every text
bears the visible trace of history, of meanings both lost and gained in
translation. Unlike everyday conversations subjected to the pressures of
social decorum, texts can be reproduced, reread, cited, and annotated by
every user. Because a majority of ESL and EFL learners learn English
through texts of various sorts, it should be interesting to examine what
role textuality plays in the native non-native relationship and what effect

written language has on the development of a learner's social and cultural identity.

The Textual Identity of the Non-Native Speaker

In a widely cited article, Peirce (1995) described a study she conducted on recent immigrants at Ontario College in Newtown, Canada. After having taught a 6-month ESL course, Peirce went on to study five of the women participants over a period of 12 months. The women were asked to keep records of their interactions with anglophone Canadians and to write diaries in which they would reflect on their language learning experiences in the home, workplace, and community. The study also made use of written questionnaires and of individual and group interviews. Peirce found in the written testimonies evidence of a complex relation between social identity, personal investment, and language learning, and of the admirable ability of some of the women immigrants, such as Martina from the Czech Republic, to capitalize on their multiple identities to make their voices heard in Canadian society.

However, one important aspect of this study has been little commented upon: for a whole year, these women engaged in a highly literate reflection on themselves and their relation to the English language. The awareness of their multiple identities as immigrants, mothers, wives, workers, and learners, came to them through writing. Let us look, for example, at Martina's March 8, 1991, diary entry, as cited by Peirce:

> The first time I was very nervous and afraid to talk on the phone. When the phone rang, everybody in my family was busy and my daughter had to answer it. After ESL course when we moved and our landlords tried to persuade me that we have to pay for whole year, I got upset and I talked with him on the phone over one hour and I didn't think about the tenses rules. I had known that I couldn't give up. My children were very surprised when they heard me. (1995, p. 22)

This diary entry not only describes the event but gives it a meaning that might be different from the one Martina experienced only confusedly at the moment. A telephone call experienced in a particular context acquires another logic when it gets languaged after the fact in a diary entry destined to be read by a researcher who had also been Martina's ESL teacher. This is not to say that Martina is not "telling the truth," only that her written text constructs, narrows down, clarifies, and focuses the truth of the event in quite a different manner than it was lived at the time. An oral rendition of the same story might have also put the accents quite differently from what we now see on the page.

For example, the coordinating conjunction between the two clauses "I talked with him on the phone over one hour *and* I did not think about the tenses rules" effectively juxtaposes and links pragmatic need (first clause) and formal grammar (second clause), the rules of political power and the rules of linguistic usage, Martina as tenant and Martina as learner of English. In essence, what Martina's text states is: "Although my use of past tenses is mostly correct in this diary entry, tenses didn't really matter in my altercation with my landlord. ESL courses might be as important in helping you stand up to your landlord as in teaching you the rules of the English language." What is interesting is that Martina voices here in near correct English the futility of English grammar and wields English grammar to denounce the abuses made by landlords through the medium of English grammar. Indeed, apart from the incorrect "I had known," her diary entry makes skillful use of English syntax to interpret her experience and impose that interpretation on the researcher.

To cite another example, the choice of information structure in the sentence—positive information ("I talked with him over one hour") followed by negative information ("and I didn't think about the tenses rules")—is a choice made by Martina as a writer, who thereby manages to highlight her pride in her achievement in such a way that the reader cannot but interpret the "and" as a concessive ("in spite of the fact that") rather than as an additive conjunction. Had she written "I talked with him on the phone over one hour, but my English grammar was incorrect because I was so upset," the reader might interpret Martina's entry not as a triumphant feat of self-assertion but as a failure to live up to the standards set by her ESL teacher. By crafting her English sentences the way she did, Martina crafted a self she would live by in the real world of landlords, employers, and bureaucrats. Indeed, the interpretation given by Peirce of the exchange between Martina and her landlord relies among other things on the implicit causal link expressed by the information structure of Martina's diary entry. Peirce writes: "Martina had to [defend the family's rights against unscrupulous social practices] . . . *regardless of her command of the English tense system*" (1995, p. 22, our emphasis). The use of regardless here picks up on the implicature entailed by Martina's and in her diary entry.

We would like to argue that writing was a decisive factor in the way Martina got a handle on the events of her life in Canada. By representing lived experience in the public form of a diary for the benefit of the researcher, Martina developed a social persona that evidently enabled her to assert herself in Canadian society (see, for instance, Luke, 1996). This self-representation is not a natural process of familiarization with the spoken style of native speakers; it is associated with the highly self-conscious, rhetorical use of the foreign language by a non-native who, by appropriating for herself a language she views as foreign, actualizes on paper a social reality that was only potentially there. Martina's experience is similar in this regard to that of Rodriguez, who writes in *Hunger of Memory* (1992) that "I became a man by becoming a public man (p. 7) . . . I sit here in silence writing this small volume of words, and it seems to me the most public thing I ever have done . . . I am making my personal life public" (p. 177). Like Rodriguez, it is by creating a textual identity for herself that Martina develops the successful personal and social identity necessary to survive in the new country.

Of course, the power of the written word to change attitudes and mind-sets is not inherent in the English language. One could argue that Martina's written narrative seems to echo prior narratives of individual self-assertion and survival in the face of societal odds—heroic narratives that are all too familiar to native speakers of English raised on *The Little Engine that Could* and later on *Star Wars*. By writing, and thus imposing meaning and value on a multifarious and often contradictory flow of experienced events, Martina, one could argue, falls prey to the dominant belief, very often expressed through the English language, in the ability of the individual to change herself and others through sheer moral determination and free will. Writing is no insurance against conformity to a dominant ideology.

But, then, the English language is also the language of less individualistic, heroic narratives like those of Salman Rushdie, Woyle Soyinka, or Chinua Achebe, who write English counternarratives of sorts. These and other non-native writers stretch the limits of the sayable in the foreign tongue. For example, the immigrant Italian writer Gino Chiellino, writing in German in Germany, is eloquent about the increasing number of foreign writers in Germany:

> Perhaps these authors write in German because they need to find another "German" language, a language not available in contemporary German, in order to write about what they experience in the foreign culture. This point seems to be quite significant, much more so than secondary literature or criticism have been willing or able to recognize (1995, p. 44) . . . It is only by maintaining his or her difference that the foreign author writing in German can contribute to dislocating the German language. [Comment by my German editor: according to the

dictionary, 'to dislocate' is to 'radically disrupt.' Surely that is not a desirable goal. I suggest 'contribute to extending the boundaries of national goals!"] (p. 28).

What writing can do is hold together, without resolving it, the fundamental tension inherent in the non-native writing condition: the adherence to correct English usage *and* the refusal to abide by any one "correct" norm of use. The building of textual homes is not given with the mastery of the English syntax; it is a subversive art, to be acquired and developed.

Building Textual Homes

Martina's languaging experience as a diary writer is eventually the stuff that literature is made of, especially literary works written by poets and novelists who write in a language that is foreign to them. In her widely acclaimed autobiography *Lost in Translation* (1989), the Polish immigrant to Canada Eva Hoffman writes about the potential generative powers of the foreign language diary. Caught in the dilemma between writing in Polish—"the language of [her] untranslatable past," and English—the language of her current school exercises, she finally opts for English.

> If I'm to write about the present, I have to write in the language of the present, even if it's not the language of the self . . . The diary is an earnest attempt to create a part of my persona that I imagine I would have grown into in Polish. In the solitude of this most private act, I write, in my public language, in order to update what might have been my other self. The diary is about me and not about me at all . . . I learn English through writing, and, in turn, writing gives me a written self . . . For a while, this impersonal self, this cultural negative capability, becomes the truest thing about me. When I write, I have a real existence that is proper to the activity of writing—an existence that takes place midway between me and the sphere of artifice, art, pure language. This language is beginning to invent another me. (p. 121)

This "me" is quite different from that of a familiar user of the language, unless that user has consciously defamiliarized his or her own language, as poets are wont to do. The experience of foreignness, of what Bakhtin called "outsideness" or "transgredience," is so much a condition of creativity (Holquist, 1990, p. 26) that some writers even tend to cultivate it as a kind of voluntary linguistic exile.

Voluntary exile? Does not this sound like a contradiction in terms? True, according to the dictionary, exile means "punishment or expulsion from one's native land by authoritative decree" and can therefore hardly be voluntary. And yet, this apparent contradiction might reveal the potential of written language for being a kind of third place, a "tierce place" (Serres, 1991, p. 78), that non-native speakers can create to express meanings not usually found under the pen of native writers. For example, a non-native writer might write about exile and not mean involuntary expulsion but rather a conscious refusal to take roots, a creative need for distance from both one's native language and the foreign tongue as it is used by native speakers. Sebbar described this exile as follows:

> If I speak of exile, it is the only place from where I can speak the contradictions, the division . . . the cultural crossings; I live, I write, in these points of juncture or disjuncture, so how could I decline a simple identity . . . I am a French writer, with a French mother and an Algerian father, and the topics of my books are not my identity; they are the signs of my history as a hybrid, as a mestizo, obsessed by the surrealist encounter of the Other and the Same, by the cross . . . between tradition and modernity, between East and West. (Sebbar & Huston, 1986, p. 126; our translation)

About her diary writing, she writes: "Here is for me, and without my having neither sought it nor provoked it . . . the tangible, concrete, materially voluptuous sign of exile." (Sebbar & Huston, 1986, p. 9; our translation). Some non-native writers of English, like the Irishman Joyce or the Nigerian Soyinka, express their own "exiled" perspective by stretching English lexicon and syntax to the limits of the intelligible.

A third place is thus an eminently relational concept, suspended between irreconcilable polarities. It is carved out here by the creative act of writing. Hoffman describes this place as the awareness that comes from the double tension between the standard English idiom spoken by native speakers and her writing in that language:

> Refracted through the double distance of English and writing, this self—my English self—becomes oddly objective; more than anything, it perceives. It exists more easily in the abstract sphere of thought and observations than in the world. . . . It seems that when I write (or, for that matter, think) in English, I am unable to use the word "I." I do not go as far as the schizophrenic "she"—

but I am driven, as by a compulsion, to the double, the Siamese-twin "you." (Hoffman, 1989, p. 121)

This in-between place should not be viewed as the static synthesis of what immigrants brought along with them and what they found in the new country, but a constantly maintained sense of difference. As Chiellino states, "Difference is the source of creativity which is lost as soon as the boundary between the familiar and the foreign is blurred" (1995, p. 51).

Textual Identities of the Third Kind

We have seen that textuality itself can serve as a catalyst for expressing thoughts and experiences unique to the non-native speaker and to his or her place between native and non-native cultures. Writing can be a rich, painful, and exhilarating experience that can help define the relationship of non-native writers to their native speaking environment.

We now turn to the effect that written texts can have on the social and cultural identity of non-native readers. In the following, we consider in some detail the case of an immigrant adolescent to the United States.[1]

Willis, a 16-year-old high school junior, emigrated from Hong Kong to California with his parents and his older sister before Hong Kong reverted to Mainland China. When asked about his immigration experience, Willis said that "his family's identity[2] had fallen" after immigration because of their lack of fluency in English: "We don't know how to talk." However, coming to live in the United States provided more political security for his family and educational opportunities for himself, he said.

Willis' schooling experiences were not without obstacles. Like many other immigrant students in the United States, he felt marginalized both academically and socially in school (Olsen, 1995). When he entered

---

[1] This forms part of an ongoing study on the cross-cultural literacy practices of immigrant adolescents in the United States. We wish to thank Willis for the insights we have gained from his testimony.

[2] The use of the term *identity* in the mouth of a recent adolescent immigrant might be surprising. Willis has obviously projected on that fashionable term the loss of pride, the disorientation, and the humiliations endured by new immigrants to a foreign country.

middle school, he was placed in a low-level class after being tested on English and Chinese. Although he did well on the Chinese part, his poor English assessment results led him into a very elementary class with other immigrant students, where, he said, he learned nothing at all for an entire year. After four years of ESL and bilingual programs, Willis transferred to the regular classes.

He mentioned that he once fought with the school counselor to get into the regular and honors classes; the counselor had originally placed him in some ESL sheltered classes for the convenience of scheduling. He said he was afraid that having too many sheltered classes on his transcript would affect future college admission. He was also taking a number of literature classes because, he said, he had been taunted by his peers for being an ESL student for too long and he had to catch up.

On several occasions, he expressed anger over how some students laughed at him and other Chinese immigrants for their heavy accents and lack of fluency in English and tried to imitate their speech disparagingly. He described the experience of one of his classmates:

> Like Feng Jin, he is in 12th grade. He always speaks Chinese, and he speaks English with a heavy accent. He doesn't read very well in English, but it's not really that bad. But then, those people always laugh at him, and imitate his voice, and they imitate in a really disgusting way. He is actually very angry with them, but he always tries hard to keep it down. He has told me, "When it gets to a point I can't stand it any more, I'm gonna knock them over real bad."[3]

Willis added that it was because of this discrimination that Chinese did not mix well with their English-speaking U.S. peers. Although he had made great leaps in his studies, he did not participate much in the social life of the school. He was unable to make friends with students from other races in the classrooms or school clubs; he only made friends with other Asians. One of his favorite pastimes outside school was reading comic books, especially Japanese comics, which could take up most of his evenings at home and night trips on the city buses.

The Japanese comic books that Willis and some of his Chinese peers read were translated into Chinese and copyrighted in Hong Kong. The

---

[3] All quotations of Willis' words are excerpts from recorded conversations and interviews conducted with Eva Lam originally in Cantonese. Italicized words are code-switches to English by Willis himself; CAPS indicate emphatic stress.

trading and circulation of comic books among these teenagers is a frequent practice, although the amount of personal possession of comics varies from person to person. Willis had one of the largest collections of comic books among his peers and was often sought for borrowing. In his judgement, both the ideas and artistic quality of the Japanese comics were superior to those in the United States and Hong Kong. He had started taking some Japanese language classes offered in his high school in anticipation of reading the comics in their original version.

An analysis of the translated Japanese comic books shows a cross-cultural mixture of signs and images. As a text that originates in Japanese society, the Japanese comics undoubtedly encode many of the beliefs, values, behaviors, and material conditions of Japanese life. These appear, for example, in the titles of people (part of Japanese honorifics), the terminology for different social institutions (such as schools and government offices), and the untranslated written artifacts in the stories (receipts and bulletins, for example). However, in their Chinese translation, these inscriptions of Japanese culture are shadowed by the Chinese cultural resonances signified in the Chinese linguistic code. Although much of the translation is in standard written Chinese, it is also interspersed with a considerable amount of Cantonese vernacular language because Hong Kong is the main market for such comics. Moreover, in many of these books, different types of Westernized or Americanized images appear in parts of the texts—in English words in the table of contents, in the sketches of the authors and characters (one picture shows the author with a cup of coffee and a donut in hand), and in the contents and settings of the stories (one story depicts a group of teenagers performing a Western drama in a European-style mansion in Japan). Hence, the Chinese version of Japanese comics, as a hybrid textual form, constitutes a transnational popular youth culture that is as intriguing and pleasurable in its multiple layers of meaning as Borges' Chinese encyclopedia translated from the Spanish into French.

The distribution of different varieties of comics across national boundaries have, on the one hand, generated a high degree of cross-cultural exchange and fusion, and, on the other, facilitated a process of sociocultural critique through the comparison and contrast of different national varieties. Willis' reading of Japanese comics and his critical comparison of comics across cultures (discussed later) were situated within the larger social practice of reading comics of both the United States and Hong Kong varieties among his peers on both sides of the Pacific.

On several occasions, during both casual conversations and more focused interviews, Willis contrasted the different varieties of comics on the professional attitude, creativity, artistry, and cultural character of the people who produced them. He mentioned how, compared to the artistic design of the Japanese comics, those in Hong Kong were lower in quality due to their pursuit of quick profits:

> The difference between the comics of the Hong Kong people and the Japanese people is in the BACKGROUND. Those [artists] who are well-known in Japan are never so lazy [sloppy]. But those in Hong Kong, because they want to turn things out really fast, so they are more lazy.

As for the U.S. comics, Willis criticized them for their extreme self-glorification and lack of creativity:

> I really don't appreciate those, because . . . their heroes seem like they will never, never be defeated, even if they are beaten up like CRAZY . . . in several episodes, in the end they are bound to win again . . . Even if they have *tragedy ending*, they will still make themselves . . . very ARROGANT. Like *"X-man," "Swamps,"* *"Spiderman," "Batman,"* I can't bear to read them . . . What the Americans come up with are only . . . if it is not about the hero saving the pretty girl, then it is about . . . victory and glory. And no matter what, they are fighting all over the place and beating up one another . . . And they make THEMSELVES, THEMSELVES . . . the heroes. For example, the United States has also a produced a version of the *"Streetfighter"* [comic and video game, original version from Japan]. The main character in the *"Streetfighter"* isn't *Gaile*—seems like it should be *Waile*, a Japanese fellow. They [Americans] make *Gaile* the main character, the strongest one in the whole *story*, and how he is *hero*, things like that.

By contrast, in talking about Japanese comics, Willis mentioned a list of distinguishing characteristics—creativity, variety, educational quality, poignancy—that he could identify with and quite strongly desired.

> After reading them, you want to follow them . . . For example, like when I saw "Ding Dong" [Japanese comic book] . . . if I had this Ding Dong (chuckles), I could even control the world. What I'm saying is you fantasize together with the book . . . there are things you can think about. And sometimes there are books which contain some lessons in them, some educational stuff . . . Those books sometimes teach you perhaps not to be greedy, or, uh, uh, to be more kind to others, not to be arrogant, stuff like

that. Sometimes they would . . . like "Kam Tin Yat"[4] . . . after reading it, you will feel that you can think more. Those books would sometimes talk about some FACTS. I mean, like those things you don't usually learn at school, you can sometimes learn from reading those books . . . Those that fantasize oneself as the hero, although I haven't really done so myself. But, but those can be, uh, pretty *attractive* too . . . And their stories are a lot more attractive. They have some that are really intriguing. And some are . . . as you read it, you feel a little sad, and things like that. How will you ever feel sad when you read *"X-men?"* One falls dead and another rushes up, one falls dead and another rushes up. That's the difference.

A closer look at Willis' discourse on comics shows us how each text positions Willis differently as a reader and offers him a different sociocultural identity. His use of personal pronouns is one way in which he indexes his relationship to American and Hong Kong cultures. The use of third-person collective pronominal forms—"they" and "those people" to designate the people in Hong Kong, "they" and "themselves" to designate the Americans—set both up as distinct objects of criticism. The repeated and emphatic stress on the reflexive pronoun "themselves" serves to accentuate the self-centeredness and self-aggrandizement of the American psyche. While Willis is distancing himself from these two groups through third person pronouns, he identifies himself with other readers of Japanese comics through the use of second and first person pronouns. These pronouns express a distinct personal relationship to the Japanese experience as illustrated in the Japanese comics.

The different social realities depicted in these comics are revealed through Willis' use of modality. The hype of American rhetoric resonates through his use in Cantonese of emphatic modifiers such as "very," "usually," "never," and the superlatives "strongest" and "greatest." Such modifiers give a factual and categorical quality to his statements. The automaticity, almost robot-like behavior of American characters is also emphasized through the repetition of words and phrases, such as "beaten up like crazy" and "one falls dead and another rushes up." In contrast to these, Willis' description of Japanese comics is much more nuanced. Here, modal auxiliaries and adverbs "could," "would,"

---

[4] The teenage male protagonist in one of Willis' favorite Japanese comic series. Though branded as a poor student in school, Kam Tin Yat is able to demonstrate his intelligence and passion for justice in solving many puzzling criminal cases.

"sometimes," "perhaps," and the conditional "if" ("if I had this Ding Dong"), serve to create a relativized world of possibility and human contingency; the verb "want" ("you want to follow them") expresses Willis' desire to make this possibility a reality.

By projecting himself into the textual community of the Japanese comics, Willis, a non-native reader, has discovered a new self aligned with what he perceives as the Japanese "hero," distanced from both the American and the Hong Kong "heroes." Comparing the depictions of heroes in the different societies, Willis said:

> The U.S. [hero] is the most . . . upright and courageous one. There are the good guys and the bad guys, and nothing else. The ones in Hong Kong, there is this group and that group, the good guys and bad guys, and some sort of in-between . . . As for the Japanese characters, they won't be drawn . . . all handsome and stuff. They have some who are ugly, silly, and tall, and short. The American ones are like . . . if you are not smart enough you are ruled out of the game, that's what is in the story . . . The Japanese hero . . . like "Kam Tin Yat," you can hardly call him a hero . . . He sometimes acts like an idiot and does some stupid things, like he would trip over while walking along the street (laughs) . . . I can't imagine the U.S. will produce a character like that, almost impossible.

It is clear that Willis found the Japanese notion of *hero* in the texts he read more appealing than in either the United States or the Hong Kong counterparts. Indeed, Willis' difficulty in equating the Japanese male protagonist with the U.S. English word *hero* harks back to the difficulties we had at the beginning of this chapter in fitting Borges' taxonomy into our cognitive and linguistic categories; it echoes the qualms of non-native writers like Eva Hoffman trying to fit her non-native experiences into the language of English native speakers. Here, whereas the nature of the Hong Kong hero is nondescript (possibly reflecting the lack of clear status and autonomy of Hong Kong society), and the U.S. hero is the quintessential good guy with a standard form and character (suggesting perhaps the monolithic construction of a U.S. national culture that marginalizes what it views as "other"), Willis sees the Japanese hero as the common folk, the less than perfect people, who live through predicaments in life with thoughtfulness and a sense of humor. Willis' place is indeed an in-between place. Between the impossibility of identifying with the native Hong Kong person he used to be, and his refusal to identify with the standardized U.S. person whose English he now speaks, Willis finds his place, as a non-native, among the common folk hero in the textual world of Japanese comics.

The role of reading and writing in the social construction of self has been pointed out in a growing body of research on literacy practices in the native language (see, for example, Cherland, 1994; Mahiri & Sablo, 1997). These studies show how people represent themselves or develop certain kinds of ethnic or gendered identity through the practices of reading and writing in their first language within a given society. In Willis' case, his identity was constructed intertextually, through the reading of popular cultural texts from Hong Kong, the United States, and Japanese societies of which he was variously a native and a non-native participant. As Fiske noted, the meanings of popular texts are created intertextually; they occur "at the moment of reading where the social relationships of the reader meet the discursive structure of the text" (Fiske, 1989, p. 122). Willis' reading practice is situated in a larger transnational discourse of comics that allows for the juxtaposition of different world views and social practices. The global circulation of cultural forms has resulted in an interpenetration of the global and the local (Appadurai, 1996; Wilson & Dissanayake, 1996), where the self is now fashioned from the "flow of [global and local] signs and images which saturate the fabric of everyday life in contemporary society" (Featherstone, 1992, p. 168). And the imagination has become an important site where people find their mode of cultural belonging. As Grossberg said recently: "It is not *where* people belong that is important, but *how* people belong—the various ways people are attached and attach themselves affectively into the world" (1997). For Willis, this attachment occurred through what we could call the "textual home" of a global popular culture.

Willis' participation in the popular discourse of comics was both a private enjoyment and a claim for a public persona. As a non-native reader, he appropriated a textual identity from the Japanese comics, and used it as a third place from which to reflect in an official interview with the researcher on the cultural practices of both the United States and Hong Kong societies. By creating this position for himself, Willis was able to verbalize the arbitrary nature of the linguistic and cultural norms of the two societies.

Conclusion

In this chapter we explored the potential of written texts to help non-native speakers define their relation toward the native speakers whose language they are using and to offer them what we called "textual identities of the third kind."

The frustrations and humiliations experienced by immigrants like Martina and Willis and the eventual sense of pride they gained by writing and reading texts in the foreign language were echoed and confirmed in the autobiographies of professional non-native writers like Eva Hoffman, Leila Sebbar, and others. What all these experiences had in common was first, the sense of security that the written medium provides non-native speakers. Unlike the evanescent spoken word with its social pressure to conform and its highly conventionalized rituals of everyday life that might make non-native speakers the targets of scorn and ridicule, the written word offers them the possibility of expressing and reflecting upon their unique experience as immigrants or foreigners. In addition, texts have the power to give them a public voice that may be distinct from both their native, private voice, and the dominant discourse of the native-speaking majority. Finally, written texts offer non-native speakers opportunities for finding textual homes outside the boundaries of local or national communities. The uses of literacy in today's global, multicultural economy are likely to alter our notions of who is native and who is non-native. Indeed they make non-nativeness in the sense of "outsideness" one of the most important criteria of creativity and innovation.

If reading and writing are meant primarily to help learners develop a secure, public persona and to give them access to a larger community of text producers and consumers through the medium of English as an International Language, it is important that language teachers themselves cultivate both an insider's and an outsider's attitude toward English, whether they be native or non-native speakers of the language. Such a position of defamiliarization in Foucault's sense, of "exile" in Sebbar's words, implies a tension between the standardized, native norms of the English language and the ability of the non-native writer/reader to see through these norms and to test their limits. Rather than being used primarily for socializing the non-natives into the ways of the standardized natives, the written language can offer the opportunity to express human thoughts and feelings that non-native speakers have experienced particularly acutely. It is in such textual spaces that native and non-native users of English may encounter one another and discover that they are all, in fact, "foreigners to themselves" (Kristeva, 1988/1991).

References

Appadurai, A. (1996). *Modernity at large: Cultural dimensions of globalization.* Minneapolis: University of Minnesota Press.

Cherland, M. R. (1994). *Private practices: Girls reading fiction and constructing identity.* London: Taylor & Francis.

Chiellino, G. (1995). *Fremde. Discourse on the Foreign.* Toronto, Canada: Guernica.

Featherstone, M. (1992). Postmodernism and the aestheticization of everyday life. In S. Lash & J. Friedman (Eds.), *Modernity and identity* (pp. 265–290). Oxford, England: Blackwell.

Fiske, J. (1989). *Understanding popular culture.* Boston: Unwin Hyman.

Foucault, M. (1970). *The order of things. An archaeology of the human sciences* (Trans.) New York: Random House. (Original work published 1966)

Grossberg, L. (1997, May). *Globalization, media, and agency.* Paper given at the transnational and transdisciplinary workshop on the Relocation of Languages and Cultures at Duke University, Durham, NC.

Hoffman, E. (1989). *Lost in translation.* New York: Penguin.

Holquist, M. (1990). *Dialogism: Bakhtin and his world.* London: Routledge.

Kramsch, C. (1997). The privilege of the non-native speaker. *PMLA, 112* (3), 359–369.

Kristeva, J. (1988/1991). *Strangers to ourselves* (L. S. Roudiez, Trans.). New York: Columbia University. (Original work published 1988)

Luke, A. (1996). Genres of power? Literacy education and the production of capital. In G. William & R. Hasan (Eds.), *Literacy in society* (pp. 308–338). New York: Longman.

Mahiri, J., & Sablo, S. (1997). Writing for their lives: The non-school literacy of California's urban African American youth. *Journal of Negro Education, 65,* 164–180.

Olsen, L. M. (1995). *From nation to race: The Americanization of immigrants in the high school of the 1990s.* Unpublished doctoral dissertation, University of California, Berkeley.

Ong, W. J. (1982). *Orality and literacy: The technologizing of the word.* London: Methuen.

Peirce, B. N. (1995). Social identity, investment, and language learning. *TESOL Quarterly, 29,* 9–32.

Rodriguez, R. (1982). *Hunger of memory.* Boston: Godline.

Sebbar, L., & Huston, N. (19–86). *Lettres parisiennes.* [Parisian letters]. Paris: Barrault.

Serres, M. (1991/1997). *The troubadour of knowledge* (S. F. Glaser & W. Paulson, Trans.). Ann Arbor: University of Michigan Press. (Original work published 1991)

Wilson, R., & Dissanayake, W. (Eds.). (1996). *Global, local: Cultural production and the transnational imaginary.* Durham, NC: Duke University Press.

PART TWO

Sociopolitical Concerns

It was stated in the Introduction that no issue is more troubling to NNSs teaching in ESL contexts than that of discrimination in employment. Originating with the Makarere Conference tenet that the ideal English teacher is a native speaker (the "native speaker fallacy") and continued by the Chomskyan notion of the native speaker as an ideal informant on a language, the discrimination faced by NNSs in employment is also being justified under the pretext that ESL students prefer to be taught by NSs.[1] Despite the ineffectiveness of so-called Native English Speaker or Expatriate Teacher programs, the preference for NS teachers is evident in EFL contexts, too (see Boyle, 1997, for a critique of the Expatriate English Teachers Scheme in Hong Kong).

In addition to discrimination in employment, NNSs also face numerous other challenges. Their credentials from the Periphery are questioned, their accents are derided, and they are often marginalized in the profession.

In Chapter 6, Suresh Canagarajah unravels the causes and consequences of the native speaker fallacy in order to understand it from a larger social perspective. Tracing the marginalization of speakers of other Englishes in the TESOL profession to the fallacy, Canagarajah first examines the linguistic basis of the fallacy by critiquing its Chomskyan origins and arguing for new terminology to reflect the linguistic competence of postcolonial English speakers. He also questions the application of the fallacy to ESL pedagogy, pointing out that a knowledge of other languages (by NNS teachers) can foster more effective language teaching. Canagarajah then explores the political implications of the fallacy in the context of "English only" ideologies,

---

[1] However, if the preference of students is the criterion for employing ESL teachers in the United States, then southern and midwestern males should probably be the preferred types. In a study of learner attitudes toward regional accents, males with southern or midwestern accents scored higher than northern males and females from the north, the south, and midwest on a variety of characteristics ranging from "very intelligent" to "professional" and "extrovert" (Alford & Strother, 1990).

"Standard English," and difficulties faced by Periphery teachers in finding employment in the Center. He then discusses the irony of Periphery teachers trained in the Center being denied employment whereas Center teachers have near free access to jobs in the Periphery. Further discussing the political implications of the native speaker fallacy, Canagarajah shows how the fallacy prevents Periphery teachers from developing their expertise in accordance with local needs because expertise in ELT is closely associated with NSs, and how the fallacy affects auxiliary services such as the production of textbook and teaching aids. In conclusion, Canagarajah advocates a reconfiguration of the relationship between Periphery and Center ELT professionals. Using linguistics theories, pedagogical approaches, and his personal experience, and writing in his usual incisive style, Canagarajah exposes the hidden economic, ideological, and political reasons that underlie the NS-NNS division.

In the next chapter, Nuzhat Amin states that little attention has been paid to how the race, ethnicity, culture, and gender of teachers impact on the classroom. She claims that critical theory in ESL is written from the viewpoint of White teachers. Positioning herself as an immigrant woman teacher from a minority group, Amin argues that the native speaker construct acts in concert with sexism and racism to disempower such teachers in Canada. Based on her interviews with minority women teachers of ESL who were recent immigrants to Canada, Amin claims that Canadian ESL students make two major assumptions of the ideal ESL teacher. The first is that only Whites can be native speakers of English and the second is that only NSs know proper Canadian English. Amin argues that the concept of the NS as White influences all aspects of Canadian ESL programs and, because most ESL teachers are women, this is an issue of greater concern to women than men. Citing a study of six leading Canadian newspapers that showed that there was little neutral coverage of minorities, Amin argues that this is an indication of the dominant (White) groups' negative perception of minorities in Canada, a perception that has been passed to ESL students.

In Chapter 7, Masaki Oda switches the focus of the discussion from the Center to the Periphery, taking a closer look at how NSs from the Center extend their influence to ELT professional organizations in the Periphery. Oda describes how some ELT organizations and affiliates in non-English speaking countries, such as the Japan Association for Language Teaching (JALT), perpetuate the dominant role of NSs in the profession to the extent that English-speaking monolinguals are more highly valued, and thus given more power, than local (bilingual) professionals. Oda closely examines JALT's officers' duties and its conduct of elections and conferences, award of grants, and decision making to show how the discourse is dominated by monolingual English NSs. Oda also reports on a survey conducted among 29 TESOL affiliates in EFL countries and shows that, although 81% of their membership consists of NNSs, twice as many (expatriate) NSs are represented in their decision-making bodies than local NNSs. In these affiliates, the language used for communication, business meetings, and the election of officers is also mainly English. Oda concludes his chapter with a discussion of language and power within the ELT profession and argues that the power imbalance between the NS and NNS membership will have negative effects on the ELT profession.

References

Alford, R., & Strother, J. (1990). Attitudes of native and nonnative speakers toward selected regional accents of U.S. English. *TESOL Quarterly, 24,* 479–495.

Boyle, J. (1997). Native-speaker English teachers in Hong Kong. *Language and Education, 11,* 163–181.

CHAPTER 6

Interrogating the "Native Speaker Fallacy": Non-Linguistic Roots, Non-Pedagogical Results

A. Suresh Canagarajah
Baruch College of the City University of New York

Surfing absentmindedly through the electronic forum for second language teachers (TESL-L) one day, I was struck by a desperate e-mail from a Korean graduate student. She said, "I am finishing my MA in TESL at the end of this semester at xxx University in Boston, and I hope to return to my country. But I cannot hope to find a teaching position back home. They don't hire non-native speakers. What are the prospects for finding jobs here in the United States? Can someone give me some clues about job openings here?" I knew the sad reality of the job market in the United States and considered it kindness not to reply. I could only imagine her consternation when even in the West, advertisement after advertisement confronts her with the fact that only those who are "native English speakers" or those with "native English competence" can apply for the available positions. Fresh from graduate school, certified with a Masters or a doctorate in applied linguistics, and groomed for a career in language teaching by a reputed university, the non-native ESL teacher often discovers a gloomy professional future.

This story confronts us with the absurdity of an educational system that prepares one for a profession for which it disqualifies the person at the same time. There are many ironies and contradictions here. Why would an educational system train someone painstakingly for a job it considers unsuitable by its own definition of the ideal English instructor? Why would an educational system teach current linguistic axioms in its course work (i.e., that the superiority of dialects is a nonlinguistic issue and that matters of accent and even pronunciation are surface structure features that do not indicate one's competence in the grammatical deep structure of the language), only to refuse to implement these in its employment practices? At a time when graduate programs in TESOL are a booming business enterprise with students from many countries trained in the West for a life in the teaching profession, such gatekeeping practices in employment raise disturbing questions. With the TESOL convention choosing "Connecting our Global Community" as its theme for 1998 and the ESOL establishment actively expanding its organizational base to the remotest parts of the world, the professional status of speakers of other Englishes remains an embarrassing contradiction to resolve. When teachers from other English speech communities are marginalized professionally, the global claims of the TESOL establishment raise much suspicion.

The notion that the ideal teacher of English is a native speaker of that language is labeled by Phillipson (1992) the "native speaker fallacy." As in other applied linguistic concepts, this notion too may be provided impressive linguistic or pedagogical justifications backed by empirical research evidence. I discuss why these purported reasons do not hold water and how this notion in fact constitutes a fallacy. I proceed to argue that there are hidden economic, ideological, and political motivations that underlie this widespread assumption. Any attempt to reconfigure the relationship between the native and non-native speaker professionals in ELT has to first grapple with these nonlinguistic and nonpedagogical motivations. My aim in this chapter is to unravel the nexus of causes and consequences of the native speaker fallacy in order to understand it from a larger sociopolitical perspective. I go on to articulate the pedagogical and linguistic strengths non-native speaker teachers bring to the profession and the domains in which their expertise may be indispensable.

The Linguistics of This Fallacy

Noam Chomsky's linguistic concepts lie at the heart of the discourse that promotes the superiority of the native speaker teacher. The Chomskyan notion that the native speaker is the authority on the language and that he or she is the ideal informant provides an understandable advantage to the native speaker in grammaticality judgments. However, the very label native speaker is questionable. With the existence of indigenized variants of English developed in postcolonial communities, many here would consider themselves native speakers of these Englishes. Some in these communities acquire English (as a first language) simultaneously with one or more other local languages to develop a fascinating multilingual competence. These are native speakers of English—just as they are native speakers of one or more local languages. To use the terminology developed by Hamers and Blanc (1989), we may call them *balanced bilinguals* who have acquired *simultaneous bilingualism* in a case of *childhood bilinguality*. That is, these speakers have acquired two or more languages in parallel since their earliest days of linguistic development with an almost equal level of competence in the respective languages. We must also acknowledge the fact that many in postcolonial communities speak English as the dominant or sole language of proficiency (even though their English might show influences from local culture and the vernacular). In fact, Chomsky's native speaker of a homogeneous speech community is an idealized construction. In the hybrid postcolonial age we live in today, one has to develop the heteroglossic competence to cope with the realities of language diversity, contact, and mixing.

For these reasons, we have to develop new terminology to reflect the complex linguistic competence of postcolonial English speakers. Continued use of the label *native speaker* will only serve to reinforce the spurious Chomskyan notion. Less problematic are the labels *Center speakers of English* and *Periphery speakers of English,* partly borrowed from B. Kachru (1986) and partly based on terminology used in politicaleconomy for these two set of communities. The label *Center* is a construct from political economy and refers to the industrially/economically advanced communities of the West, which sustain their ideological hegemony by keeping less-developed communities in Periphery status (see Frank, 1969; Wallerstein, 1991). Foremost among the Center nations are the communities of North America, Britain, Australia, and New Zealand, which claim ownership over English. Periphery speakers of English are defined in this chapter as historically recent users of this language, many of whom would display sound multilingual competence in many codes—including the Center's standard dialects as well as their indigenized variants of English—which they would use in contextually appropriate ways. There are of course others in the Periphery whose competence is dominantly in the vernacular, with lesser degrees of proficiency in Center or Periphery variants of English.

It is important to note that the native speaker fallacy is linguistically anachronistic. It flies in the face of some basic linguistic concepts developed through research and accepted by contemporary scholars. Thus it creates a disjunction between research awareness and professional practice in ELT. For instance, we take for granted that all languages and dialects are of equal status; that there are no linguistic reasons for the superiority of one dialect or language over the other; that languages in situations of contact will always undergo modes of indigenization or vernacularization; that language learning is a creative cognitive and social process that has its own trajectory not fully dependent on the teacher (much less the teacher's accent); that the contextually relevant variants of the language have to be used in different situations; and that language change or diversification cannot be stopped by attempts at purification or standardization. However, the native speaker fallacy goes against these basic assumptions. It is based on the view that the language of the native speaker is superior and/or normative irrespective of the diverse contexts of communication; that the corruption of the language can be arrested by the prescriptive role of the native speaker teacher, and that language acquisition is conditioned (in behaviorist terms) by the dialect of the teacher to which the student is exposed. Thus this fallacy enforces traditionalism in our profession.

Although the superiority of the native speaker generates a whole set of linguistic problems, its application in the pedagogical domain is even more questionable. Is a native speaker necessarily a good teacher? Does the fact that one displays good pronunciation and correct grammar (these value-ridden notions will themselves be challenged) make one a successful teacher of that language? Language teaching is an art, a science, and a skill that requires complex pedagogical preparation and practice. Therefore, not all speakers may make good teachers of their first language. On the other hand, it is possible to make a case that speakers with multilingual competence, even in a situation where the language is a foreign or second language, may make successful language teachers. Their proficiency in more than one language system develops a deep metalinguistic knowledge and complex language awareness. It is for these reasons that Britten (1985) paradoxically argued that such multilingual speakers may have a sounder grasp of English grammar and even be more effective teachers of the language than the so-called native speakers.

In fact, there is evidence to suggest that the use and awareness of other dialects/languages can help a person facilitate the process of second language acquisition (SLA) much better. There is growing realization that the first language is not a problem but a resource in SLA (see Y. Kachru, 1994; Sridhar, 1994). First language can help build a cognitive bridge to the second language, apart from addressing student concerns regarding language maintenance, identity conflict, and cultural clash. Periphery speakers can use their vernacular competence to relate English better to students from their own communities and help them integrate English more effectively into their existing linguistic repertoire. Auerbach et al. (1996) showed, from participatory research in ESL classes in the Boston area community centers, that teachers from the communities of the immigrant students are able to do a good job in relating English literacy to the challenges, needs, and aspirations of the learners and facilitate second language acquisition. Their insider status in the community provides them an intimate awareness of the learning styles, language attitudes, and functional needs of the students so that they can develop an effective curriculum and pedagogy. (See also Kamhi-Stein, Chap. 10, this volume, for the inspiring role of non-native teachers as positive models for their ESL students.)

If the superior claims of the native speaker teacher do not hold water, why does this notion carry such importance in our profession? It is here that we realize the ideological value of this concept. Even if the concept does not have any linguistic or pedagogical validity, the political and economic consequences deriving from this notion are attractive to those from the dominant speech communities. Such is the force of the economic and political interests behind the ESL enterprise that even basic linguistic notions may be suppressed or distorted to support these ulterior motives.

The Political Economy of the Fallacy

We need to consider the native speaker fallacy in the context of the English-only ideologies that are gaining ground in Center communities these days (see Lucas & Katz, 1994). Phillipson finds the native speaker fallacy to be enjoying popularity in the context of demands that the medium of teaching should be English only. According to what Phillipson (1992) labeled *the monolingual fallacy*, L1 is not considered to play a useful function in the acquisition of English and is considered to harm the process of second language acquisition. There is thus a backlash against the accommodation of multilingualism and cultural diversity in schools and institutions while English is being legislated as the sole language of interaction/communication in these situations. This movement is an attempt to protect the interests and values of Center speakers of English, which are perceived to be threatened by the democratization of the social mainstream with the inclusion of other languages and language groups. Groups such as U.S. English are lobbying for a constitutional amendment that would establish English as the official language of the United States. The House of Representatives of the U.S. Congress has passed a bill that makes English the official language. In the debate on the bill, the speaker of the House, Newt Gingrich, referring to bilingual educational programs stated,

> This isn't bilingualism. This is a level of confusion, which if it was allowed to develop for another 20 or 30 years would literally lead, I think, to the decay of the core parts of our civilization. . . . Is there a thing we call American? Is it unique? It is vital historically to assert and establish that English is the common

language at the heart of our civilization. (see Schmitt, 1996, p. A10).

In such a context, the bilingual/multilingual Periphery English teachers may be considered a hindrance to socializing students into monolingual schools and social institutions. Their multilingualism in fact becomes a liability as it could encourage the very processes of ethnic/linguistic diversity that the mainstream feels threatened by.

We should also note the movements insisting on standardizing English in order to understand the idealization of native speaker teachers. It is in the context of arguing for standard English that Quirk (1990) endorsed the value of native speaker teachers. It is feared that Periphery variants of English will spoil the purity of English and affect mutual intelligibility among speakers of the language. Native speaker teachers, on the other hand, will serve a useful function in containing the development of indigenized variants of English and restricting the further diversification of the language. More positively, they would spread the Center variants of English to new learners and thus contribute to the dominance of these standard dialects. Therefore, native speaker teachers can be expected to play a helping role in the linguistic hegemony of Center Englishes over Periphery variants.

Furthermore, because teachers of English are not expected to possess a knowledge of Periphery languages or Periphery Englishes in order to be good teachers, the professional gate is opened wide for a cadre of Center teachers. At a time when English teaching jobs are hard to come by, the native speaker fallacy creates a global demand for Center teachers. The professional license these traveling teachers need in order to qualify as ESL instructors is virtually their identity as native speakers. An ESL teaching job is their birthright. The beneficial consequences of the native speaker fallacy will be appreciated by Center teachers especially at a time of reduced funding for ESL/bilingual education in many institutions and the continuing recession/downsizing in Western societies. Many English majors and Ph.D.'s are joining the ranks of the unemployed in the Center.

The native speaker fallacy not only helps preserve the few jobs available in the Center for native speakers but also to monopolize the ESL teaching jobs in the Periphery. One has only to eavesdrop on the electronic forum TESL-JB (devoted to employment issues in ESL) to read the often frantic messages by U.S. and British teachers on the prospects of finding jobs in Korea, Japan, China, or the Middle East. Fortunately for them, these countries very specifically advertise that "only native speakers" will be considered for employment. In fact, among the worst culprits to popularize and/or legitimize the native speaker fallacy are the Periphery academic institutions themselves. That Center variants of English should be the norm and that Center speakers of that language are the models seem to have been effectively internalized in these Periphery communities. This goes to show the international hegemony of this discourse. Ironically, even those whose interests may be harmed by this pedagogical assumption implement it unquestioningly.

Whereas Center-based teachers are assured of ESL jobs in the Periphery communities, Periphery teachers find it difficult to teach in the Center. The native speaker fallacy protects jobs for Center teachers in their home institutions. This should be seen from the perspective of protectionism in trade and employment that is gaining favor in the United States and many other Center communities these days. There is a widely shared feeling that the jobs and products of the Center communities should be protected from foreign competition. It might appear that the native speaker fallacy has done for ELT, more effectively and far ahead of time, what other industries are attempting to do in their own fields to protect jobs for Center-based professionals/workers. I must grant that in some Center communities there is greater flexibility than in some Periphery institutions when we consider their advertisement for professionals with native linguistic ability rather than an identity as a native speaker. It is this leeway that enables Periphery professionals like me to receive appointments in Center academic institutions. However, native linguistic ability is often interpreted narrowly to mean Center-based pronunciation or accent and does not include the deep structural features like grammatical competence. Because the manifestation of native linguistic ability is determined by superficial linguistic signs, even such flexible terminology is inadequate to guarantee teaching positions for Periphery professionals.

In the context of such a job market, we have to ask some disturbing questions on the place of teacher training for Periphery scholars/professionals in Center academic institutions. There are many graduate students from Asian, African, and Latin American countries undergoing training in U.S., Canadian, and British institutions today. Although these institutions are generating enough money through programs like MA's in TESL and Ph.D.'s in foreign language education, for what purpose are these foreign scholars being trained? Have these institutions considered carefully the employment prospects for the students they train as teachers? If after their training these teachers would be subject to the native speaker fallacy when they apply for teaching jobs, these programs are training them for a life of unemployment. It is indeed tragic that persons who have spent valuable time and money on professional training should end up disqualified from practicing that job for spurious reasons. In the light of such an obvious contradiction (i.e., training Periphery scholars for language teaching while also subscribing to the native speaker fallacy that denies them job opportunities), perhaps the only rationale for such training programs is the pecuniary motive. There is a double whammy here: not only do Center institutions make money on training Periphery teachers, they eventually exclude them from these professions in order to monopolize the jobs.

The native speaker fallacy also contributes to the narrow definition of expertise in ELT. If it is one's accent and pronunciation that qualify one to be a teacher, then the sense of professionalism developed in ESL is flimsy. In effect, teaching is defined primarily in terms of linguistic considerations. Imagine the level of expected professionalism if, even now, Center subjects who travel to the Periphery for a variety of personal reasons are often pressed into service as English teachers by virtue of their native speaker status. Such undue emphasis on the linguistic status/proficiency of the teachers excuse them from understanding the local languages, cultures, and social conditions of the communities where they are teaching. They are not under any compulsion to develop their pedagogical practice in terms of the larger social, political, and cultural conditions of the communities where their students come from. It is not surprising then that Pennycook (1994) and Phillipson (1992) find the professional base of ELT very narrow. They find that teacher educational programs do not provide adequate orientation in sociology, cultural studies, or even foreign languages to those trained. If teaching is defined on the basis of one's linguistic identity, the other dimensions of instructional competence may not receive adequate attention. Therefore, unless the native speaker fallacy is effectively challenged and dismissed, we may not develop a formidable sense of professionalism in ELT that orientates to language learning and the language learner in a holistic sense.

The narrow sense of professionalism has a different consequence for Periphery teachers. It prevents them from developing their expertise in ways relevant to their local community needs, apart from forcing them to be obsessed with native-like pronunciation or other narrow linguistic proprieties. Many Periphery professionals feel compelled to spend undue time repairing their pronunciation or performing other cosmetic changes to sound native. Their predominant concern is in effect "How can I lose my accent?" rather than "How can I be a successful teacher?" The anxiety and inhibitions about their pronunciation can make them lose their grip on the instructional process or lack rapport with their students. Merrit and her team of researchers pointed out from ethnographic observations in African classrooms that local teachers display a "linguistic insecurity" deriving from their concerns about "proper English" (Merrit, Cleghorn, Abagi, & Bunyi, 1992). This affects their pedagogical effectiveness in the classroom. The researchers suggest that they would be more effective teachers if they can only assume that their own variants of English and the ubiquitous mixed codes (i.e., mixing of Swahili and English) are pedagogically valuable for both content instruction and second language acquisition. The debunking of the native speaker fallacy can therefore liberate Periphery teachers to give more attention to the other serious concerns relating to their professional practice—such as the learning styles of their students, and the cultural traditions, social conditions, and economic needs of their communities. They should also negotiate the complex language attitudes, hybrid codes, and sociolinguistic patterns developing in their communities as they engage in language teaching.

Furthermore, we must consider the situation in ELT where expertise is defined and dominated by native speakers. In fact teacher trainers, curriculum developers, and testing experts are predominantly from the Center. Language teaching consultants have to make periodic trips from Center academic institutions to guide, counsel, and train Periphery professionals on the latest developments in teaching. The native speaker fallacy appears to legitimize this dominance of Center professionals/scholars in the circles of expertise. However, the constructs and notions developed by such experts are not always relevant to the realities of international ELT enterprise. Center experts cannot relate well to the complex social, cultural, and pedagogical challenges played out in Periphery classrooms. In fact, Phillipson (1992) characterized the governing assumption of Center language teaching circles in the following manner: "Part of the professional identity and image of the Center applied linguistics institutions is that their skills are universally relevant" (p. 238). Similarly, Widdowson summed up the assumptions motivating Center pedagogical activities in Periphery contexts with thinly veiled sarcasm in an interview conducted by Phillipson: "We've always tended to make the same basic error, which is to assume that somehow it is the local conditions that have to be adjusted to the packaged set of concepts we bring with us rather than attempt to look into the real issues, practical as well as ideological, of implementation and innovation within those contexts" (quoted in Phillipson, 1992, p. 260). This is a policy of convenience. Because Center professionals know best their own conditions of work, it is advantageous for them to promote these as universally applicable. It is by challenging the dominance of the native speaker expert and letting more Periphery teachers enter the professional inner circles that we can theorize the radically different realities found in Periphery classrooms.

The native speaker fallacy eventually feeds into the auxiliary pedagogical services associated with the ELT enterprise—such as the production of textbooks and other teaching aids. Because it is less complicated to rely on the competencies and background of native speaker teachers, publishing houses in the Center find it convenient to produce textbooks and audiovisual aids based on their own norms and expectations. Such textbooks would use discourses, situations, and cultural content familiar to native speakers as the publishers can confidently assume that the teachers who use these books worldwide—that is, those from their own communities—would be able to understand the content and teach it without problem to local students. Similarly, audiotapes provided for listening comprehension and speaking instruction carry British or U.S. English. Testing services such as TOEFL also treat U.S. English as the norm. Using other languages, dialects, and discourses in such material would put the largely monolingual Center teachers and examiners at a disadvantage. The native speaker fallacy together with the monolingual fallacy thus saves textbook publishers precious money because they do not have to employ those fluent with other languages/dialects for producing ELT material. Imagine what it would take to recruit speakers of languages spoken in all the communities where ESL is taught in order to produce textbooks relevant to their unique situations! It is therefore economically advantageous for these publishing houses to refrain from using indigenous languages and local English dialects in the material produced for the Periphery.

All this makes Periphery scholars and communities more and more dependent on the Center-based ELT establishment. The legitimization of the Center norms and competencies through the native speaker fallacy— including the concomitant dominance of Center professionals in the development of expertise, professionalization, and production of teaching materials—makes Periphery teachers look up to the Center for professional advancement and assistance. This has serious implications for their professional identity. Their autonomy as a discourse community is also affected. They are in fact torn between Center norms and Periphery practice; Center expectations and Periphery classroom conditions; Center prescriptions and Periphery realities. This leads to a schizophrenic state of teaching practice. There are many contradictions that characterize the everyday teaching experience of Periphery teachers—as I witnessed in Sri Lankan English-teaching circles. They may profess Center pedagogical fashions, but practice local/traditional approaches in the classroom. They may believe that the sole medium of ESL courses should be English only, but practice considerable code switching in the classroom. They may reward standard British/U.S. English in examinations, but use Sri Lankan English for classroom communication. Such tensions pose severe constraints on their ability to develop an independent professional identity and pedagogical discourse. Periphery teachers need to be empowered to theorize the realities and needs of their local classrooms in terms of the indigenous pedagogical and linguistic traditions.

We must not fail to note how the native speaker fallacy prevents the democratization of the TESOL establishment. The fallacy prevents the critical development of the TESOL professional community and its discourses as it denies the participation of Periphery teachers on equal terms. This is not simply a question of more inclusive treatment of Periphery professionals in the ELT establishment; much more is at stake. The very terms and notions that define our understanding of language teaching and second language acquisition are impoverished because the unique insights Periphery professionals can provide from their experience and background are suppressed. Periphery professionals can shed new light on teaching that may critically redefine the assumptions and practices of TESOL. To provide just a single example, Y. Kachru (1994) and Sridhar (1994) alerted us to what they call the "monolingual bias" in SLA models. They argued that the assumptions of SLA, as they are conceived in the 1990s, are based on the monolingual norms existing in Center communities. Such notions do not relate to the dynamic multilingualism existing in Periphery communities where speakers acquire English together with some other local languages and use it as part of an integrated repertoire with other codes and discourses. They call for a new paradigm for language acquisition that takes into account such postcolonial contexts of hybrid communication. Many such theoretical, research, and pedagogical contributions that may be made by professionals from the Periphery will be silenced if they are not accommodated on equal terms in the professional community.

It is important therefore to take stock of the material and ideological consequences of this fallacy that dominate the profession so much that even basic research findings are suppressed. As ELT becomes a profit-making multinational industry in the hands of Center agencies, there are obvious economic benefits involved here. The fallacy also furthers the ideological hegemony of the Center. Although traveling teachers from the Center would carry western ideologies directly into Periphery classrooms and communities, the cultural/pedagogical practices they promote through their textbooks, teaching materials, and methods would conduct this ideological domination more subtly. Conducting language teaching by treating Center dialects and discourses as the norm is an important form of political control over the Periphery. This is especially significant when the Periphery threatens to nativize English according to its own needs and traditions. It is no exaggeration that the ELT enterprise can carry out Center hegemony in politicoeconomic terms in Periphery communities, reproducing Center ideologies and institutions globally (as argued by Pennycook, 1994; Phillipson, 1992). It is through ideologies such as the native speaker fallacy that the Center is able to reap the material benefits envisioned through English. The chairman of the British Council stated in his Annual Report 1983-1984 (with a use of telling images): "Our language is our greatest asset, greater than North Sea Oil, and the supply is inexhaustible; furthermore, while we do not have a monopoly, our particular brand remains highly sought after. I am glad to say that those who guide the fortunes of this country share my conviction in the need to invest in, and exploit to the full, this invisible, God-given asset" (quoted in Phillipson, 1992, p. 144–45). One cannot miss the very direct connection drawn here by this responsible cultural officer between his particular brand of English, foreign investment, and material rewards.

Reconfiguring the Professional World

Before concluding, I wish to outline more balanced ways of understanding the roles and responsibilities of Center and Periphery English teachers. Creating changes in our profession and in the classroom can go a long way toward empowering Periphery communities and instilling democratic practices in our classrooms and communities. If the types of economic and political domination described above can be accomplished through unfair pedagogical practices, changing the professional world should in turn have an impact on the larger sociopolitical realities.

Lest my argument in the preceding section be misconstrued, I must state that the case I am making here is not for setting aside Center positions for Periphery professionals or for placing restrictions on the employability of Center professionals in the Periphery. Even the good old laissez faire exchange practices should suffice: free competition, free movement, equal sharing of products and ideas, and open employment prospects for both Center and Periphery ELT professionals. It is such democratic practices that will ensure a healthy sharing of experiences, views, and expertise that can set our profession on solid intellectual and pedagogical footing. The native speaker fallacy affects the egalitarian nature of these interactions and exchanges, helping Center professionals monopolize these resources and, thus, serving to impoverish our profession.

As we reconfigure the relationship between Center and Periphery professionals, it is good to observe some basic pedagogical distinctions well known in our circles. Distinguishing ESL and EFL situations, we can say that Periphery professionals have an advantage in teaching students in communities where English is learned as a second or widely used language for intracommunity purposes (often with indigenous communicative norms). On the other hand, Center professionals may make a greater contribution for students learning English as a foreign language for use in Center communities for institutional/formal purposes or for specialized purposes in restricted contexts of use (i.e., English for Specific Purposes). Hence a second distinction: English for intranational uses in Periphery communities (whose discourses and conventions Periphery professionals know firsthand) and English for international use where mutual intelligibility is important. Furthermore, even in the Center, a Periphery professional may teach courses on English literacy (even if he or she does not have a British or U.S. accent) as formal written English has codes and conventions that are internationally shared. As in all languages, English prose has relatively more in common than speech across different dialect users. Teaching of speaking for formal/institutional purposes in international contexts might require the services of Center professionals to develop the skills appropriate for the specific Center community the student hopes to interact with. If using the native linguistic norm as a blanket requirement for all communicative situations is unwise, so is the insistence on the authority of the native speaker teacher for all language teaching/learning contexts.

Widdowson (1996) pointed to certain developments in the pedagogical domain that might turn out to provide more authority and demand for Periphery professionals. He referred to pedagogical practices such as learner-centered, self-directed, and collaborative teaching approaches, which he interprets as encouraging the autonomy of the learner. These pedagogical approaches conflict with the demand for authenticity in language learning. Widdowson (1994) interpreted authentic use as having to do with the uses and structures of English in the traditional native speaker communities. He therefore argues: "A pedagogy which combines authenticity of use with autonomy of learning is a contradiction. You cannot have it both ways" (p. 387). In fact, autonomous learning by Periphery students in terms relevant to their needs, values, traditions, and aspirations will contribute to developing appropriate forms of English that are authentic in their own context—making them move away from Center notions of authentic English. The fact is that the expectation of authentic use privileges the professionalism of native speaker teachers and the textbooks, curriculum, and expertise developed in Center communities. However, if one values the strategies and styles of learning the students themselves bring to SLA in order to acquire the language efficiently in terms of their own communicative needs, he or she cannot impose on the students the authority of native speaker teachers or native Englishes. Widdowson argued that autonomy of learning would in fact privilege the expertise of Periphery teachers. It is they who know best the typical learning styles, strategies, needs, and contexts of use of second language students and can thus facilitate their language acquisition in ways that suit their interests.

It is possible that some may consider my argument for more professional opportunities for non-native teachers in the Center as motivated by vested interests. They might wonder why these teachers cannot go back to their own Periphery communities for jobs but attempt to teach in the Center. In response, I first observe that in the postcolonial world where there is great fluidity in migration and settlement patterns, it is impossible to deny the presence of teachers and students from Periphery communities in the Center. Furthermore, the claims of Widdowson and Auerbach's experience in Boston show that non-native teachers have a positive role to play in the socialization and language acquisition of members of their own communities in Center locations. At a deeper level, my critique is of the discourse that marginalizes non-native teachers whether in the Center or the Periphery. The unequal employment opportunities for native and non-native teachers whether in Center or Periphery communities is only a surface manifestation of this discourse. The deconstruction of this discourse will hopefully lead to a healthy critique of the narrow-minded distinctions made in the professional world and enable more democratic professional practices.

We can only imagine the sociopolitical consequences of empowering Periphery teachers of English. It is not only that teachers will use pedagogies and material that are socially and culturally relevant for their students, but also that they will feel more comfortable about using language teaching to negotiate the sociopolitical realities of their communities through a more critical and transformative pedagogy. The English language and its discourses will themselves undergo considerable changes. English will be nativized more constructively and consciously to complement the local needs and aspirations. If English language teaching in Periphery communities is to be conducted in a socially responsible and politically empowering manner, the authority for conceiving and implementing the curriculum and pedagogy should be passed on to the local teachers themselves.

Epilogue

It is suitable to end with a story, having started this chapter with one. This story makes a provocative point on the pedagogical possibilities that are available for Periphery teachers. Although I have argued that being multilingual provides certain pedagogical advantages for Periphery teachers, I want to take my argument a step further here. The professional world is perhaps ready to ponder how even those Periphery professionals who are not perfectly competent in the deep structure of the English grammatical system may serve as successful teachers. To appreciate the significance of this story, we must first note that despite the intent of the native speaker fallacy, there are not enough Center teachers to cater to the needs of English teaching worldwide. Therefore more than 80% of the ELT professionals internationally are non-native speakers. These are the teachers working in the remote corners of the world in small village classrooms, often meeting under trees in farms and fields away from the eyes of the professional pundits of the Center. These English teachers are village elders, parents, and priests who may often possess only a smattering of English. I am not ashamed to say that it is such a charismatic rural teacher who initiated my own learning of the language that has sustained me to this point in earning a doctorate in English linguistics and serving in the faculty of an English department. Obviously, much more than proper English or the Queen's accent were required by my village schoolteacher to do the magic of providing a solid foundation for my English education. My teacher instilled in me his own curiosity toward the language, the ability to intuit linguistic rules from observation of actual usage, a metalinguistic awareness of the system behind languages, and the ability to creatively negotiate meaning with speakers and texts. These are the secrets of successful language acquisition that were passed on to me by my village teacher. This solid training on learner strategies still sustains me as I continue to explore both my vernacular and English. At a time when learner strategy training and self-directed learning are fashionable concepts, it should not be difficult to understand the extreme case of a Periphery teacher with "poor" grammar and "bad" pronunciation functioning as a good teacher. Paradoxically, such a teacher may lead the student to acquire (if need be) even Center versions of English. It is through such language teaching practices that non-native teachers in remote parts of the world succeed in teaching appropriate English to many students today—whatever the pundits in the Center may prescribe.

References

Auerbach, E., Barahona, B., Midy, J., Vaquerano, F., Zambrano, A., & Arnaud, J. (1996). *Adult ESL/Literacy from the community to the community: A guidebook for participatory literacy training*. Mahwah, NJ: Lawrence Erlbaum Associates.

Britten, D. (1985). Teacher training in ELT. *Language Teaching, 18*, 112–128.

Frank, A. G. (1969). *Latin America: Underdevelopment or revolution*. New York: Monthly Review Press.

Hamers, J., & Blanc, M. H. A. (1989). *Bilinguality and bilingualism*. Cambridge, England: Cambridge University Press.

Kachru, B. B. (1986). *The alchemy of English: The spread, functions and models of non-native Englishes*. Oxford, England: Pergamon.

Kachru, Y. (1994). Monolingual bias in SLA research. *TESOL Quarterly, 28*, 795–800.

Lucas, T., & Katz, A. (1994). Reframing the debate: The roles of native languages in English-only programs for language minority students. *TESOL Quarterly, 28*, 537–562.

Merrit, M., Cleghorn, A., Abagi, J., & Bunyi, G. (1992). Socialising multilingualism: Determinants of codeswitching in Kenyan primary classrooms. In C. Eastman (Ed.), *Codeswitching* (pp. 103–122). Clevedon, England: Multilingual Matters.

Pennycook, A. (1994). *The cultural politics of English as an international language*. London: Longman.

Phillipson, R. (1992). *Linguistic imperialism*. Oxford, England: Oxford University Press.

Quirk, R. (1990). Language varieties and standard language. *English Today, 21*, 3–10.

Schmitt, E. (1996, September 2). House approves measure on official U.S. language. *New York Times*, p. A10.

Sridhar, S. N. (1994). A reality check for SLA theories. *TESOL Quarterly, 28*, 800–805.

Wallerstein, I. (1991). *Geopolitics and geoculture*. Cambridge, England: Cambridge University Press.

Widdowson, H. G. (1994). The ownership of English. *TESOL Quarterly, 28*, 377–392.

Widdowson, H. G. (1996). Authenticity and autonomy in ELT. *ELT Journal, 50*, 67–68.

CHAPTER 7

Minority Women Teachers of ESL: Negotiating White English[*]

Nuzhat Amin
Ontario Institute for Studies in Education
University of Toronto

The Context

In the field of English as a Second Language (ESL), much attention has been and continues to be paid to the race, ethnicity, culture, and gender of the learners, but far less attention has been given to how these variables in the teacher may impact on the classroom. Thus, the different experience of visible minority teachers has been left unaddressed by most writers on ESL. Even in critical writing on ESL (see, for instance, Cummins, 1989; Peirce, 1993; Rockhill & Tomic, 1995), the teacher is positioned as White and an implicit juxtaposition is made between the powerful (White) ESL teacher and the powerless (mainly non-White) minority student. This is so because critical theory, which addresses the inequalities that are perpetuated in the ESL classroom, is written from the perspective of White teachers. Kamhi-Stein and Thomas (Chap. 10, and Chap. i, respectively, this volume) make similar points. For example, Kamhi-Stein says that in TESOL, the issue of minority teacher representation is a "non-issue," and Thomas says that although TESOL has a diverse membership, in some cases the presence of non-native teachers is "totally ignored" within TESOL.

In this chapter, I position myself as a visible minority immigrant woman and as a teacher of adult ESL students in Toronto, Canada. I bring to this chapter an experiential basis that is different from that of White writers on this subject. Building on my own experience and the findings of a study that I conducted on minority ESL teachers in 1994 in

---

[*] Some parts of this chapter have appeared in *TESOL Quarterly*. See Amin (1997).

Toronto, I explain the ways in which the minority female teacher is disempowered in our profession. I consider the disempowerment of the minority ESL teacher to be an issue that primarily concerns women.

Perhaps because teaching ESL in Canada is by and large a low-paid occupation, with very little security, the majority of teachers are women—or is ESL a low-paid profession because the majority of teachers are women? Although this chapter focuses on minority immigrant women, I suggest that their experiences in the ESL classroom have commonalities with the experiences of minority women born in Canada. I show that there are biases inherent in the ESL profession that privilege the White teacher and that make it difficult for non-White teachers to make much headway in the profession. More specifically, I address assumptions regarding the ownership of the English language that permeate the ESL profession and that work in concert with sexism and racism to disempower the minority teacher.

I have pointed out that the experience of minority teachers has not been acknowledged by writers of ESL, and so, in order to show the processes by which the minority teacher is disempowered, I describe my experience and research in this field.[1]

Stereotype of Authentic ESL Teacher

In 1994, during a pilot study I conducted in Toronto, I interviewed five minority women teachers who were teaching or had taught a class of male and female adult ESL students from different racial, cultural, and linguistic backgrounds. I chose as my participants women who, like myself, had immigrated to Canada as adults. The 2-hour, semistructured interviews consisted of 25 questions about the teachers' perceptions of their students' ideal ESL teacher. The findings of the study indicated that some ESL students make two major assumptions. The first is that only White people can be native speakers of English and the second is that only native speakers know "real," "proper," "Canadian" English. My participants reported that their students were vague about what Canadian English is but they seemed to be clear that a non-White teacher could not teach them Canadian English. My participants said that they were constantly judged and compared unfavorably with White teachers

---

[1]   I am using the terms "visible minority," "minority," "woman of color, "and "non-White woman" interchangeably in this chapter.

and that they felt disempowered by their students' stereotype of an authentic ESL teacher (Amin, 1994).

The findings of my study corroborated my own experience. I am an ethnic Pakistani; I went to English language schools in postcolonial Pakistan and immigrated to Canada as an adult armed with two Master's degrees—in English literature and in English language—and university teaching experience. I have taught ESL to adults in Toronto in both credit and noncredit courses in programs run by community colleges and by school boards. There are many differences in these programs in terms of goals, curriculum, and duration. The students in these programs vary in terms of age, gender, ethnicity, linguistic background, level of education, ability in English, and length of stay in Canada. But a common thread in these very differing teaching situations is that many of my students have voiced their assumptions that I am not a native speaker of English and therefore not a "real" ESL teacher. The overriding impression that I am left with is that my students feel shortchanged by having a minority woman as their teacher and that they feel that I am occupying the teacher's position because the school cannot find a real ESL teacher.

The discourse of these programs is such that the majority of the students, both male and female, show a decided preference for White teachers over non-White teachers. To illustrate how this is expressed, I describe one incident. At the end of one 8-week session where I was teaching a Level Two class in a noncredit program, I gave a few students the choice of moving to a Level Three or staying in a Level Two class for the next session. My experience with students from these countries had been that they dreaded being considered failures—a concept I am familiar with from my education in Pakistan. Therefore, I expected a great deal of resistance from them to staying in the same level. To my surprise, all the students I talked to, both male and female, readily agreed to do the Level Two course again. Then I was approached by other students, who I had assigned to a Level Three class, who told me that they too felt they would benefit from staying on in a Level Two class. I finally pieced together what was happening. My students had found out that a White woman was teaching the Level Two class in the next session and a non-White woman was teaching the Level Three class. My students had made their decision based entirely on the teacher's race. It would seem that this is not an isolated case; the teacher-participants in my study described similar experiences and other minority teachers (for example, Braine, Chap. 2, and Thomas, Chap. 1, this volume) describe incidents in which their students showed attitudes to their minority teachers that were not dissimilar to those of my students.

Privileging the Native Speaker

The findings of my study, like my experience, corroborate the point made by Rockhill and Tomic (1995) that the referent of ESL in Canada continues to be "White, Anglo, male" (p. 210). In this section I argue that the concept of the native speaker as White pervades all aspects of ESL programs in Canada as it influences the teaching, classroom materials, and the relations between the teacher and learners.

In what way is it disempowering for an ESL teacher to be considered a non-native speaker of English? The answer is simple: it is because the referent of the ESL classroom is the (White) native speaker. Ferguson (1992) referred to this phenomenon when he states that linguists have long given a special place to the native speaker as the only truly valid and reliable source of language data (p. xiii). Ferguson alluded to the "mystique" that the native speaker whose mother tongue is English enjoys in the linguistic community (p. xiii), a mystique which, as I have pointed out elsewhere (see Amin, 1997), insinuates that a native speaker has more ownership of English than a non-native speaker. But as my study indicates, the native speaker has such a mystique not only among linguists but also among ESL students in Canada.

Ferguson is but one sociolinguist who refers to the preference that is given to the native speaker. Widdowson made a similar point. Referring to the English-language teaching profession, he said that "there is no doubt that native speakers of English are deferred to in our profession. What they say is invested with both authenticity and authority" (1994, p. 386). Further, "native-speaker expertise is assumed to extend to the teaching of the language" (p. 387) so that native speakers "not only have a patent on proper English, but on proper ways of teaching it as well" (pp. 387–88). This association of the native speaker with owning the subject matter of the ESL classroom—that is, the English language—and having the expertise to teach this subject matter positions the minority teacher as an unauthentic teacher because he or she is constructed as a non-native speaker on the basis of not being White.

As I pointed out at the beginning of this chapter, the majority of ESL teachers are women and hence I consider issues arising out of being constructed as a non-native speaker primarily to concern minority women, and not minority men. I do not want to attempt a separate analysis of race and of gender, for, as minority women have stressed, their experiences cannot be neatly fragmented by gender, race, and class (see Das Gupta, 1991); but I would like to point out some possible differences between the experiences of minority men and minority women ESL teachers. Here, I briefly refer to the point made by Widdowson—that the teacher who is a native speaker is awarded "authenticity and authority." The operative word from a gender perspective is "authority"—the teacher's authority is an issue that women professors, including minority women professors, have discussed, an issue that I elaborate on in later in this chapter. In short, women professors cannot command the same authority as men professors. As ESL's referent is White, Anglo, male, I suggest that a non-White male, though not as authentic a teacher as a White male in the students' eyes, would still command the authority that his gender confers on him.

Native Speaker and White Accents

The opinions of ESL students reflect dominant stereotypes of minorities' speech, perceptions that pervade second language education as well as the society we live in. One such dominant perception, as I have pointed out, is that the native speaker is White; another such perception is that the native speaker has a particular accent. I consider myself to be a native speaker on the grounds that English is the language I know best, but my colleagues—teachers of English and ESL, linguists, and applied linguists—usually position me as a non-native speaker, I suggest, because I am non-White and because I have a Pakistani accent. When I self-identify as a native speaker, there is a look of bewilderment, disbelief, and embarrassment on their faces. They, too, are reflecting an unsaid tenet of the ESL profession and a dominant belief of Canadian society—that only a White accent qualifies one to be a native speaker. My pilot study indicated that accents associated with White English-speaking countries of the First World such as Britain, the United States, and Canada have a higher status than accents associated with non-White countries such as India, Kenya and Singapore (Amin, 1994).[2]

This is so because, as Edwards (1979) pointed out, views of language often correspond to views of the social status of language users, and, as Ng (1990) stated, immigrant women from non-White countries have a low status in Canada, a point I return to later in this chapter. Edwards (1979) added that "the language, dialect or accent employed provides a simple label which evokes a social stereotype which goes far beyond language itself" (p. 79). Although both Edwards and Ng are

---

[2] There is also a hierarchy among accents associated with White English-speaking countries.

writing in the Canadian context, researchers in the United States have come to similar conclusions about the status ascribed to people on the basis of their accents as well as about popular conceptions of what an accent is and who has one. For example, Thuy (1979) stated: "The accent with which a foreign born person speaks English can create a favorable or unfavorable impression on a number of Anglo-Americans" (p. 5). He adds that if one speaks with an accent influenced by a prestige language or with an accent peculiar to an ethnic group that is historically successful in the United States, this accent is "readily considered a stamp of approval, if not a symbol of prestige and respect" (p. 5). On the other hand, Thuy continued, the foreign accent that is peculiar to the language of a less successful or respected minority group can "lead to some sort of stigma" (p. 5). Whereas Thuy addressed why some accents are liked and others are not, Matsuda (1991) articulated what a non-accent is: "Everyone has an accent," she says, "but when an employer refuses to hire a person 'with an accent,' they [sic] are referring to a hidden norm of non-accent . . . People in power are perceived as speaking normal, unaccented English. Any speech that is different from that constructed norm is called an accent" (p. 1361). In the course of her work as a law professor, Matsuda listened to a number of stories about people who had been born outside the United States and who had been denied a particular job in the United States because of having a heavy accent, and came to the conclusion that "accent discrimination is commonplace, natural, and socially acceptable" (p. 1348).

In light of Matsuda's observations, especially on perceptions about unaccented English, who has an accent in Canada? And who does not? Understandably, immigrant women from non-White countries have accents that are different from Canada's constructed norm, and hence they are told that they have accents. For example, I am constantly being asked questions about my accent by colleagues who appear to think—much as Matsuda pointed out—that they either do not have an accent or that they have the right accent.

This preference for White accents is reflected in the teaching materials of the ESL classroom. Until the 1980s, British accents were highly valued in the Canadian ESL classroom but more recently U.S. and Canadian accents are increasingly being held up as the model. However, in my experience a non-White accent, say, an Indian accent or a Trinidadian accent, is never held up as a model. It is therefore not surprising that ESL students should feel that they are being shortchanged by a non-White teacher with an accent that is considered nonstandard by society and by the ESL classroom. Immigrant teachers from non-White countries are further disempowered because whenever a native speaker is required, for instance, for making teaching materials such as audiotapes for the language laboratory, their accent disqualifies them from being considered for such projects; in effect, they are disqualified by their race and accent from being considered authentic English teachers. Hence the native speaker construct acts in concert with the sexism and racism that permeates the ESL classroom, an issue I now address.

Minority Teachers on Their Disempowerment

Ng (1991), a Toronto-based academic whose research focuses on minority women, described how sexism and racism, as relations of domination and subordination that have developed over time and which saturate all interactional contexts, are operative in educational settings.[3] As a woman and a university teacher, one's power and authority is undermined constantly by existing gender relations that operate in the society at large. "For a racial minority female teacher, the devaluation of her authority and credibility is compounded by her race and ethnicity" (p. 105). Even when minority teachers have been granted institutional power, other practices are at work in the university setting that "strip minority teachers of their right to speak and act as figures of authority" (pp. 105–106). What are some of the ramifications for the classroom when students question the legitimacy of a minority woman in the position of teacher? One direct ramification of such sexism and racism is voiced by Montreal-based scholar Hoodfar (1992), who said that she faces different reactions than do most mainstream teachers at the university where she teaches. In her words, "The legitimacy of my occupying the powerful position of teacher in a classroom is, at best, shaky" (p. 310).

This nonacceptance has day-to-day ramifications on the teacher and on the classroom. Antiracist feminist scholars Bannerji and Ng point out that most minority teachers, and especially those who are new to the profession, have to invest a great deal of energy in establishing themselves as legitimate teachers, both in the eyes of their students and other teachers (quoted in Hoodfar, 1992, p. 310). Hoodfar added that she is conscious that she, like most other minority teachers at the early stages of their career, is "even less secure than junior White male or female teachers" (p. 315). My experiences are similar to those of Hoodfar, who says that her authority and knowledge are easily questioned and that

---

[3] Ng's use of the term *minority* encompasses racial minorities as well as women, whereas the other writers referred to in this chapter and I use this term to mean only racial minorities.

many of the students' questions and class interventions are designed to discredit her. I am constantly being challenged on the rules of English grammar, and it seems to me that some of my students are waiting for me to make a mistake. When they try to bait me with questions about minor, irrelevant rules of grammar, I win grudging acceptance because I am able to answer these questions. I recognize these questions for what they are—not genuine information questions but tests of my legitimacy (see Medgyes, Chap. 12, this volume, for descriptions of similar experiences with students).

It seems then that the experience of non-White women teachers in the ESL classroom and in a university setting is so different from that of their White colleagues that they have to use a different pedagogy. In the Teaching of English as a Second Language (TESL) courses that I took in a Toronto academy, we were advised by experienced White teachers to show our humanity to our students by saying "I don't know the answer to that question, but I will find out." My White colleagues tell me that they use this strategy, and it does indeed make their relationship with their students stronger because it humanizes the teacher. However, this strategy has not worked for me. My interpretation is that by saying "I don't know the answer," I am merely confirming what the students think of me or of any minority woman in the position of teacher: that she is not a legitimate teacher. Hence I try to avoid situations where I do not know the answer. I spend long hours preparing my lessons, and I also try to anticipate my students' questions. I am suggesting that I devote more time to preparing my lessons and that I am under greater pressure in the classroom than my White colleagues. And just like me, the teacher participants in my pilot study said they had to know all the rules of English grammar because they felt they were being constantly judged, tested, and compared unfavorably with their White colleagues.

Ramifications

In this discussion I have shown some of the biases inherent in the ESL profession that favor the White teacher and make the non-White teacher, especially the non-White immigrant woman teacher, look illegitimate. What suggestions can I make to address this situation? One course of action that Cheshire (1991), Ferguson (1992), and Kachru (1992) suggested is to drop the concept of the native speaker.[4] I consider that to

---

[4] They are making this call for pragmatic reasons—that the terms *native speaker* and *mother tongue* do not make sense in the context of English being a world language.

be a step in the right direction. In addition, the unspoken assumptions about who is a valid speaker of English, a valid English-language teacher, in fact, a valid teacher, that pervades the ESL classroom need to be articulated and addressed. It is The ESL class that reflects at the micro level the prejudices that exist outside the classroom. As Edwards (1979) argued, social prejudices directed toward language varieties are long-standing, and there is little reason to suppose that such prejudices will rapidly disappear because views of language often correspond with views of the social status of language users. An indicator of the low status of minorities is their representation in the Canadian media. Miller and Prince (1994) of Toronto-based Ryerson Polytechnic University's Journalism department, commented:

> When you read the largest newspapers in five of Canada's most cosmopolitan cities, it's easy to form the following impression of visible minorities: Half are either athletes or entertainers: if they're in the news otherwise, they're probably in trouble of some sort; and few make any contribution to business or have noteworthy lifestyles. (p. 1)

These are some of the findings of a content analysis done in the fall of 1993 at Ryerson: the study examined 2,141 photographs and 895 local news stories carried in a random week's editions of six major Canadian daily newspapers—*Vancouver Sun, Calgary Herald, Winnipeg Free Press, Toronto Star, Toronto Sun,* and *Montreal Gazette.* According to *Statistics Canada,* these cities include some of the country's highest concentrations of aboriginals and visible minorities, ranging from 26.8% in Toronto to 12.8% in Montreal. According to the 1991 census, visible minorities and aboriginals make up 13.2% of the national population (cited in Miller & Prince, 1994, p. 1).

The Ryerson study was undertaken to find answers to two questions: Are non-Whites in each city receiving the amount of news coverage that their numbers seem to warrant? And, are pictures of minorities appearing in representative numbers throughout the newspapers (pp. 1–2)? Pictures and stories were evaluated for tone; they were deemed positive if they showed achievement, negative if they depicted minorities as criminals or in stereotypical ways, and neutral if they reflected the participation of minorities in everyday life, such as taking part in a street poll (p. 3). In a week's sampling of Canada's six biggest newspapers, the researchers found that of the 895 local, staff-written stories that appeared on the news pages of the six papers during the week, only 14%, or a total of 128 stories, featured minorities or involved minority issues. The tone of minority news content in the six newspapers was more negative (49%) than positive (42%), and there were only 12 neutral stories. This part of the study focused only on local news and did not look at the sports or entertainment pages or at the stories supplied by wire services, thus giving the researchers a good indication of how the six newspapers cover diversity "in their own backyards" (pp. 3–6).

The findings of the Ryerson study are an indicator of the dominant group's negative perception of minorities in Canada. More specifically, according to Ng (1990), the dominant group's negative perception of minority women is seen in the way the term *immigrant women* is generally used; it embodies "class, ethnic and racial biases" as it is equated with "visible minority women, their stereotype being of women who either do not speak English or speak it with an accent other than British or American, and women who have low-paid, low-status jobs" (p. 21).

I have encountered such commonsense racism even at my faculty, which has a reputation for being enlightened, progressive, and forward looking. I have met well-meaning educators here who use the term immigrant woman in the way Ng (1990) described it. Recently, a colleague asked me to participate in her presentation on students who had their education outside Canada. The group of four students who were supposed to interview me looked stupefied when they met me. At the end of a 20-minute interview, one member of the group, a high school teacher who was at my faculty for that year with the expressed aim of educating himself on racial issues, admitted to the class that I was not his idea of an immigrant woman. When another student—one who appeared to be familiar with Ng's work on this subject—asked if his idea of an immigrant woman was that of someone who spoke broken English and worked as a cleaning woman, the teacher sheepishly concurred. The group members also conceded that their idea of a foreign student was an English learner, not an English teacher.

If such prejudices exist against minority women, especially against those of us who have immigrated here, even in an enlightened graduate school, how can ESL students be expected to accept their minority women teachers? "We usually learn to value what we see valued and to undermine what we see undermined," observes Thomas (Chap. 1, this volume) by way of explaining that the marginalization of the non-native teacher by non-native students has to be seen within the context of the non-native teacher's marginalization by colleagues and by the profession. I would add to Thomas' observation that in addition, ESL students in Canada are cognizant of the message that Canadian society is giving them about who is important and who is not important. Their response to their minority women teachers is forged in the structural context of a society in which we communicate the message that important people are White, Anglo, and male. In the classroom, we have to address and challenge our students' perceptions of an ideal ESL teacher and thus try to unravel their sexism and racism. But that is only a small beginning. A bigger step toward the empowerment of the minority woman ESL teacher would be when Canadian society interrogates and challenges the low status that it attributes to minority women. And a much bigger step toward the empowerment of the minority woman ESL teacher would be when Canadian society ascribes a higher status to minority women.

References

Amin, N. (1994). *Minority women teachers on ownership of English.* Unpublished master's research paper, University of Toronto, Toronto, Ontario, Canada.

Amin, N. (1997). Race and the identity of the non-native ESL teacher. *TESOL Quarterly, 31,* 580–583.

Cheshire, J. (1991). Introduction: Sociolinguistics and English around the world. In J. Cheshire (Ed.), *English around the world: Sociolinguistic perspectives* (pp. 1–12). Cambridge, England: Cambridge University Press.

Cummins, J. (1989). *Empowering minority students.* Sacramento, CA: California Association for Bilingual Education.

Das Gupta, T. (1991). Introduction and overview. In J. Vorst et al. (Eds.), *Race, class, gender: Bonds and barriers* (pp. 1–11). Toronto, Canada: Garamond.

Edwards, J. R. (1979). *Language and disadvantage.* London: Edward Arnold.

Ferguson, C. A. (1992). Foreword. In B. B. Kachru (Ed.), *The other tongue: English across cultures* (pp. xiii–xvii). Urbana, IL: University of Illinois Press.

Hoodfar, H. (1992). Feminist anthropology and critical pedagogy: The anthropology of classrooms' excluded voices. *Canadian Journal of Education, 17,* 303–320.

Kachru, B. B. (1992). (Ed.) *The other tongue: English across cultures.* Urbana, IL: University of Illinois Press.

Matsuda, M. (1991). Voices of America: Accent, antidiscrimination, law, and a jurisprudence for the last reconstruction. *The Yale Law Journal, 100,* 1329–1407.

Miller, J., & Prince, K. (1994). *The imperfect mirror: Analysis of minority pictures and news in six Canadian newspapers.* Toronto, Canada: School of Journalism, Ryerson Polytechnic University.

Ng, R. (1990). Racism, sexism, and visible minority immigrant women in Canada. *Zeitschrift der Gesellschaft fuer Kanada-Studien, 10*(2), 21–34.

Ng, R. (1991). Teaching against the grain: Contradictions for minority teachers. In J. Gaskell & A. McLaren (Eds.), *Women and education* (pp. 99–115). Calgary, Canada: Detselig Enterprises.

Peirce, B. N. (1993). *Language learning, social identity, and immigrant women.* Unpublished doctoral dissertation, University of Toronto, Toronto, Ontario, Canada.

Rockhill, K., & Tomic, P. (1995). Situating ESL between speech and silence. In J. Gaskell & J. Willinsky (Eds.), *Gender in/forms curriculum: From enrichment to transformation* (pp. 209–229). New York: Teachers College Press.

Thuy, V. G. (1979). *Bilingual education: A necessity or a luxury?* Palo Alto, CA: R and E Research.

Widdowson, H. G. (1994). The ownership of English. *TESOL Quarterly, 28,* 377–388.

CHAPTER 8

English Only or English Plus?
The Language(s) of EFL Organizations

Masaki Oda
Tamagawa University

Throughout the history of ELT, professional organizations have played important roles in promoting the profession. As Howatt (1984) stated, a number of major organizations were set up in English-speaking countries in the late 1960s as "further markers of professional cohesion" (p. 224). Phillipson (1992) and Pennycook (1993) discussed the significant impact of professional organizations, information centers such as the British Council and the U.S. Information Agency, and assistance from Western governments on host EFL communities. However, only a scrutiny of how an ELT organization relates to the international and local professional communities would reveal the complicated nature of NS-NNS power relationship in the ELT profession.

This chapter deals with the situation within the Japan Association for Language Teaching (JALT), the second largest TESOL affiliate in the world and the local branch of the International Association of Teachers of English as a Foreign Language (IATEFL). I first discuss JALT's internal language policy, its effects on the ELT profession in Japan, JALT's attempts to overcome some of the resultant problems, and what remains be done. I also relate the issues in JALT to my previous study of the language policies of TESOL affiliates in EFL contexts (Oda, 1994c) and conclude with a description of the negative consequences of the dominance of NSs in the ELT professional community, particularly in EFL contexts.

JALT and Its Language Policy: Background

In 1996, with more than 4,000 members, JALT was the second largest TESOL affiliate in the world and the third largest language teaching association in Japan. About 45% of the JALT members were Japanese nationals and 55% were non-Japanese nationals. Most of the latter were NSs of English.

Although it was originally started as an organization of EFL teachers in the mid-1970s, JALT is no longer exclusively for ELT professionals. It now includes language teaching professionals at all levels, from private tutors to teachers from elementary to tertiary level, and teachers of various languages such as English, German, Chinese, as well as Japanese as a Second Language. In fact, JALT approved a special interest group in Japanese as a Second Language in 1992 and another group of teachers of languages other than English has filed a petition for its formal recognition as a special interest group within JALT.

JALT's top decision-making body consists of seven nationally elected officers along with several national-level board and committee chairs appointed by the president. In April, 1997, there were 38 geographically based "full" chapters and three affiliate chapters listed on its directory. Each full chapter sends a representative who is a voting member to the National Executive Board. There are three voting representatives from 12 national special interest groups (N-SIGs).

JALT has a monthly publication, *The Language Teacher*, a more research-oriented biannual journal, *The JALT Journal*, and some other publications, all of which are distributed to its members. Its annual international conference attracts more than 2,000 participants.

English has been used as the de facto official language of JALT since its founding. This has been considered appropriate as English is the only language everyone in the organization understands and thus a neutral choice. The exclusive use of English in JALT has, therefore, been legitimized with an assumption that it is beneficial to everyone in the organization. For many years, the dominant status of English in JALT has not been questioned, although the number of members who neither teach English nor are NSs of English has increased over the years. It was only in the early 1990s that some members publicly expressed their concerns regarding the status of English in JALT and its negative consequences for the organization.

In 1994, JALT was to vote on a revised Constitution and Bylaws at its annual meeting, including a clause describing the status of the two languages, Japanese and English. After several heated debates and revisions, the proposed language clause was finalized as follows: "For administration purposes, the working languages of JALT shall be English and/or Japanese" (*JALT Information and Directory*, 1997).

Many NNSs of English have been disadvantaged in JALT. Although NS members have never been required to be proficient in Japanese, the language of the local community, NNS members, most of whom are native speakers of Japanese, have had to be competent in English to fully participate in the organization's activities. Moreover, native-like proficiency in English has been crucial for those NNS members who participate in the decision-making processes of the organization because most of the meetings are conducted in English and important information is disseminated in English only. This de facto English only policy had never been publicly criticized until the author argued for the necessity of a bilingual policy in JALT for its internal and external purposes (Oda, 1994b).

At its 20th annual conference in October, 1994, the revised constitution and bylaws of JALT, including the working language clause, were ratified. However, despite the fact that the working languages of the organization are defined, a large part of JALT's activities are still conducted monolingually in English. This includes dissemination of important information to members who have no interest in ELT, such as teachers of Japanese as a second language or teachers of French as a foreign language.

More Than Just a Linguistic Problem

Between the fall, 1994 and the spring, 1996, a series of opinion articles appeared in *The Language Teacher* (Marshall, 1994; Oda, 1994a, 1995; Jannuzi 1995, 1996). The main issue of the debate was whether JALT should use only English. Both Marshall and Jannuzi supported an English-only policy whereas the author (Oda, 1994a) supported the bilingual (English-Japanese) working language policy.

The supporters of the English-only policy argued that English "is the single most important language for international, cross-cultural communications, education, academia, language teaching, etc." (Jannuzi, 1995, p. 44, summarizing Marshall) and thus it should be the only language of the organization. In response, the author argued that this was "a value judgment more than an objective fact" (Oda, 1995, p. 33). The rationale behind the author's argument against the English-only policy in JALT was that, as a Japan-based professional organization of second/foreign language teaching, JALT would not be able to function without Japanese. The author also argued that using Japanese as one of the languages of the organization would not exclude the use of English.

Unfortunately, the supporters of the English-only policy misunderstood the author's position: many assumed that the author was promoting a "Japanese only" policy and referred to various historical events related to linguistic imperialism by the Japanese government such as Japan's suppression of its Korean, Ainu, and Okinawan minorities (see Jannuzi, 1995).

Ironically, besides the issues of the debate themselves, the language of the debate disadvantaged the author, a native speaker of Japanese. Although *The Language Teacher* permits submissions in Japanese, the author was not able to use the option as Marshall and Jannuzi may not have been able to read Japanese. The use of English by the author may have also distanced him from 45% of the JALT members who are Japanese nationals and native speakers of Japanese. Although some Japanese members may have had opinions on the issue, it may have been difficult for them to follow a debate conducted in a foreign language, thereby making them nonparticipants in the debate.

Language and Power in JALT

In a large volunteer organization such as JALT, there needs to be a system that ensures that the minimum effort leads to the maximum benefit. Thus, it is natural to assume that using a single language is more economical than using two or more languages. However, a disadvantage of using English within the organization is that it would restrict members whose primary language is not English from being involved in its decision-making processes and administration. Consequently, it would create an unequal division of power based on language background.

The author presents some examples both at macrolevel (organizational structure) and microlevel (actual language use) that illustrate the negative consequences of having only one working language in an organization that has members with different language backgrounds.

The strongest argument for having one working language of the organization lies in its economy. It is derived from a pragmatic point of view in which matters are handled in the most appropriate manner under actual conditions rather than following a general principle. As JALT is open to those involved with foreign language teaching in Japan, it must have close ties with the Japanese community. Having English as the only working language or English monolingualism of the organization would severely restrict communication with the community that the organization is meant to serve. Although English can be used at the informal level, it would not be an acceptable language for official communication with the local community.

As the following cases show, the promotion of English monolingualism within JALT may have been accomplished through the reorganization of JALT's structure and the restriction of information to members who used a language other than English.

Case 1: Officers' Duties

Currently, there is no language proficiency requirement to become a JALT officer even at the highest decision-making level. There are no monolingual Japanese-speaking officers either at national and chapter levels of JALT because they all have to participate in meetings that are often conducted in English. Although officers are expected to perform their duties both in English and Japanese, it is possible for a monolingual NSs of English to hold office.

Case 2: Elections

In 1994, the nominations and elections committee of JALT decided to publish candidates' statements both in English and Japanese on the grounds that it would give better access to information. The committee asked candidates to submit their statement in English and had them translated into Japanese. NNSs including Japanese speaking candidates were also asked to submit their statements in English so that the committee would translate them into Japanese. Those who benefited the most from this service were monolingual English-speaking candidates.

Case 3: Conferences

JALT's annual international conference attracts around 2,000 participants and has approximately 400 presentations. Although presentations can be made in any languages including English and Japanese, presenters have to submit a data sheet in English. In addition, the title of presentations must be in English. This may discourage presentations in languages other than English thus disadvantaging NNSs of English. English could thus become an obstacle to submitting a proposal.

Case 4: Research Grants

JALT provides research grants to its members. Although its announcements are given in both English and Japanese, the applicants are advised to submit proposals in English, as the guidelines are not available in Japanese. This applies to presentations on teaching Japanese as a second language as well.

Case 5: Decision Making

Most decision making in JALT takes place at meetings at various levels. English is used as the language of meetings based on the assumption that it is the only language every participant understands and thus is fair to everybody. *Robert's Rules of Order* (Robert, 1970; De Vries, 1990) is used as the standard parliamentary procedure of the organization because it is "the standard parliamentary procedure" in English-speaking countries. This creates two distinct problems. First, NNSs are forced to use English to participate in decision making because it is the only language understood by English-speaking monolinguals who constitute roughly half of the decision-making bodies. Second, the fact that *Robert's Rules* is used is certainly a disadvantage to most NNSs as they would require time to get accustomed to the procedure itself (see Takahashi, 1991).

NNSs of English participating in JALT decision making must overcome other language obstacles, too. As most documents are in English, NNS participants have disadvantages to begin with, especially when they have to read and understand the documents under time pressure. In meetings, they have to follow spontaneous verbal interactions in English while simultaneously observing *Robert's Rules.*

When the discussion gets heated, some NS participants take undue advantage of minor shortcomings in the language use of NNSs. The following question and answer session from a JALT meeting is one example.

Speaker B (NS):	When was the application for the JSC filled?
Speaker A (NNS):	On the 30th of the last month. [Speaker A meant the 13th]
Speaker B (NS):	February 30th? I don't understand what he's talking about?
Speaker A (NNS):	No. THIRTEENTH.
Speaker B (NS):	Oh, I did not know February 30th existed in the Japanese calendar.

It is contextually clear that Speaker A meant the 13th, because February 30th does not exist. However, this type of verbal exchange is very common in the meetings of the organization and, in fact, the strategy has been successfully used to discourage NNSs from participating actively in meetings (see Takahashi, 1991). The deliberate use of complex structures such as double negatives (for example, "it is not unlikely" instead of "it is likely"), culturally loaded metaphors (for example, "this is like [the name of a soap opera character on American TV]"), and the use of slang are also common.

Much time is spent discussing the wording of what is to be recorded in the minutes. It is certainly a disadvantage for NNS participants to argue over the wording of English with those who are supposed to have an innate intuition of the English language. NNSs often have to agree without further debate when the phrase "We don't say it" is used by a NS.

JALT's Attempts to Deal With the Language Issue

So far, the author has discussed the various language-related problems in JALT resulting from the English-only policy of the organization. However, in 1994, a majority of JALT members voted for the revised constitution, which includes the bilingual language clause. In fact, many of those who supported the bilingual policy were NSs of English.

Since 1994, the bilingual policy has been successfully implemented in some areas. In publications, the editors of *The Language Teacher* and *The JALT Journal* have added NNSs to their editorial boards. In *The Language Teacher,* the editor has gradually added Japanese-speaking coeditors to columns in order to encourage submissions in Japanese. Some JALT chapters have started organizing presentations in Japanese or at least allowed questions in Japanese at the end of a presentation in English. Plenary sessions at the international conference were simultaneously interpreted in 1995 and 1996.

In the decision-making process, some officers have prepared written reports in two languages. In addition, the national elected officers have decided to have an interpreter at its Executive Board Meetings and Annual General Meetings. However, interpreters who are familiar with the organization as well as *Robert's Rules of Order* have not been easy to find.

In 1997, three years after the members voted for the bilingual policy, all seven nationally elected officers and five of the seven appointed sub-committee chairs are NSs of English (*JALT Information and Directory,* 1997). Few of them appear to be competent in Japanese.

Is JALT Different From Other TESOL Affiliates?

As described in the previous sections, the language policy of JALT has a complex history. However, is this a feature common to all TESOL affiliates and IATEFL branches in non-English-dominant contexts, or is it peculiar to JALT? In the case of TESOL, its affiliates are defined as "[g]eographically based, autonomous organizations that support the mission of TESOL" (Teachers of English to Speakers of Other Languages [TESOL], 1995, p. 475). It is essential for these affiliates to support the following TESOL mission statement, and act accordingly:

> TESOL's mission is to strengthen the effective teaching and learning of English around the world while respecting individual's language rights. TESOL promotes scholarship, disseminates information, and strengthens instruction and research. (TESOL, 1997, p. 357).

The mission statement states that TESOL and its affiliates are supposed to promote ELT but in no way demote the languages of the learners and of the local community. I now examine the issues raised in the previous sections, referring to my study on language policy of TESOL affiliates in EFL contexts.

TESOL Affiliate Survey

A preliminary survey was conducted among 29 TESOL affiliates in EFL countries by the author in late 1993 (Oda, 1994c). Although some may categorize the affiliates in Quebec and Puerto Rico as ESL organizations, they were included in this survey because their local languages, French and Spanish, are more dominant than English in their communities. Out of the 29 TESOL affiliates, 16 (55%) participated in the survey. The 16 affiliates include 4 in Asia, 4 in Central America and the Caribbean, 4 in South America, 2 in Europe, and 1 each from North America and Africa. In this section, I present those figures relevant to the discussion.

Procedure

Each of the affiliates was sent a questionnaire and asked to respond to 26 questions concerning the characteristics of the organization as well as the relationship between English and the local languages in various domains and activities such as the constitutions and bylaws, administrative meetings, elections, internal affairs, external affairs, conferences, and newsletters. The questionnaire was filled out by TESOL liaison officers in 4 of affiliates or other officers including affiliate presidents, public relations chairs, or secretaries in 12 affiliates.

Characteristics of the Affiliates

The 16 affiliates that responded to the survey varied in size and status in the local academic communities. The size of the affiliates ranged from 100 to 5,400 members. Two of them are organizations for foreign language teaching in general, while others are exclusively for EFL professionals. It should also be noted that six (37.5%) of them are the only professional ELT organizations in their communities.

Table 8.1 below shows the composition of affiliate membership by first language (L1) groups. The table shows that 19% of the entire membership of the 16 affiliates are NSs. Although this figure was based on responses to the question asking how the membership population is distributed among the three groups, it is still reliable enough to contrast with the fact that approximately 45% of JALT members are NSs as stated earlier in this chapter, and 89% of TESOL members "speak English as a first language" ("Members profiled," 1997). The figures also indicate that NNS teachers are actively involved in TESOL affiliate activities.

Decision-Making Bodies

In order for a professional ELT organization to carry out its mission successfully, the role of its decision-making body is crucial. The group decides how to obtain relevant information, what information to disseminate to members, and aspects of ELT to be emphasized in its activities. As a whole, the decision-making body of each organization must be fully familiar with the field of ELT in the local community.

As Table 8.1 indicates, 36% of the members of the affiliates' highest decision making bodies are NSs of English and the rest (64%) are NNSs. This shows that JALT is not a typical TESOL affiliate in this respect as 100% of the members of its highest decision-making body are NSs of English. Although it is not shown in Table 8.2, there are four affiliates with no NS of English in their highest decision-making bodies.

Overall, the NS-NNS ratio was 19:81 for the general membership of the affiliates, in contrast to the 36:64 ratio in the highest decision-making bodies. In other words, NSs of English are represented approximately twice as often in the highest decision-making bodies of the affiliates as NNSs. It should, however, be noted that their native language itself is not an important factor in the decision-making process; what is of greater significance is the number of NSs of English in the highest decision-making bodies who are also competent in the languages of the local communities they serve.

Table 8.1 First Language of the General Membership of TESOL Affiliates
and of their Highest Decision-Making Bodies

Language Group	Composition	
	General Membership*	Highest Decision-Making Body**
English	19%	36%
Local language(s)	80%	63%
Other language(s)	1%	1%

*N = 16, **N=170

The percentages of the NS members of the affiliates' highest decision-making bodies who are competent in the local language(s) indicate that, in many affiliates, it is possible for a monolingual NS of English to hold a position in the bodies. If the four affiliates that had no NS in their decision-making bodies are excluded, the survey results show that 57% of the NS members are competent in the local language(s); this rises to 82% (57% + 25%) if those who speak but cannot read/write the language(s) are added. It should be noted that the definition of competency varies and some respondents may not wish to admit that some members of their highest decision-making bodies are, in fact, unable to communicate in the local languages.

For the same reason, the author was not able to ask members of the highest decision-making body of JALT, all of whom are NSs of English, if they are functionally competent in Japanese. Since October 1994, when its two working languages were defined in its bylaws, there have been few written reports and no report given directly (i.e., without having someone translate) by any of the NS officers of JALT.

Administration

In EFL contexts, the role of local language(s) is more important for the affiliates' administration than in ESL contexts. The more the affiliate is willing to be involved in the community, the more it needs the local language(s). Table 8.2 shows the language(s) used in formal internal and external communication by the affiliates.

English is the only language of internal communication in 10 (62%) of the affiliates surveyed. In fact, eight of these affiliates declared English as their official language. As for external communication, however, only three use English as the only language; two of them operate in communities where both English and another local language are used in daily communication. In the case of JALT, English and Japanese are defined as its working languages for administration as mentioned earlier. JALT uses Japanese for external communication with boards of education, government authorities, mass media, and so forth. when necessary. However, translations and negotiations in Japanese are usually done by an ad hoc assembly of bilingual members, most of whom are NNSs without any authority for decision making.

Table 8.2 Language(s) Used for Communication in TESOL Affiliates

Language(s)	Internal Use	External Use
English Only	10 (62%)	3 (18%)
English and local language(s)	5 (31%)	4 (25%)
Local language(s) only	1 (6%)	9 (56%)

N = 16

Table 8.3 shows the language(s) used for conducting business meetings, taking minutes, and making motions at the meetings. In addition to the eight affiliates who declared English as their only official language, there are two affiliates in which business meetings are conducted monolingually in English. In contrast, five (31%) affiliates conduct their meetings multilingually.

Among these 10 affiliates, 9 take minutes only in English and 1 in both English and the local language. All six affiliates whose meetings are conducted either multilingually or in the local language(s) take minutes in the local language(s). It is noteworthy that most of these affiliates are in Spanish-speaking communities in Central or South America where the local authorities require them to submit their minutes in Spanish to be officially recognized as academic organizations.

Only five affiliates (31%) allow the members to make motions in the local language(s). This may be related to the language used at the meeting as well as the fact that many of them use *Robert's Rules of Order* as the standard procedure for meetings. In the case of JALT, despite the bilingual working-language policy, meetings are still conducted monolingually in English and motions and minutes are entirely in English.

Table 8.3 Language(s) Used for Business Meetings in TESOL Affiliates

Language/Domain	Meetings	Minutes	Motions
English	10 (62%)	9 (56%)	11 (68%)
English and local Language(s)	5 (31%)	1 (6%)	4 (25%)
Local language(s)	1 (6%)	6 (37%)	1 (6%)

N = 16

Election of Officers

Many TESOL affiliates elect members to their highest decision-making bodies. As the election is among the most important events of an affiliate, the general members must be fully informed about the candidates as well as the procedures. Table 8.4 shows the languages used in various contexts related to elections.

Two affiliates responded that they did not hold elections and only three (18%) said that the candidates' profiles were given to the voters in the local language(s). Three (18%) affiliates provide information to their members only in English despite the fact that English is not their declared official language. In the EFL contexts where these affiliates are located, English is not the language of daily communication, making it necessary for the officers responsible for external communication to be proficient in the local language to carry out their duties satisfactorily. However, only one (6%) affiliate said a knowledge of the local language was required of all of its officers, and one affiliate said it was a requirement for particular positions. In other words, it is possible for English-speaking monolinguals to occupy a majority of the highest decision-making positions of TESOL affiliates, as in the case of JALT.

Conferences and Newsletters

For general membership, attending conferences and getting information through newsletters are among the most typical reasons to join TESOL affiliates. Conferences also provide an excellent opportunity for those members who want to share ideas with other EFL professionals. In most of the affiliates, conference presentations are made only in English. As they are organizations for ELT, it is natural that English be the language for presentations. However, many affiliates responded that NS presenters made a considerably larger number of presentations. One of the possible reasons is that essential information for participation, such as Call for Proposals, are give to the members only in English in 12 affiliates (75%). Three (18%) affiliates said that they give such information in English with a short summary in the local languages; however, only one (6%) gives multilingual information.

Table 8.4 Languages for Elections

Language(s)	Profile	Procedure	Ballot
English Only	11 (68%)	10 (62%)	10 (62%)
English and local language(s)*	2 (12%)	3 (18%)	2 (12%)
Local language(s) only	1 (6%)	1 (6%)	2 (12%)
N/A (No election)	2 (12%)	2 (12%)	2 (12%)

$N = 16$; *This category includes English and a brief summary in the local language(s).

Summary of the Survey

The results of the survey lead to several conclusions. First, English is the dominant language in most of the affiliates surveyed. This may be justified because English is the language taught by most members of the affiliates. Nevertheless, it is also possible to argue that the dominance of English may create an unequal division of power within the affiliate for NSs and NNSs of English. From the survey, it is also apparent that NSs are more involved in the decision-making processes of the affiliates.

JALT may not be a typical TESOL affiliate in EFL contexts. As stated earlier, JALT has made efforts to implement its bilingual policy in administration since 1994. Nevertheless, the historical dominance of English has been an obstacle to such efforts. In EFL contexts, there needs to be a place for NSs to exchange ideas and obtain information about the profession, yet it does not mean that TESOL affiliates or any ELT organizations should become a place to maintain power of NSs in the ELT profession.

Language and Power in the ELT Profession

Skutnabb-Kangas (1994) used an "A team and B team" metaphor to illustrate the relationship of power between two groups. She stated that those who belong to the A team have "more access to structural power and material resources than their numbers would justify" (p. 9) and those who belong to the B team have "less access to structural power and material resources than their fair share" (p. 9). Language is one factor that can create such an imbalance.

In the ELT profession, English is likely to serve as the dominant language. Although there are ELT professionals as well as learners with diverse first languages, English is the target language to be taught. In the contexts of EFL, however, the dominant language of the communities is not English. This would create a situation in which those who are not proficient in the local language(s) have limited access to structural power and material resources in the host communities. Consequently, NSs of English may not have as much opportunity to exercise their power as they might in ESL contexts. Nevertheless, from the survey discussed earlier, it is apparent that some TESOL affiliates give power to NSs regardless of proficiency in the local language(s). In other words, the system guarantees NSs membership in the A team, whereas NNSs are relegated to the B team.

The domination of the A team over the B team in the affiliates is not always overt. In order to present a paper at a conference, an affiliate member has to submit a proposal in English, prepare the presentation in English, and deal with follow-up questions in English. This could discourage dialogues among the local ELT professionals in the local language(s).

In many TESOL affiliates, proposals are vetted before inclusion in conference programs. Those affiliates who declare English as their only official language assume that the presentations will be in English and affiliates in which English is the de facto official language expect the presentations to be in English. This goes against the mission of TESOL to promote the ELT profession, because it is unlikely that local NNS teachers would derive the maximum benefit from the information disseminated by the affiliates only in English.

The power of English is often used to maintain the Team B status of NNSs in the affiliates. As seen from the survey, administrative information is given to the members only in English in most of the affiliates. In business meetings, NNSs may have some difficulty in following spontaneous discussions in English.

The power relationship between NSs and NNSs in one ELT organization, as in JALT in Japan, could sometimes influence the ELT profession as a whole. Every year, when TESOL and IATEFL hold their annual conferences, official representatives from their international affiliates or branches participate in various functions at the conferences. In the case of TESOL, JALT has been the only affiliate from Japan. In the past ten years, nine of the official representatives sent by JALT to the annual TESOL Convention were NSs, and some representatives had taught in Japan for only a few years. Most important, only a very few had enough command of Japanese to obtain thorough information about ELT in Japan to be disseminated at the convention.

The author once received a comment from a referee of a professional journal on a manuscript he had submitted. The referee wanted the author to consider revising a section in which the author had stated that "In Japan, many secondary school students take English, because it is the only foreign language available in most of the schools" to "English is required in Japanese secondary schools." The referee stated that "people from JALT" he or she met at TESOL conferences had said so. However, English is not a required language at Japanese secondary schools. This may have been a case of one referee, yet it illustrates the impact of affiliate representatives on TESOL members.

Conclusion

In this chapter, the author discussed the role of TESOL affiliates in EFL contexts with special attention to the language issues of JALT. It can be concluded that the unequal power relationship between NSs and NNSs is intact, with a strong support from the prevailing assumptions that "English is best taught monolingually" and that "The ideal teacher of English is a native speaker" (see Phillipson, 1992), or that "English is natural, neutral and beneficial" (see Pennycook, 1993). NS teachers, including those who are monolinguals, appear to be given a privileged status in the profession. Many TESOL affiliates are controlled by NS professionals who are not necessarily more qualified as language teaching professionals than their NNS counterparts.

There have been discussions on whether NSs are really better than NNSs as ESL/EFL teachers. Some have argued that in certain contexts, NNSs have advantages over NSs (see Medgyes, 1992; Widdowson, 1992). As Rampton (1990) suggested, it is more important for an ESL/EFL teacher to be an accomplished user of English, an expert, rather than being advantaged as a NS. In addition, a knowledge of the learners is crucial to be a successful teacher. This would include the teacher's understanding of the classroom culture that provides the "tradition and recipe for both teachers and students in the sense that there are tacit understandings about what sort of behavior is acceptable" (Holliday, 1994, p. 24). This would lead the author to argue that it may be difficult for monolingual NS EFL teachers to meet the above criteria for a successful teacher.

In fact, this has been a major obstacle for the affiliates to carry out TESOL's mission. Without a proper awareness of the local linguistic, cultural, and social settings, the affiliates could be perceived as promoting linguistic or cultural imperialism within the EFL communities. Therefore, proficiency in the local language(s) is crucial for those at the leadership of TESOL affiliates. In addition, the fact that English monolingualism is practiced in many of the TESOL affiliates suggests that NNS professionals' individual language rights are being violated, thereby contradicting TESOL's mission statement.

References

De Vries, M. A. (1990). *The new Robert's rules of order.* New York: Signet Books.

Holliday, A. (1994). *Appropriate methodology and social context.* Cambridge, England: Cambridge University Press.

Howatt, A. P. R. (1984). *A history of English language Teaching.* Oxford, England: Oxford University Press.

JALT Information and Directory. (1997). Tokyo: Japan Association for Language Teaching.

Jannuzi, C. (1995). The languages of JALT: A view from the provinces. *The Language Teacher, 19*(2), 44–45.

Jannuzi, C. (1996). Who misunderstands whom? Another reply to Oda. *The Language Teacher, 20*(4), 27, 29.

Marshall, R. (1994). Whither the languages of JALT? *The Language Teacher, 18*(9), 26–27.

Medgyes, P. (1992). Native or non-native: Who's worth more? *ELT Journal, 46,* 340–349.

Members profiled in 1997 survey. (1997, June/July). *TESOL Matters, 7*(3), 16.

Oda, M. (1994a). Against linguicism: A reply to Richard Marshall. *The Language Teacher, 18* (11), 39–40.

Oda, M. (1994b, April 5) Public relations chair report. *The Language Teacher: JALT News Suppl.*

Oda, M. (1994c, March). *TESOL affiliates: Promoting English or demoting local languages?* Paper presented at the Twenty-Eighth Annual TESOL Convention, Baltimore, MD.

Oda, M. (1995). More on the languages of JALT: A reply to Charles Jannuzi. *The Language Teacher, 19*(12), 32–33.

Pennycook, A. (1993) *The cultural politics of English as an international language.* Essex, England: Longman.

Phillipson, R. (1992). *Linguistic imperialism.* Oxford, England: Oxford University Press.

Rampton, M. B. H. (1990). Displacing the 'native speaker': Expertise, affiliation, and inheritance. *ELT Journal, 44,* 97–101.

Robert, H. M. (1970). *Robert's rules of order* (Rev. ed.). Glenview, IL: Scott, Foresman.

Skutnabb-Kangas, T. (1994, March). *The politics of language standards.* Paper presented at the Twenty-Eighth Annual TESOL Convention, Baltimore, MD.

Takahashi, J. (1991). Kokusai Kaigi ni Miru Nihonjin no Ibunka Koushou. [Cross-cultural negotiation strategies by Japanese participants at international meetings]. In J. Takahashi, O. Nakayama, K. Midouoka, and F. Watanabe (Eds.), *Ibunka e no Sutorategii* (pp. 181–201). Tokyo: Kawashima Shoten.

Teachers of English to Speakers of Other Languages, Inc. (1995). The twenty-ninth annual convention and exposition [Convention Handbook]. Alexandria, VA: Author.

Teachers of English to Speakers of Other Languages (1997). The thirty-first annual convention and exposition [Convention Handbook]. Alexandria, VA: Author.

Widdowson, H. G. (1992). ELT and EL teachers. *ELT Journal, 46,* 333–336.

PART THREE

Implications for Teacher Education

Just as in sociopolitical concerns, the NS-NNS dichotomy has created a strong and lasting impact on teacher education. However, only a few empirical studies have examined the issue in an ELT context. Keiko Samimy and Janina Brutt-Griffler (Chap. 9) extend Medgyes' (1994) survey by examining the effects of the dichotomy on 17 NNS students enrolled in a graduate TESOL course titled "Issues and Concerns Related to NNS Professionals." The two-fold study first examines the students' self-perceptions in terms of linguistic and pedagogical competence and then explores the students' perceptions and beliefs on the NS-NNS issue. The data is collected via a hybrid of qualitative and quantitative approaches. Samimy and Brutt-Griffler conclude that the participants saw themselves differently from their NS counterparts in their English proficiency and pedagogy, recognized the multidimensionality of the ELT professional, and linked success in the profession to specific sociocultural and linguistic contexts. Although the participants acknowledged the native speaker construct, its significance in ELT was left in doubt.

Whereas Samimy and Brutt-Griffler focused on one teacher preparation course, Lia Kamhi-Stein (Chap. 10) argues that with the increase in the numbers of NNSs enrolled in TESOL MA programs, there is a need to modify the whole curriculum to integrate discussions related to NNS issues in TESOL. She then describes how issues related to NNSs are integrated across the curriculum in a TESOL teacher preparation program that enrolls a high percentage of NNSs. Using her own background as a teacher in Argentina and graduate studentship and teacher trainer roles in the United States as a backdrop, Kamhi-Stein describes how the powerful influence of a role model can be used to improve the self-image of NNSs. She then details how these NNS issues are integrated to the curriculum through classroom activities (such as analyzing the language histories of the teacher trainees and conducting classroom-centered research on NNSs) as well as out-of-class activities (such as providing teacher trainees with opportunities for professional growth and engaging in advocacy activities on behalf of themselves).

Throughout Kamhi-Stein's chapter, the reader discerns the powerful influence that NNS teacher educators can exert on NNS teacher trainees.

In Chapter 11, Jun Liu returns to the theme expounded by Samimy and Brutt-Griffler by describing the impact of NNS teachers on ESL learners—as seen from the teachers' viewpoint. Seven non-native ELT teachers from a variety of cultural and linguistic backgrounds are placed on a NS-NNS continuum instead of a dichotomy. Using a case study approach, extensive data relating to their self-perceptions on the continuum and to their impact on ESL students is presented. By using direct quotes extensively, Liu provides insights to the teachers' expectations and their responses to their influence on students. Liu concludes that when the self-expectations of the teachers on the NS-NNS continuum match those of their students, students tend to appreciate their teachers' competence and achievement as learners of English. Liu also notes that students are influenced by the teachers' ethnic background, skin color, and physical appearance when placing the latter on the NS-NNS continuum: a White may be categorized as a NS whereas an Asian with a longer exposure to English may not. Liu argues that by accepting the continuum (instead of a dichotomy), social context cues such as skin color and physical characteristics will play a lesser role in the measurement of a NNS teachers' ability.

In Chapter 12, Peter Medgyes takes a different view, arguing for the maintenance of the NS-NNS dichotomy. Although acknowledging the innate advantages of NNS teachers, Medgyes states that NSs have a better knowledge of English. To be effective, self-confident, and satisfied professionals, NNS teachers need to be near-NSs and ambassadors of the language, and therefore language training is of paramount importance during their training. In support of these views, Medgyes narrates his personal experiences both within and outside the language classroom. Medgyes then discusses which variety of English should be taught by NNS teachers, and in the absence of a clearly defined "International English," states that the obvious choice would be between the British and the U.S. varieties. He then illustrates the bond between language and culture by narrating another personal experience and states that bilinguals are the best ambassadors between peoples and cultures. Using his experience as a teacher-educator in Hungary to substantiate his viewpoints, Medgyes argues that teacher educators have the responsibility of transforming English teachers to ambassadors of English.

In the final chapter, Dilin Liu uses his background as a teacher educator in the United States to argue that the needs of NNS teacher trainees are not met in teacher education programs in North America, the

United Kingdom, and Australia, and to offer suggestions to remedy the situation. Liu states that although nearly 40% of the teacher trainees in these countries are NNS international students, they are often given the same training that NSs receive. Arguing that ethnocentric ideologies such as new teaching methods are to be blamed for this situation, Liu specifies L2 acquisition theories, TESOL methodologies, language improvement courses, and cultural understanding as the areas that most need attention. For instance, Liu argues that methods and teaching styles developed for process-oriented, student-centered classrooms are unsuitable for Asia, where English teaching is still product-oriented and teacher centered. Further, although many NNSs need help in improving their English ("language training," according to Medgyes in Chap. 12, this volume), they are instead taught grammar courses that enhance their explicit knowledge of language rules instead of their language ability. Liu concludes that with increased cultural sensitivity and increased effort, teacher educators in the West will be able to better meet the needs of NNS international teacher trainees.

References

Medgyes, P. (1994). *The non-native teacher*. London: Macmillan.

CHAPTER 9

To Be a Native or Non-Native Speaker: Perceptions of "Non-Native" Students in a Graduate TESOL Program

Keiko K. Samimy and Janina Brutt-Griffler
The Ohio State University

English has become a *lingua franca* among literate educated people and is the most widely learned foreign language in the world. Although comprehensive statistics on the number of students learning the language are difficult to come by, the fact that "there are now at least four non-native speakers of English for every native speaker" (B. Kachru, 1996, p. 241) points to the importance of the learning of English in the second and foreign language contexts. And given that distribution of English acquisition, there inevitably arises the question: Who is best suited to teach these students, the native or the non-native English-speaking teacher?

Although ELT professionals and scholars have voiced differing opinions on issues related to nativeness (for example, Davies, 1991; B. Kachru, 1992; Medgyes, 1994; Phillipson, 1992; Rampton, 1990), empirical studies on beliefs and/or perceptions of non-native professionals on those particular questions are extremely scarce (except in Medgyes, 1992; Reves & Medgyes, 1994). As the number of non-native English-speaking professionals increases in ELT, it is critical for us to conduct a systematic inquiry about the issues and concerns that they have regarding their profession. Such inquiry will not only reveal non-native speakers' voices but also raise our collective consciousness as ELT professionals, both native and non-native speakers of English.

Theoretical Background

Native versus Non-Native Dichotomy: Subject of Scholarly Debate

As Medgyes (1994) noted, the scholarly debate over the question of the native non-native dichotomy has generated a number of controversial issues in applied linguistics. Among them, three are relevant here. First, the native/non-native dichotomy has been challenged on sociolinguistic grounds from the standpoint of the sociohistorical development of English (B. Kachru & Nelson, 1996; B. Kachru, 1986, 1992). Second, an approach has been advocated that sees the native speaker identity as a sociolinguistic construct that can be overcome within certain circumstances (Davies, 1991). In a third approach, the dichotomy is more or less maintained (Medgyes, 1994).

B. Kachru and Nelson (1996) approached the issue from the sociolinguistic implications of the historical spread of English. They introduce the notions of history and language change to the questions of nativeness and reject the notion of innateness in language usage. Thus, from a historical perspective, every language variety can develop its linguistic and sociolinguistic norms that meet the needs of a particular speech community. B. Kachru (1986) further argued that the sociolinguistic innovations should not be construed as a sign of language deficiency, as they would be if they are judged from a hegemonic perspective, which maintains the dichotomy of the native versus non-native perspective by seeing the "idealized" native norm or "mother English" as a point of reference. Rather, such sociolinguistic innovations are functionally and contextually productive and a sign of linguistic nativization and acculturation in "un-English" contexts (B. Kachru, 1986, 1992).

B. Kachru and Nelson (1996) rejected the notion of the perpetuation of the dichotomy at the national and individual level. They state: "[I]n thinking of a country as an ESL country or of an ESL speaker, for example, we perpetuate the dichotomy of native versus non-native, 'us versus them'" (p. 79). The spread of English in its sociohistorical context has created different varieties of English, and highly proficient speakers and professionals in the area of English studies and second and foreign language education. To view them through the lens of the native versus non-native dichotomy is to accept "a linguistic caste system" and maintain a monocultural and monolingual point of reference (B. Kachru & Nelson, 1996).

In the second approach, Davies (1991) also emphasized the sociolinguistic aspect by placing the construct of native and non-native speaker within social and power relations. To Davies, "[T]he distinction native speaker-non-native speaker, like all majority-minority relations, is at bottom one of confidence and identity" (pp. 166–167). Significantly, Davies sees "the native speaker boundary" as one attributable as much to non-native speakers as to native speakers while acknowledging that determining the native speaker construct is a difficult, if not an impossible, task for linguists. He notes that the definition of a native speaker tends to be circular: the native speaker is defined as he or she who is perceived as not being a non-native speaker, whereas the non-native speaker is defined solely as not being a native speaker. Davies' own definition of a native speaker emphasizes the importance of early language acquisition. Although he sees the construct of the native speaker as more of "a useful myth" with limited validity, he nevertheless contends that for L2 learners "the native speaker must represent a model and a goal" (p. 165).

But Davies does not assert absolute validity for the native speaker construct. He explicitly rejected the idea that the "native speaker is uniquely and permanently different from a non-native speaker" (1991, p. 45). For Davies, it is clear that the L2 learner can acquire native linguistic competence of the language even if he or she is outside of the L1 environment. In that sense, non-native speakers can "choose native speaker membership" (p. 165).

The third position on the question of native versus non-native speaker considers the question specifically in its application to the ELT profession. In his treatment of the question of the non-native teacher of English, Medgyes (1992, 1994) adopted the native/non-native contrast as a clear categorical distinction. He asserted that the native speakers' linguistic competence constitutes an "advantage . . . so substantial that it cannot be outweighed by other factors prevalent in the learning situation, whether it be motivation, aptitude, perseverance, experience, education, or anything else" (1992, p. 342). The non-native speaker labors eternally under a "linguistic handicap" (1994, p. 103) while progressing along the interlanguage continuum. He sees native speakers as those who "have acquired English in comparison with non-native speakers who are still acquiring" (p. 12). In short, non-native speakers, unlike native speakers, are permanent learners. At the same time, he describes the non-native speaker's handicap as "relative": "By offering this compromise, [he lets] non-native speakers into the much coveted land of native-like proficiency" (p. 13). Yet, even if they acquire "native-like" proficiency, Medgyes still labels non-native speakers as "pseudo-native speakers," perhaps due to the phonological or colloquial variability in their usage of the language.

Medgyes, however, does not conclude from this that native speakers are necessarily more effective English language teachers; he pointed out that non-native teachers have "an equal chance of success" (1994, p. 103) "on their own terms" (p. 76). For example, non-native speakers show empathy, provide a good model for imitation, and teach "effective language learning strategies," to name just a few (p. 69). In practice,

Medgyes encourages collaboration between native and non-native teachers.

Native Versus Non-Native Dichotomy: Empirical Studies

As mentioned, there is a scarcity of empirical studies that explore the differences between native and non-native teachers of English. There is a particular need for such studies in the area of self-perception or self-image as ELT professionals.

Challenging "liberal-minded" researchers who argue that there are far more important issues than differential English competencies between native and non-native speakers, Medgyes (1994) conducted an international survey to examine two hypotheses: (1) that native English speaker teachers (NESTs) and non-NESTs differ in terms of their language competence and teaching practice; and (2) that the discrepancy in language competence accounts for most of the differences found in their teaching practice. A survey questionnaire was circulated among 216 native and non-native teachers working in 10 countries. The survey revealed that 68% of the respondents perceived differences between native and non-native teachers of English in the way they teach and only 15% saw no differences. Medgyes concluded that the differences found in their teaching were also closely related to their linguistic competencies.

Using the same data set collected from the international survey, Reves and Medgyes (1994) conducted a further analysis to ascertain causal relationships among variables such as non-NESTs' command of English, the differences between NESTs and non-NESTs, and the self-image assumed by the latter. The authors hypothesized that non-NESTs' command of English vis-à-vis NESTs affects their self-image as professionals and, in turn, influences the way they teach. Based on the results obtained from the correlational analysis, the authors conclude that the factors that are essential in the "causal chain" are non-NESTs' teaching qualifications, the time non-NESTs spend in an English-speaking country, and the frequency of non-NESTs' contact with native speakers of English. Based on their findings, the authors make two recommendations in order to "salvage the non-NESTSs' self-perceptions" (p. 364). First, the linguistic deficit on the part of the non-NESTs "have to be openly acknowledged and legitimized" (p. 364); second, non-NESTs need to work on their command of English "to minimize the deficiencies so as to approximate their proficiency, as much as possible, to that of the NESTs'" (p. 364).

The Study

Because teachers' beliefs and self-perceptions often influence the way they teach (Richards & Lockhart, 1994), it is important to investigate their self-image as ELT professionals. In particular, is the low self-image of non-native speaking ELT professionals a result of their low language proficiency, as indicated in Reves and Medgyes (1994)? Given the dearth of empirical research on this topic, the present study aims to document perceptions of non-native TESOL graduate students regarding the native versus non-native issues in teaching English. It employs, as part of its research methodology, the instrument of data collection from Medgyes' (1994) study. In addition, the research questions posed in the this study were similar: How do non-native TESOL graduate students perceive themselves as ELT professionals? Do they think that there are differences between native and non-native speakers of English in their teaching behavior? If so, what are they? Do they feel that they are handicapped because they are not native speakers of English? If so, in what way? What are some of their concerns as ELT professionals?

The present study, however, extends considerably beyond Medgyes' approach in that alongside the quantitative data collected by using the questionnaire, it included data from classroom discussions, in-depth interviews, and autobiographical accounts of the participants. The hybrid use of a quantitative and qualitative approaches helped to increase the validity and reliability of the study. Other differences lie in the sample size as well as in the composition of the subjects or participants of the study. This study focused on a group of 17 participants. Moreover, whereas 77% of Medgyes' subjects had never been in an English-speaking country or had been there less than 3 months, all the participants in the present study were enrolled in an MA or Ph.D. program in TESOL at a large Midwestern university in the United States.

The study was conducted in two phases. The first phase examined how the participants perceived themselves as professionals in terms of their linguistic competence, communicative competence, teaching methodologies/techniques and so forth vis-à-vis native English-speaking professionals. The questionnaire (Medgyes, 1994) employed to collect the relevant data was intended for NNS professionals and contained 23 questions, most of which are closed-ended. In this study, the participants were free to identify themselves or remain anonymous. The questionnaire was distributed at the beginning of the academic quarter. The second phase involved in-depth exploration of the NNS professionals' perceptions and beliefs on the issues of nativeness versus non-nativeness in the profession via interviews and the analysis of their autobiographical accounts related to their experiences of learning and teaching English. The interviews took place throughout the academic quarter depending on the availability of the participants.

Seventeen non-native English speaking graduate students participated in the study. They were all enrolled in a graduate seminar titled "Issues and Concerns Related to NNS Professionals." As mentioned, the participants were pursuing either a MA or a Ph.D. in TESOL. Their length of stay in the United States varied from 1 to 4 years and they represented eight countries: Korea, Japan, Turkey, Surinam, China, Togo, Burkinafaso, and Russia. The gender ratio was approximately the same.

The graduate seminar met once a week for two and one half hours for 10 weeks. The syllabus consisted of a group discussion based on assigned readings, lectures by guest speakers, and oral presentations. The main textbook was *The Non-native Teacher* by Medgyes (1994) which was supplemented by selected articles such as "The Ownership of English" by Widdowson (1994), "English as an International Language" by Strevens (1992), "Models for Non-Native English" by B. Kachru (1992), "Culture, Style, and Discourse: Expanding Noetics of English" by Y. Kachru (1992), "Testing English as a World Language: Issues in Assessing Non-native Proficiency" by Lowenberg (1992), and "My Language, Your Culture: Whose Communicative Competence?" by Nelson (1992). The guest speakers were invited to share their experiences as coordinators, academic specialists, or as graduate teaching associates from the ESL programs (Composition and Spoken English) on campus. The titles of their lectures were "Voice, Self, and Authority in Academic Writing," "The International TA Experience and the Problem of Presence," "Recognizing the Strengths of the NNS ESL Teacher," "Confessions of an International TA," and "International English: Cultural and Linguistic Models and Their Relevance to NNS Professionals." During the final week of the course, the students were asked to make a short presentation based on their retrospective and introspective reflection on their experience as an EFL learner as well as a teacher.

Results

Background Information

In terms of the length of their EFL teacher education (see Table 9.1),

Table 9.1 Duration of Participants' EFL Teacher Education

Number of participants	Years of EFL education	Percentage
2	10 - 12	12
2	7 - 9	12
11	4 - 6	64
2	1 - 3	12

N = 17

12% of them had between 10 to 12 years; 12% 7 to 9 years; 64% 4-6 years; and 12%, 1 to 3 years. There were no participants who had no formal training in EFL. Sixty-two percent of them had more than 5 years of teaching experience, 12% less than 5 years, 24% less than 3 years, and only 12% had less than 1 year (see Table 9.2). Most of them had taught either at the college or secondary school level; only a few had taught at vocational schools. Forty-seven percent of them had on the average more than 35 students in their classes, whereas only 16% of them had a small class size of 15 to 20 students. As the descriptive statistics show, more than half of the participants had 4 to 6 years of formal training in EFL and more than 5 years of teaching experience.

Table 9.2 Duration of Participants' English Teaching Experience

Number of participants	EFL teaching experience	Percentage
2	less than 1 year	12
1	1 year	6
3	less than 3 years	18
0	3 years	0
2	less than 5 years	12
1	5 years	6
8	more than 5 years	46

With respect to the institutions in which these participants had taught, 53% had no NESTs and 41% of the schools employed some. Sixty-five percent of the participants stated that there was no organized cooperation between native and non-native speaker teachers of English in their countries, whereas 29% responded that there was some.

At the time of the study, all the participants resided in a Midwestern city in the United States. The average length of stay varied from 1 to 4 years. When they were asked to indicate how often they spoke English with native speakers, 53% of them said everyday; 12%, once or twice a week; 6%, rarely; and the rest did not respond.

To summarize, in terms of teaching experience and formal teacher training, the participants in the this study were a rather sophisticated group of non-native speakers of English.

Linguistic and Pedagogical Issues

In comparison with fellow non-native teachers of English in their countries, 20% of the participants rated their command of English as "excellent," 73% as "good" or "average," and 13% of them rated themselves as "poor" (Table 9.3). Among the areas of difficulties in the use of English were fluency, writing, vocabulary, cultural knowledge, carrying on a dialogue, using new vocabulary, understanding jokes, and reading between the lines. However, when they were asked to what extent the difficulties hindered them in their teaching, 6% of them responded "not at all," 54% "a little," 12% "quite a bit," 6% "very much," and 24% had no response (see Table 9.4). When the participants were asked whether they saw any differences between NESTs and non-NESTS in their teaching of English as a foreign language (EFL), 88% of them responded positively whereas only 6% responded negatively (Table 9.5).

Table 9.3 Participants' Rating of their Command of English

Number of participants	Response	Percentage
3	excellent	29
8	good	53
3	average	20
2	poor	13
0	very poor	0

Table 9.4 Participants' Perception of How Language Command Affects their Teaching

Number of participants	Response	Percentage
1	not at all	6
9	a little	54
2	quite a bit	12
1	very much	6
0	extremely	0
4	no response	24

They noted the differences in the area of linguistic competence in English, teaching methods, and general characteristics. As can be seen in Table 9.6, the participants characterized native speakers as being informal, flexible, self-confident, fluent, and accurate users of English, whereas non-native teachers were characterized as being more sensitive to their students' needs, efficient, aware of negative transfer in learners' interlanguage, able to use learners' L1 as a medium, and tending to rely on textbooks.

To the question, "Who do you think is more successful in teaching EFL?" 58% of the participants responded "both," 24% said "non-natives," and 12% responded "natives." Those who responded "both" explained their position by saying that it depends on the goal, age, and levels of students as well as on the individual teacher and his or her personal factors/abilities. One participant commented that the "successful teacher never depends on 'nativeness'."

Table 9.5 Perceptions of Differences between Non-Native and Native English Speaking Teachers

Number of participants	Response	Percentage
15	Yes	88
1	No	6
1	No response	6

Table 6: Perceived Differences in Between Native and Non-native English Speaking Teachers

Native English-speaking teachers	Non-Native English-speaking teachers
• Informal, fluent, accurate • Use different techniques, methods, approaches • Flexible • Use conversational English • Know subtleties of the language • Use authentic English, provide positive feedback • Communication not exam preparation	• Rely on textbooks, materials • Apply difference between L1 & L2 • Use L1 as a medium • Aware of negative transfer, psychological aspects of learning • Sensitive to the needs of students • More efficient • Know students' background • Exam preparation

Native speaking teachers were perceived to be more successful because of their use of authentic English, whereas those who responded that non-native teachers were more successful gave reasons such as sensitivity to the students' needs and greater efficiency.

To the question, "What do you consider the main aims/objectives of your teaching EFL?" 47% of the participants responded that their primary aim was to teach communicative English; 17% stated that their goal was to increase their students' cultural understanding of the target language and culture; another 17% gave their aim as increasing their students' grammatical competence. Finally, 6% responded that their main aim/objective was to help their students pass entrance examinations.

An analysis of the quantitative data collected via the questionnaire seems to indicate that the majority of the participants observed differences between native and non-native speakers of English in their teaching behavior. They did not, however, necessarily think that the native English-speaking teachers were superior to their non-native speaking counterpart. Instead, they argued that successful teaching depends on numerous factors such as the goals and objectives of a program, age, and level of students as well as individual teachers' personality and skills.

Interviews

In order to better understand the results obtained from the questionnaire, interviews were conducted. The participants were grouped according to their native country and each group was interviewed by a researcher for approximately one hour or longer depending on the number of participants in the group. The interviews were semistructured: a set of questions was prepared by the researcher beforehand, although some flexibility was allowed. Some of the questions were as follows: What are your concerns as non-native English-speaking teachers of English? Do you feel that you are disadvantaged because English is not your first language? What do you think your unique contributions might be as non-native English-speaking professionals?

In the following section, some highlights from the interviews are presented according to the research questions.

What are some of your concerns as a NNS English teacher?

Although some of the interviewees felt that lack of native-like proficiency in English is an important concern, many participants argued that it may not be the most important issue for EFL professionals. They were more concerned with the English curriculum, preservice teacher education, and professional development. Participants from Korea and Japan, for example, voiced their concern regarding the negative impact entrance examinations have on their English curricula. Although a listening comprehension component was added to the English portion of the exam recently, the emphasis was still on grammar and reading. They all agreed that the washback effect is enormous in the way English is being taught at secondary and high school levels. "This is very frustrating because we should be teaching how to communicate in English rather than teaching how to conjugate the verbs in English," stated one Korean participant.

Another important concern was raised by a group of Korean participants as to the quality of preservice teacher education in Korea. They stated, "We took courses such as linguistics, literature, education, speaking, and listening at the university, but no TESOL methodology courses were offered." This lack of preparation forces many new teachers to teach English in the same way they were taught as students, relying on more traditional methods than communicative approaches. Similarly, the Japanese participants argued: "How can we teach communicative English when we were never taught how to communicate in English?" To supplement the lack of communicative skills in English among teachers, the ministries of education of Japan and Korea have been actively recruiting native speakers of English to teach in their countries.

The participants from Japan and Korea, however, expressed some reservations about it because "often they [the native speakers] are not well-qualified; they are hired simply because they are native speakers of English. The government should invest more money in educating non-native speaker teachers in their country rather than bringing in native speakers from other countries. What the government is doing offers only a short-term solution. English teachers should be homegrown."

In terms of professional development, a participant from a Latin American country expressed her frustration for the lack of support and resources available to English teachers. According to her, "It is very difficult to keep up with what is happening in our field. We have very little support from the government to attend TESOL conferences, for example. In fact, we are still using the same textbooks that we used 20 years ago. There is not enough awareness as to how difficult it is to teach English in the Third World countries. We are more concerned with the development of the country. People are too busy just surviving."

Do you feel that you are disadvantaged in your profession because you are not a native speaker of English?

Overall, most of the participants did not feel particularly disadvantaged in their work as EFL teachers because of their non-nativeness. On the contrary, during the interviews, they communicated a sense of confidence and self-esteem as professionals. One Turkish participant, for example, stated: "I put value on myself. I had limited resources and exposure to the target language and little contact with native speakers. But I learned English nonetheless. No one can understand our culture, our students, their attitudes, and behavior better than Turkish teachers." Her statement echoes what Edge (1988) had experienced as a native speaker teacher of English in Turkey.

> When I stood in front of a class of Turkish schoolchildren, there was clearly a very restricted sense in which I could act as a model for them in social, cultural, emotional, or experiential terms, with regard either to their past or their future. The person who could act as such a model would be a Turkish teacher; and if we believe that reference to the social, cultural, and emotional experiences, awareness, and aspirations of our pupils is important in learning, then this is the ideal model (p. 155).

Another participant who was an English teacher in Russia stated: "In Russia, I never had a problem professionally because I am not a native speaker. In fact, I was highly regarded as a professional in the community. There were not many native speakers around to feel competitive toward them." A participant from a West African country who has 25 years of teaching experience agreed: "I was maybe lucky enough to accumulate a lot of experience from different places and different training institutions. But even from the start, I never felt the lack of native-like proficiency as a serious pedagogical handicap. I don't think anyone has ever questioned my competence just because of my non-native background."

There are some instances, however, where non-native professionals felt subservient to native speakers due to linguistic and sociopolitical power dynamics. One participant commented: "As a professional representing my government's interests, I have to discuss with the British and the American colleagues and consider them as 'the owners' of the language. This, added to the fact that they are the owners of the resources and of the knowledge base, put the scale in their favor in the power relationship games. I feel I do not have absolute autonomy."

Many of the participants in the study, as mentioned earlier, possessed a high level of English proficiency and many years of teacher education and teaching experience. They did not seem to feel particularly disadvantaged as English teachers in their home countries. However, life in ESL contexts has challenged them professionally and personally. According to a participant from a West African country, "I always feel like a learner here because there are so many realities which talk to you everywhere. It might be cultural aspects you don't understand, or administrative procedures to go through at the bank or at the Immigration Services, or subtle racial implications at the medical center. As a non-native speaker, my professional competence was questioned to some degree when I came to pursue my MA in an American university. I was required to take English 101 class based on the fact that my TOEFL score was 584." Similarly, a participant from an Asian country shared his experience living in the United States: "Back home I was somebody [a professor], here I am nobody. I am just a student. I felt that I don't have an important role to play here." Another participant from a West African country recounted his initial frustration and disappointment during his stay in England: "I was frustrated for being able to understand my instructors in class and yet unable to understand my interlocutors both in Grays and in London. Can you imagine? An English teacher who cannot understand the English spoken by the very speakers of the language! I had the impression that I had been telling lies to my students, teaching them some language that I thought was English but that in fact was not."

These experiences reveal that even those who perceived themselves as competent and successful English teachers in their home countries found their confidence and self-identity challenged in ESL contexts. Self-image or self-esteem as professionals, then, may be very context dependent. The cited instances seem to indicate that contextual factors— sociocultural, interpersonal, and linguistic, among others—greatly influence, albeit temporarily, the way one perceives himself or herself as a person or as an ELT professional.

What do you think your contributions might be as a non-native speaker of English in ELT?

Many participants talked about their role as "teacher educators" upon their return to their respective countries. They plan to (1) emphasize the distinction between teaching in the ESL and EFL contexts so that EFL teachers can identify clearly objectives and goals of English teaching; (2) help EFL teachers to assess the appropriateness of materials according to their settings and their students' needs; (3) make study or work abroad a mandatory component of teacher education; (4) create opportunities for in-service teachers to work with teachers from various English-speaking countries such as India, Singapore, and Philippines, and (5) introduce integrative and creative methods of evaluation, such as such as portfolio assessment, in schools.

Moreover, several participants felt that EFL teachers were not actively contributing to research and/or publications in the field. They felt that many research findings were from ESL contexts. In fact, they believed that ESL/EFL differences are not adequately dealt with in ELT. Yet, due to the lack of a research tradition in some educational systems, "among the teachers there is an attitude of 'we are not a member of the club' with a subsequent total dependency on annual seminars organized by the British Council and the American Cultural Center." One participant suggested that EFL teacher development programs need to aim at developing self-awareness among teachers. He added, "It is crucial to make EFL autonomous, by encouraging local research, with teachers collaborating with other researchers to establish an EFL knowledge base." Another participant echoed this sentiment: "It is high time non-native teachers began getting more involved in linguistic research and publications. I realize I have been inactive for a long time, but I believe it is never too late. Non-native teachers should let their voices be heard. Our contribution is indispensable."

Native or Non-Native: Is that Still the Question?

This study examined the way non-native TESOL graduate students perceived themselves as ELT professionals vis-à-vis native speakers of

English. The first part of the study investigated the participants' perceptions and/or evaluations of themselves as EFL teachers in terms of their linguistic competence, communicative competence, and teaching behaviors in relation to native speaker teachers. The analysis of the descriptive statistics seems to indicate that the participants saw themselves differently from their native speaker counterparts. The perceived differences lay not only in their English proficiency but also in their teaching. The participants, for example, characterized native speaking English teachers as "informal, flexible, and confident" whereas non-native speaking teachers were characterized as "sensitive to the students' needs, efficient, and dependent on textbooks." The observed differences, however, did not suggest that native speaker teachers are necessarily better than the non-native counterparts. In other words, to the critical question, "Who do you think is more successful in teaching EFL?" more than half the participants responded "both." Although 24% favored non-native English speakers, only 12% saw native speakers as superior. Moreover, the general consensus to the question was, "It all depends." That is to say, who is more successful depends on learner factors (age, motivation, goals/objectives, aptitude), teacher factors (knowledge, skills, training, experience, personality), and contextual factors (ESL vs. EFL context, amount of available input, degree of contact with native speakers, availability of authentic materials). Thus, the participants of the study recognized the multidimensionality of the ELT professional; significantly, they linked the notion of success in the profession to the dynamics and demands of a particular sociocultural and linguistic context, thereby allowing for sociocultural and individual flexibility and pluralism in the profession.

The responses to the questionnaire were similar to those in Reves and Medgyes (1994) in that the participants in the two studies did see the differences between native and non-native teachers with regard to their linguistic as well as pedagogical behavior. Furthermore, to the question of who is more successful, both groups of participants responded in the descending order of both, non-native speakers, and native speakers.

Despite the similarities observed from the quantitative data, the analysis of the qualitative data in the present study led us to a different conclusion from that of Reves and Medgyes (1994). Namely, unlike the causal relationship that they established between NNS professionals' command of English and impoverished self-image, the results of this study seem to suggest otherwise. In other words, although the construct of native speaker is recognized and is psychologically real in the participants' consciousness, they did not express a sense of inferiority vis-à-vis native speaker professionals. In fact, one of the participants made the following comment, which epitomizes the sentiment of the majority of the participants: "To me, the NS/NNS dichotomy debate is a waste of resources. Our profession must be more pragmatic in our approach towards teaching English. The majority of teachers of English in the world, and certainly in Korea, will continue to be non-native speakers. Thus, the question, 'How can non-native speaker teachers become more like native speaker teachers?' misses the point. The guiding question in EFL teacher development in Korea [for example] must acknowledge the real status of the teacher pool. Thus, the question should be stated as 'How can the present and future teachers be helped to become all they can be as Korean people who teach English to other Korean people?'"

The question of whether native or non-native speakers are better language teachers appeared to be rather irrelevant if not counter-productive. A more relevant question, according to the participants in the study, was how qualified an individual is as an EFL teacher. The participants' views might be reflected in what Rampton (1990) called expertise. Unlike the construct of nativeness, Rampton argues that "expertise is learned, not fixed or innate" (p. 98) and that "the notion of experts shifts the emphasis from 'who you are' to 'what you know'" (p. 99). Thus, the construct of *expertise* diminishes undue prejudices and discriminations against non-native speaker professionals and challenges the notion that the ideal teacher of English is a native speaker (see Phillipson, 1992).

So where do we go from here? As mentioned, all the participants in the study were enrolled in a graduate seminar called "Issues and Concerns Related to NNS Professionals." Many participants felt that the opportunity to share their experiences with other non-native speaker professionals during the seminar empowered them personally and professionally.

Further, several implications can be drawn from the study. First, the "native speaker fallacy" (Phillipson, 1992) needs to be examined critically in the existing TESOL programs, especially in Center countries, in order to raise the collective consciousness of teacher trainees, native and non-native alike. Second, in TESOL methodologies, more emphasis needs to be placed on the multidimensionality and expertise than on nativeness or authenticity. Finally, as the number of non-native speakers increases in TESOL graduate programs in Center countries, a special course or seminar needs to be added to the existing curricula in order to discuss specific issues and concerns related to ELT professionals from diverse cultural and linguistic backgrounds. Such a course would benefit both native and non-native TESOL graduate students.

No doubt, the debate over the relative merits of native and non-native teachers of English will continue. While we sort out conceptual and pragmatic issues, ELT professionals should, first, continue to sharpen their expertise (linguistic, pedagogical knowledge, and skills), and second, seek or create opportunities to discuss issues related to professionals from diverse, multilingual contexts to raise their own consciousness and awareness. They can then become catalysts to the better understanding of the issues related to both non-native and native ELT professionals.

References

Davies, A. (1991). *The native speaker in applied linguistics.* Edinburgh, England: Edinburgh University Press.

Edge, J. (1988). Natives, speakers, and models. *JALT Journal, 9,* 153–157.

Kachru, B. B. (1986). *The alchemy of English: The spread, functions and models of non-native Englishes.* Oxford, England: Pergamon.

Kachru, B. B. (1992). *The other tongue: English across cultures* (2nd ed.). Urbana: University of Illinois Press.

Kachru, B. B. (1996). The paradigms of marginality. *World Englishes, 15,* 241–255.

Kachru, B. B., & Nelson, C. L. (1996). World Englishes. In S. L. McKay & N. H. Hornberger (Eds.), *Sociolinguistics and language teaching* (pp. 71–102). Cambridge, England: Cambridge University Press.

Kachru, Y. (1992). Culture, style, and discourse: Expanding noetics of English. In B. B. Kachru (Ed.), *The other tongue* (pp. 340–352). Urbana: University of Illinois Press.

Lowenberg, P. H. (1992). Testing English as a world language: Issues in assessing non-native proficiency. In B. B. Kachru (Ed.), *The other tongue* (pp. 108–121). Urbana: University of Illinois Press.

Medgyes, P. (1992). Native or non-native: Who's worth more? *ELT Journal, 46,* 340–349.

Medgyes, P. (1994). *The non-native teacher.* London: Macmillan.

Nelson, C. L. (1992). My language, your culture: Whose communicative competence? In B. B. Kachru (Ed.), *The other tongue* (pp. 327–339). Urbana: University of Illinois Press.

Phillipson, R. (1992). *Linguistic imperialism.* Oxford, England: Oxford University Press.

Rampton, M. B. H. (1990). Displacing the 'native speaker': Expertise, affiliation, and inheritance. *ELT Journal, 44,* 97–101.

Reves, T., & Medgyes, P. (1994). The non-native English speaking EFL/ESL teacher's self-image: An international survey. *System, 22,* 353–367.

Richards, J. C., & Lockhart, C. (1994). *Reflective teaching in second language classrooms.* New York: Cambridge University Press.

Strevens, P. (1992). English as an international language: Directions in the 1990s.

In B. B. Kachru (Ed.), *The other tongue* (pp. 27–47). Urbana: University of Illinois Press.

Widdowson, H. G. (1994). The ownership of English. *TESOL Quarterly, 28,* 377–381.

CHAPTER 10

Preparing Non-Native Professionals in TESOL: Implications for Teacher Education Programs

Lía D. Kamhi-Stein
California State University, Los Angeles

"I had a [student's] parent who did not want her child to be taught by an Asian person who's not a native English speaker. My student's mother wanted a blonde American as her son's teacher. What can I do? . . . The child is in an English Only class now and cannot communicate with his parents who speak only Vietnamese."

"It was my non-native speaker status that led me to teach kindergarten. I never felt that my language skills were good enough to teach older students."

"This was the first time talking about it [the status of non-native English speakers in TESOL]. Before, I felt it was only me who had the problem. When I heard other people share the same concerns, I said, it's not only me!"

"I wanted you to know how much I admire you. Sometimes I feel that my English will never be good enough to teach others, but here you are teaching how to teach. That's great!"

These four comments made by graduates of and teacher-trainees enrolled in MA TESOL programs reflective a variety of challenges faced by NNSs in the TESOL profession. These challenges may include, but are not necessarily limited to, parental distrust on the basis of ethnicity and language status, a poor self-image, and a lack of role models in the TESOL profession.

Growing numbers of NNSs are graduating from MA TESOL programs in the United States. There is a small but growing body of literature focusing on the perceived advantages and disadvantages of being a non-native English speaker in the profession (see, for example,

Medgyes, 1994; Samimy & Brutt-Griffler, Chap. 9, this volume), the attitudes of ESL and EFL students toward NNS teachers (for example, Amin, 1997; Tang, 1997), and the struggles and triumphs of non-native professionals (Braine, Chap. 2; Connor, Chap. 3; Li, Chap. 4; and Thomas, Chap. 1, this volume). However, there is little information regarding how teacher preparation programs are incorporating curricula related to non-native professionals in the TESOL field.

Samimy and Brutt-Griffler (Chap. 9, this volume) describe a TESOL education program offering a graduate seminar in which NNS students read about and discuss issues related to NNSs in the profession. In this chapter, I describe a different approach to the design of curricula related to NNSs in TESOL education programs. In this approach, the syllabi of selected courses are modified and discussions on issues related to NNSs are integrated across the curriculum. Because NNSs represent over 70% of the student population in the TESOL program described in this chapter, the cross-curricular intervention is effective in that it prevents the marginalization or isolation of issues related to NNSs.

To understand my interest in the topic of non-nativeness in English and the TESOL profession, it is necessary to explain my background. Briefly, I describe my journey from EFL student and teacher in Buenos Aires, Argentina, to teacher educator in the United States. I then present the rationale supporting the integration of discussions on issues related to NNSs across the curriculum of teacher preparation programs. Finally, I describe some of the classroom and out-of-class activities implemented in the MA TESOL program at California State University, Los Angeles (CSULA).

A Journey of Transition:
From EFL Student in Argentina
to Teacher Educator in California

I began studying EFL at the age of 9 in Buenos Aires, Argentina. Later, as a student at Universidad del Salvador, I first specialized in translation and later in Teaching English as a Foreign Language. After graduating from college, I taught at two Argentine universities, Universidad de Buenos Aires and Universidad del Salvador. Later, I began teaching at the Instituto Cultural Argentino Norteamericano (ICANA)—the Buenos Aires Binational Center (BNC)—where eventually I was appointed Academic Secretary, a supervisory position. In that capacity, together with two other colleagues, I was responsible for hiring EFL teachers as well as for their pre- and in-service training and development. In hiring teachers at the BNC, my two colleagues and I operated on the assumption that mother tongue should not be a selection criterion. Hiring decisions were made on the basis of professional preparation in TESOL and an awareness of the language needs and difficulties of EFL students.

When I migrated to the United States, although I had considerable professional experience in TESOL, my language skills in Spanish led me to consider entering an MA program in Spanish. However, because my prior professional experience and interest was in the TESOL field, I opted for entering a MA TESOL Program. While enrolled in that program, several experiences challenged my self-confidence. One was my own struggle to adapt from the Argentine school culture, which rewarded memorization and group collaboration, to the constructivist and competitive approach to education promoted in the MA TESOL Program. Further doubts about my professional future in the United States arose when, at a TESOL affiliate conference, I became aware that many administrators in California believed that only native English speakers could be good teachers of ESL.

Although I found my self-image challenged as a student in MA TESOL, I received the support and confidence of native English-speaking professionals when I entered a Ph.D. program at the University of Southern California. These professionals did not see my mother tongue as a problem; they viewed it as a resource. In fact, they believed that I could provide "underprepared" second language (L2) students enrolled in courses in English for Academic Purposes (EAP) with a model for successful language learning. In working with these L2 students, I became well aware of my role as a model not only for learning English but also for succeeding in adapting to a culture other than my own and for surviving in an academic environment that required skills that differed from those I had used in Argentina.

A Rationale for Addressing
Issues Related to NNSs in TESOL Education Programs

The integration of issues related to NNSs across the curriculum of TESOL courses is supported by two interrelated rationales. First, as noted by researchers in the field of EAP (for example, Leki & Carson, 1994; Brinton, Snow, & Wesche, 1989), the design of curricula that students, in this case teacher-trainees, may perceive as relevant to their needs and interests is believed to increase teacher-trainee motivation. In my new position as a faculty member of the MA TESOL program at CSULA, I found that many teacher-trainees, who, as already indicated, represent over 70% of the program enrollment, came to me to voice their concerns regarding their status as NNSs. These teacher-trainees have a variety of backgrounds and experiences. For example, although many of them are immigrants, others have come to the United States to pursue graduate studies in TESOL and return to their countries. Others, although born in the United States, speak another language at home. Teacher-trainees born outside the United States come from a variety of countries, such as Vietnam, Korea, China, Guatemala, Mexico, El Salvador, Spain, Iran, The Philippines, Taiwan, and Japan. These students' experiences are similar to mine. They are NNSs. Moreover, many of them are not White Anglo-Saxon and do not come from a middle class background. Given this diverse profile and the teacher-trainees' expressed interest in discussing issues related to their status as NNSs, it seemed only natural that their needs and interests would be taken into account in curriculum design.

The second rationale for integrating instruction on issues related to NNSs is supported by the notion that TESOL education programs should allow future teachers to develop an understanding of their "own assets, beliefs, and values" (Smith as cited in Bailey et al., 1996) and should promote an improvement of the teacher-trainees competencies. The cross-curricular approach to instruction provides teacher-trainees with multiple opportunities to systematically examine the non-nativeness issue in relation to theories of language acquisition, teaching methodologies and curriculum design, and cultural and social factors affecting L2 development.

In designing curricula, I was guided by the following questions: What types of discussions within the TESOL curriculum could promote an improvement in the self-image and self-perception of the NNS teacher-trainees and, at the same time, prepare them for addressing some of the situations that they are likely to encounter in their professional lives? In what ways, if any, would it be possible to increase the visibility of NNSs and the issues that concern them in the MA TESOL program as well as in professional organizations at the regional and state levels?

Integrating Issues Related to NNSs Into the TESOL Curriculum

I next describe some of the ways in which I address issues related to NNSs across the curricula of four courses that I teach, which are Educational Sociolinguistics; ESL/EFL Course, Syllabus, and Materials Design; Language Planning and Language Policy; and Practicum in ESL. I also discuss how I serve as a mentor to NNSs enrolled in the MA

TESOL program. The description focuses on nine areas organized into two categories, classroom activities and out-of-class activities.

Classroom Activities

Analyzing the Language Learning Histories of NNS Teacher-Trainees. As Phillipson (1992) argued, NNSs bring to the classroom a personal understanding of the L2 learning (and teaching) process. Therefore, in class, teacher-trainees analyze the NNSs' L2 learning experiences in relation to teaching methodologies, curriculum and materials design, and cultural and social factors affecting L2 learning.

The analysis of the L2 speakers' language learning history has two immediate benefits. First, it allows native English speaking teacher-trainees to develop a better understanding of the ESL/EFL learning process. Second, sharing their English language learning histories allows NNSs to view themselves as sources of information, and ultimately leads them to improve their self-image because they are put in a position of authority vis-à-vis their native English-speaking classmates.

Exploring the Beliefs of Teacher-Trainees. As noted by Richards and Lockhart (1994), teachers' instructional practices are the reflection of their beliefs. With this view in mind, teacher-trainees read excerpts from *Reflective Teaching in Second Language Classrooms* (Richards & Lockhart, 1994) and reflect upon the sources of their beliefs as teachers, which may arise from a combination of factors including ESL/EFL teaching and learning experiences; personality and attitudinal factors; established practices in the teachers' countries, districts, or schools; and an understanding of educational or second language theories and how these can be translated to classroom practices (see Richards & Lockhart, 1994 for a discussion on these topics). Further discussions focus on how planned and unplanned language policy in the graduate students' countries, districts, or schools may affect their classroom practices.

On occasion, some NNSs, notably from Japan, argue that because they speak what they call "a deficient variety of English," they are qualified only to play the role of assistants to native English-speaking teachers. When students make this point, I respond by acknowledging the importance of providing ESL/EFL students with good language models. Then I proceed to conduct an activity designed to emphasize the idea that the ideal teacher is not necessarily a native English speaker. Specifically, I ask students to list the qualities of a good language teacher. Among the qualifications most often mentioned by all teacher-trainees, native and non-native English speakers alike, are training in ESL/EFL pedagogy, an in-depth understanding of the English language, and knowledge of the L2 acquisition process.

Teacher-trainees also indicate that sharing their students' linguistic and cultural background contributes to a positive learning environment (a point also made by Auerbach, 1993) and allows classroom teachers to have an enhanced understanding of their students' language needs, to predict their students' language problems, and to design instruction targeting such problems. Finally, teacher-trainees argue that NNSs can function as models of successful language learning and can empathize with their students' experiences as L2 learners (Kamhi-Stein, Lee, & Lee, 1998; also see Medgyes, 1994; Tang, 1997 for a discussion on the same topic).

Challenging The Assumption That Only a White Anglo-Saxon Native English Speaker Is a Better ESL/EFL Teacher. When addressing this issue, I resort to the use of authentic case studies. The case studies selected deal with the experiences of NNS professionals whose credibility as teachers is often challenged because they have an accent and, as Rubin (1992) suggested, because they do not look "American," meaning White Anglo-Saxon. Specifically, teacher-trainees study the case of Elis, an Asian teacher born and raised in Brazil who immigrated to the United States in her early 20s and obtained her MA degree at CSULA. Elis found herself working twice as hard as any of her colleagues in order to gain the acceptance of her ESL students. After Elis wondered for some time why it was so difficult to establish her authority as a teacher, she found the answer in one of her students' journal entries: "Most Asian students think American teacher who has blue eye and brown hair is much better than Asian-looking teacher, but I don't think so." As Elis's student's journal entry suggests, she had never been exposed to an ESL teacher who was not White, much less to someone who did not speak English as a native language.

Teacher-trainees also discuss how the teacher-student relationship may be negatively affected not only by factors like ethnicity and language status, but also by gender. In class, I introduce the concept of the "triple minority,"[1] meaning a female NNS, non-White Anglo-Saxon person. Teacher-trainees then study the case of another former student, María, a Latina who attributed her lack of credibility with some of her male Latino students to the fact that she was female, looked Latina, and sometimes resorted to Spanish to clarify a difficult language concept. Some of María's male students chose to enroll in an adult education

---

[1] The term "triple minority" draws on Losey's (1995) idea of "double minority," meaning female Mexican-Americans.

course taught by a White instructor who does not speak a word of Spanish.

It is true that case studies provide teacher-trainees with valuable opportunities to reflect upon the challenges faced by minority teachers. However, as implemented in my classes, the success of case study analysis depends on the insights teacher-trainees gain from the analysis and the development of solutions or responses to the challenges faced by teachers like Elis and María.

Further class discussions focus on the fact that a lack of acceptance may not necessarily be limited to ESL/EFL students. As explained elsewhere in this chapter, it may come from program administrators in and outside the United States (see Medgyes, 1994, for a discussion on this topic). As can be observed in the following three quotations, teacher-trainees often attribute their lack of credibility with program administrators to their ethnicity and to their status as second language English speakers. "Because I'm Asian, not a lot of institutes, particularly in Japan, want to hire Asian-looking teachers." "They [institutions in Korea] want the blonde and blue-eyed [teacher], the typical stereotype of the American." "[One of the disadvantages of being a non-native English speaker is] the issue of being discriminated against because people don't believe, or do not give credit to, the amount of knowledge that you have of . . . language."

Because nativeness in English (or lack of thereof) may be an issue when applying for a teaching position, I make a point of informing teacher-trainees of the TESOL Organization resolution on non-native English speakers and discriminatory hiring practices. Specifically, the resolution states that the TESOL Organization "will make every effort to prevent such discrimination in the employment support structures operated by TESOL and its own practices" (TESOL, 1992). However, I also indicate that the statement in itself will not prevent covert discriminatory practices. Therefore, in class I make the case that NNSs should become proactive and participate in professional organizations at the regional, state, and international levels as a means to enhance the status of NNSs.

Analyzing the Language Situation in the United States From the 1700s to the 1900s, the "Official English" Movement, and the Controversy Over Bilingual Education. Teacher-trainees compare the language situation of 1776 when multilingualism was seen as a common, desirable phenomenon (Molesky, 1988) to the language situation of the mid-1800s, when, with the beginning of the Nativist movement, the idea that being alien and speaking non-English languages were symbols of being un-American (Macías, 1990). Furthermore, teacher-trainees discuss the "Official

English" movement (Crawford, 1992a, 1992b) and reflect on what counts as teaching qualifications and expertise in light of these movements. As a follow-up task, this perspective of language as a problem is contrasted with the view of language as a resource. Specifically, teacher-trainees analyze the cases of monolingual ESL/EFL teachers whose limited understanding of their students' sociocultural/linguistic situation leads them to encounter cross-cultural problems and, ultimately, to create a negative learning environment.

I should note that, although these discussions may not be relevant to NNS teacher-trainees who come to the United States with the intention of obtaining a degree and returning to their country of origin, they are critical to NNS teacher-trainees coming from an immigrant background. As noted by Auerbach (1993), immigrant teachers not only bring to the language classroom their experiences as English language learners but also share with their students their struggles as newcomers to the U.S. culture. Therefore, these shared experiences allow immigrant teachers to make curricular connections that would otherwise not be possible (Auerbach, 1993).

Doing Classroom-Centered Research on the Topic of NNSs. Teacher-trainees draw upon published investigations—focusing on the attitudes of ESL/EFL students toward NNSs (for example, Amin, 1997; Marquez, 1998; Tang, 1997) and the NNSs' perceptions about their own English language skills (Medgyes, 1994; Reves & Medgyes, 1994; Sheorey, 1986)—and conduct classroom-oriented research. Not surprisingly for a program that includes a large NNS student population, the topic of minority and NNS teachers has become a focus of deep student interest. As examples of this new area of research, I mention two ongoing studies. The first investigation (Wei, 1998) was designed to describe an ESL classroom from the point of view of a novice, NNS teacher. The second study (Kamhi-Stein et al., 1998) focused on ESL teachers and teacher-trainees in relation to their perceived L2 skills and teaching preferences. Critical to the research conducted by CSULA students is that teacher-trainees are using their findings to raise the profile of NNSs in professional conferences.

Encouraging Collaboration Between Native and NNS Teacher-Trainees. Drawing on the belief that native and non-native English speakers have a lot to learn from one another, teacher-trainees engage in collaborative projects, including evaluating ESL/EFL textbooks and developing instructional materials designed to meet the language needs of a specified student population. These collaborative projects allow non-native English speakers to excel because they have a first-hand understanding of the linguistic, social, and cultural needs of their target audience and the language teaching situation. The contributions of native English-speaking teacher-trainees are equally important because, as noted by Widdowson (1994), "they are in a better position to know what is appropriate in contexts of language use, and so to define possible target objectives" (p. 387).

Out-of-Class Activities

Providing Teacher-Trainees With Opportunities for Professional Growth. NS and NNS novice teachers alike face complex classroom demands such as managing the classroom, designing and implementing lesson plans (Almarza, 1996; Johnson, 1996) and, very often, reconciling their teaching philosophy with that of the school where they teach (Wei, 1998). In addition, novice NNS teachers sometimes suffer from a lack of confidence in their English language skills caused by their perceived language needs (Kamhi-Stein et al., 1998; Wei, 1998). Therefore, I am concerned with providing NNS teacher-trainees with experiences that allow them to begin to develop confidence in their language and teaching skills. For this purpose, prior to or along with the Practicum, I encourage NNS teacher-trainees to work for different CSULA departments where knowledge of ESL/EFL pedagogy is welcome. Given the demographics of CSULA, where approximately 70% of the entering freshmen come from non-English home backgrounds and 82% of these students are required to enroll in developmental reading and writing courses, the preparation of MA TESOL students has proven to be of critical importance because they are implementing many of the ideas to which they have been exposed in their graduate courses. In addition, NNSs serve as role models of successful language learners to the linguistically and culturally diverse CSULA student population.

Examples of some of the teaching positions held by NNS teacher-trainees include working as computer trainers at the CSULA Computer Center, teaching reading for academic purposes to underprepared L2 freshmen, or teaching database research skills to undergraduate and graduate students. Other jobs include teaching a variety of ESL classes in an after-school program offered by the Intensive English Program on campus, or working as graduate teaching assistants in special programs offered by the MA TESOL program.[2]

---

[2] Such as the Institute for Egyptian Teachers of EFL (see Kamhi-Stein & Galván, 1997).

"Easing" NNSs Into the Profession. Although the job interviewing process may be stressful for all new TESOL graduates, it is often twice as stressful for NNSs. It is not uncommon to hear that, in the course of job interviews, NNSs become self-conscious about their language skills and make grammatical mistakes that they would not make under different circumstances. Therefore, in order to ease teacher-trainees into the interviewing process, they participate in professional conference committees at the regional and state TESOL affiliate levels. In this way, teacher-trainees do not feel pressure to perform and instead network with colleagues and program administrators in a relaxed atmosphere.

NNS teacher-trainees are further eased into the TESOL profession by presenting papers at regional, state, or international conferences. For example, teacher-trainees enrolled in the class titled "ESL/EFL Course, Syllabus, and Materials Design" analyze conference abstracts. Then teacher-trainees are required to write an abstract and complete and submit the call for participation for a professional conference such as TESOL or California Teachers of English to Speakers of Other Languages (CATESOL). This requirement serves two purposes. First, it provides teacher-trainees with instruction in the skills needed to write a successful conference abstract. Second, it emphasizes the importance of professional involvement and development. Following is what a teacher-trainee had to say about the abstract requirement:

> The idea of doing [a conference presentation] as a school project . . . I would have never done one; I would have said, 'I'm a non-native English speaker . . . Let so-and-so do it.' But going through the process, this is a project that you have to do; you are capable of doing it; it actually prepares you as a non-native English speaker, exposes you to what other people are doing who are native speakers, and puts you in a position of you can do it.

Engaging in Advocacy Activities on Behalf of NNS Teacher-Trainees. In addition to the activities designed to enhance the professional preparation of NNSs, I engage in advocacy work aimed at creating forums for discussing issues related to NNSs. Some of the activities in which I have participated over the past 18 months involve giving and organizing presentations at regional, state, and international conferences in which NNS teachers and teacher-trainees address a number of their concerns, including perceptions (as self, student, or administrator) that may affect teacher effectiveness, overt and covert hiring and retention practices, and NNSs' instructional strategies. In addition, I engaged in discussions with program and district administrators regarding their expectations in teacher competencies. These discussions have resulted in the identification of a number of programs and districts interested in hiring and retaining teachers who reflect their student population.

Discussion and Conclusion

The cross-curricular approach to instruction described in this chapter reflects the thinking that giving teacher-trainees opportunities to systematically examine issues related to NNSs in regard to theories of L2 acquisition, teaching methodologies and curriculum design, and cultural and social factors affecting L1 and L2 development will result in an improvement in the self-perception of NNSs, ultimately leading to better teacher preparation. The approach to curriculum design presented in this chapter has resulted in a number of positive developments for native and NNS teacher-trainees. First, NS teacher-trainees have acquired a greater awareness of cross-cultural factors affecting L2 acquisition. In addition, NS have developed greater sensitivity to the overt and covert politics of hiring and retaining of TESOL professionals.

Second, as indicated elsewhere in this chapter, prior to integrating classroom activities addressing non-nativeness issues, individual teacher-trainees would voice their concerns to me directly and would avoid discussing the topic in public. Much like in other MA TESOL programs, the non-nativeness issue was not a topic of open discussion. Upon the implementation of the activities described in this chapter, NNSs engage in conversations with NSs regarding the challenges they faced—whether linguistic, social, or cultural—as well as their successes. As noted by several teacher-trainees, the fact that I as a NNS resorted to my own experiences as an EFL learner and an EFL/EAP instructor and teacher educator is helping to overcome their self doubts.

Third, the relevance of the topic to the lives and experiences of NNSs has led to two immediate results. First, NNSs enrolled in the TESOL program are beginning to see themselves as sources of information regarding L2 acquisition and cross-cultural issues. In turn, NNSs have seen their status elevated, and this has resulted in an improvement in their self-image. Second, native and NNS teacher-trainees are engaging in a more meaningful dialog, which has resulted in several collaborative projects such as giving conference presentations and designing classroom materials. Critical to these projects is the fact that native and non-native English speakers see themselves as equal partners, sharing their unique perspectives and learning from one another.

Fourth, interest in addressing issues related to NNSs in the TESOL program has expanded to my colleagues, and other TESOL program faculty members are addressing issues related to NNSs in their classes. In addition, the syllabus of the class titled "Theories of L2 Acquisition" is currently being revised to incorporate discussions relevant to the topic of NNSs.

Fifth, the increased visibility of NNSs and the issues that concern them have led to the development of social networks of NNSs. Specifically, novice teachers are seeking the support and advice of successful NNS professionals. For example, experienced NNS teachers are advising teacher-trainees on how to respond to or deal with possible student, peer, or administrator biases. In addition, NNS teachers are becoming "mentor teachers" to graduate students enrolled in the Practicum course. These mentor teachers are providing their students with authentic examples of success stories. Here is what a teacher-trainee enrolled in the practicum course had to say about this issue:

> It's important to have role models [referring to a NNS mentor teacher]. No matter what you learn about NNSs and how much you study issues related to NNSs, if you don't have a role model, the topic does not seem real, authentic.

Sixth, another important development arising from the higher visibility and profile of NNSs and their concerns in the MA TESOL program is that there has been a dramatic increase in the representation of NNSs in professional conferences at the regional and state levels. For example, at recent professional conferences, some NNSs reported the results of research investigating the classroom practices of and the challenges faced by novice and experienced NNS teachers. Other NNSs discussed instructional practices designed to promote the enhanced academic performance of at-risk L2 students. Still other NNSs presented curricula designed to enhance the language skills of EFL teachers. Additionally, native English-speaking program administrators discussed their hiring and retention practices regarding NNSs. Much like what happened at TESOL '96—when a colloquium organized by Braine (1996) gave birth to the idea of a NNSs Caucus within TESOL—following a colloquium at CATESOL '98, native and non-native English professionals, including teacher educators, program administrators, teachers, and graduate students, agreed that it is imperative that a NNS interest group be formed within the CATESOL organization. Such an interest group would provide a forum within the formal CATESOL structure for addressing issues related to the hiring, retention, training, and development of NNS professionals. In addition, an interest group would provide NNS professionals with a much-needed voice within the formal structure of the CATESOL organization.

Although NNS teacher-trainees and the issues that affect them are beginning to be addressed in my program as well as in other programs (see Samimy & Brutt-Griffler, Chap. 9, this volume), much needs to be done. I am convinced that it is the responsibility of NNS teacher educators to become agents of curriculum change. In this endeavor, different program models are possible. For example, some programs, with moderate numbers of NNSs in their student body, might choose to offer seminars related to NNSs in the TESOL profession (Samimy & Brutt-Griffler, Chap. 9, this volume, describe such a course). Other programs, like the one described in this chapter, in which NNSs represent a large percentage of the program enrollment, could integrate discussions on issues related to NNSs across the MA in TESOL curriculum, thereby giving voice to and elevating the status of NNSs in the program. Whatever model is adopted, the time for action is now.

References

Almarza, G. G. (1996). Student foreign language teacher's knowledge growth. In D. Freeman & J. Richards (Eds.), *Teacher learning in language teaching* (pp. 50–78). Cambridge, England: Cambridge University Press.

Amin, N. (1997). Race and the identity of the non-native ESL teacher. *TESOL Quarterly, 31,* 580–583.

Auerbach, E. (1993). Reexamining English only in the ESL classroom. *TESOL Quarterly, 27,* 9–32.

Bailey, K. M., Bergthold, B., Braunstein, B., Fleischman, N. H., Holbrook, M. P., Tuman, J., Waissbluth, X., & Zambo, L. J. (1996). The language learner's autobiography: Examining the "apprenticeship of observation." In D. Freeman & J. Richards (Eds.), *Teacher learning in language teaching* (pp. 11–29). Cambridge, England: Cambridge University Press.

Braine, G. (1996). *In their own voices: Nonnative speaker professionals in TESOL.* Colloquium presented at the annual meeting of the Teachers of English to Speakers of Other Languages, Chicago, IL.

Brinton, D. M., Snow, M. A., & Wesche, M. B. (1989). *Content-based second language instruction.* Boston: Heinle & Heinle.

Crawford, J. (1992a). *Hold your tongue: Bilingualism and the politics of "English Only."* Reading, MA: Addison-Wesley.

Crawford, J. (Ed.). (1992b). *Language loyalties: A source book on the official English controversy.* Chicago: University of Chicago Press.

Johnson, K. E. (1996). The vision versus the reality: The tensions of the TESOL practicum. In D. Freeman & J. Richards (Eds.), *Teacher learning in language teaching* (pp. 30–49). Cambridge, England: Cambridge University Press.

Kamhi-Stein, L. D., & Galván, J. L. (1997). EFL teacher development through critical reflection. *TESOL Journal, 7*(1), 12–18.

Kamhi-Stein, L. D., Lee, C., & Lee, E. (1998, April). *Listening to the voices of NNS teachers and teacher-trainees.* Paper presented at the annual meeting of the California Teachers of English to Speakers of Other Languages, Pasadena, CA.

Leki, I., & Carson, J. G. (1994). Students' perceptions of EAP writing instruction and writing needs across the disciplines. *TESOL Quarterly, 28,* 81–101.

Losey, K. M. (1995). Gender and ethnicity as factors in the development of verbal skills in bilingual Mexican American women. *TESOL Quarterly, 29,* 635–661.

Marquez, E. (1998). *ESL student attitudes and the native speaker fallacy.* Unpublished manuscript.

Macías, R. F. (1990). *Cauldron-boil & bubble: United States policy toward indigenous language groups during the nineteenth century.* Unpublished manuscript, University of Southern California, Los Angeles.

Medgyes, P. (1994). *The non-native teacher.* London: Macmillan.

Molesky, J. (1988). Understanding the American linguistic mosaic: A historical overview of language maintenance and language shift. In S. L. McKay & S. C. Wong (Eds.), *Language diversity: Problem or resource* (pp. 29–68). Boston: Heinle & Heinle.

Phillipson, R. (1992). *Linguistic imperialism.* Oxford, England: Oxford University Press.

Reves, T., & Medgyes, P. (1994). The NNS EFL/ESL teacher's self-image: An international survey. *System, 22,* 353–367.

Richards, J. C., & Lockhart, C. (1994). *Reflective teaching in second language classrooms.* Cambridge, England: Cambridge University Press.

Rubin, D. L. (1992). Nonlanguage factors affecting undergraduates' judgments of NNS teaching assistants. *Research in Higher Education, 33,* 511–531.

Sheorey, R. (1986). Error perceptions of native-speaking and non-native speaking teachers of ESL. *ELT Journal, 40,* 306–312.

Tang, C. (1997). On the power and status of non-native ESL teachers. *TESOL Quarterly, 31,* 577–580.

Teachers of English to Speakers of Other Languages, Inc. (1992, August/September). A TESOL statement on non-native speakers of English and hiring practices. *TESOL Matters, 2*(4), 23.

Wei, J. (1998, April). *A non-native speaker's view of the language classroom: A novice's perspective.* Paper presented at the annual meeting of the California Teachers of English to Speakers of Other Languages, Pasadena, CA.

Widdowson, H. G. (1994). The ownership of English. *TESOL Quarterly, 28,* 377–389.

CHAPTER 11

From Their Own Perspectives: The Impact of Non-Native ESL Professionals on Their Students

Jun Liu
The University of Arizona, Tucson

Does being a NS or a NNS of English make a difference in teaching English? The answer is yes and no. It depends on who asks the question and who answers, when, where, and why. Although there is an increasing number of NNS professionals assuming the role of English teachers in both ESL and EFL contexts all over the world, they are not always given the credit they deserve (see Thomas, Chap. 1, this volume). Further, there is insufficient literature in the field of second and foreign language learning and teaching that gives credit to NNSs as ESL professionals (see Kachru, 1992; Kresovich, 1988; McNeill, 1994; Medgyes, 1994; Rampton, 1990). Instead, much research on NNSs of English to date has, quite justifiably, focused on the experience of ESL learners and effective ways to help them learn English.

Although the majority of ESL professionals in the United States are native English speakers, there is a growing body of ESL professionals whose first language is not English. The tenet that the ideal teacher of English is a native speaker, what Phillipson (1992) termed the "native speaker fallacy," is now being questioned (see also Medgyes, 1992, and Chap. 12, this volume). Even though ESL students sometimes tend to have reservations and concerns about being taught ESL by NNSs (Liu, 1996; see also Braine, Chap. 2, and Thomas, Chap. 1, this volume) and NNSs of English sometimes have experienced undue discrimination in the hiring process (see Braine, Chap. 2, Canagarajah, Chap. 6, and Thomas, Chap. 1, this volume), the fact that the English learning experiences of ESL professionals whose native languages are not English could be helpful for ESL learners is undeniable (Medgyes, 1992; Soter, 1985; Kamhi-Stein, Chap. 10, this volume).

In order to demystify the native speaker fallacy, a few recent studies have been conducted with encouraging results. Samimy and Brutt-

Griffler (Chap. 9, this volume), for instance, examined the way non-native speaking TESOL graduate students perceived themselves as ELT professionals by using both quantitative and qualitative methods. These students thought that the question of whether native or non-native speakers are better language teachers was irrelevant. According to them, the important issue is how qualified an ESL teacher is regardless of NS/NNS status.

Although the study described in this chapter addresses the same issue, it differs from Samimy and Brutt-Griffler's study in several ways. First, unlike the participants in Samimy and Brutt-Griffler's study who perceived their impact on ESL students either retrospectively (for those with teaching experience) or futuristically (for those without teaching experience), all the participants in this study were ESL professionals teaching either as full-time academic program specialists or as part-time graduate teaching assistants. Therefore, their responses to the questions raised in interviews, both face-to-face and by e-mail, were based on their ongoing teaching experiences. Second, instead of using a hybrid method, this study was qualitative in nature simply because of my belief that the topic cannot be adequately investigated through quantitative methods. Third, in this study, the impact of NNS teachers on their ESL students was seen from the teachers' perspectives—reflectively; that is, instead of surveying students' opinions of their teachers' impact on them, the study focused on how NNS teachers perceived their impact on ESL students. Although this could be a limitation of the study, it is argued that soliciting the opinions of ESL students at random on the impact of their teachers would not show the complete picture. Instead, I believe that a more holistic perspective can be obtained by inviting these practicing teachers to reflect on their impact on ESL students.

The Study

This study was conducted over a period of 8 months (December, 1996 to July, 1997) at a major Midwestern university in the United States. Seven professionals, including two full-time teachers and five graduate teaching associates in the ESL Programs of the university (a post-admission composition program, an International Teaching Assistants (ITA) education program, and a pre-admission intensive language program), participated in the study. They represent a wide variety of cultural and linguistic experiences—Cantonese, Danish, Korean, Italian, Tagalog, Dutch (an official language in Surinam), and Kimbala (a Bantu language spoken in the former Zaire).

A letter of consent together with the proposal of this study was sent to eight potential participants in the three ESL programs, and seven agreed to participate in the study. In order to obtain informative data that truly reflects the visions and voices of NNS professionals in ESL, an e-mail discussion format was utilized to collect interview data, in addition to the traditional face-to-face interview format. By using an e-mail interview format, the participants were given sufficient time to think about and reflect upon the issues and questions raised, and interactions between the researcher and each participant were therefore extended along the continuum of topic initiation, thinking, responding, probing, and reflection.

To facilitate data analysis, the seven participants were given pseudonyms through the use of the initial letter of each participant's first language with the exception of Danish, which was abbreviated as DK in order to avoid confusion with Dutch. For example, Mr. C is the pseudonym of the participant whose first language was Cantonese. Accordingly, the seven pseudonyms were as follows: Mr. C (Cantonese), Ms. DK (Danish), Mr. D (Dutch), Mr. F (French), Ms. I (Italian), Mr. K (Korean), and Ms. T (Tagalog). As these participants came from diverse educational backgrounds and with rich experiences of language learning and teaching, their self-perceptions as NNS professionals in ESL were multidimensional and multilayered.

This chapter consists of two parts. In part one, "Teachers' Self-Perceptions," the seven participants are introduced in terms of their background and language learning experiences. Then, their diverse perspectives are synthesized in defining the term NNS professionals in ESL and in describing their self-perceptions on the NS/NNS continuum. In part two, "Emerging Perspectives and the Impact on ESL Learners," the participants' self-perceptions either as NSs or NNSs are discussed in relation to their students' perceptions of them as ESL professionals and to the impact of the perceptions of the participants on ESL learners from both the participants' and the students' points of view. Pedagogical implications are discussed and suggestions are made in the conclusion.

Part One: Teachers' Self-Perceptions

The Background of the Participants

The demographics of the participants in the study can be seen in Table 11.1 in terms of their birthplace, first language, other

Table 11.1 The Demographics of the Participants

	Mr. C	Ms. DK	Ms. I	Mr. K	Mr. D	Ms. T	Mr. F
Birthplace	Hong Kong	Denmark	Italy	Korea	Surinam	Philippines	Zaire
First language	Chinese (Cantonese)	Danish	Italian	Korean	Dutch	Tagalog	French
Other languages learned or spoken	Japanese Greek	German Japanese	Spanish French	Spanish	Sranan Spanish	Spanish	Kimbala Kikongo Lingala
Age of arrival in U.S.	23	10	6	9	30	21	35
First exposure to English	KG	5th grade	1st grade	4th grade	JH	birth	high school
Context of first exposure to English	bilingual	U.S.	U.S.	U.S.	EFL	bilingual	EFL

languages learned or spoken, age of arrival in the United States, first exposure to English, and context in which the first exposure to English took place.

As can be seen from Table 11.2, 2 of the 7 participants began learning English as a foreign language in their own countries; for example, Mr. D began in junior high school in Surinam and Mr. F in high school in the former Zaire. Three of the participants began learning English as a second language after they came to the United States with their parents at an early age.[1] The other 2 participants started learning English in a bilingual environment in which English was treated as a second language.[2] All 7 participants expressed their ideas and concerns about NNS/NS issues in teaching ESL. Additionally, they did not reach a consensus on the terminology (NS vs. NNS).

The NS/NNS Controversy

Is the term "NNS professionals in ESL" too complex? How does one define NNS professionals in ESL? In what way and to what extent do you consider yourself a NNS professional in ESL? Is there a need to distinguish NNSs from NSs in the ESL profession? The 7 participants held diverse views on these issues. Some (Ms. DK, Mr. K, and Ms. T) found it hard to accept the simplistic way of categorizing a rather complex phenomenon with a NS/NNS dichotomy and expressed difficulty in affiliating themselves with either category. However, others (Mr. C, Ms. I, Mr. D, and Mr. F) did not experience problems in defining the term and felt relatively comfortable to be or not to be associated with the category each chose, although they expressed their concerns in one way or another. However, they all agreed that because the term *NNS professional* is so complex, it is better viewed on a multidimensional and multilayered continuum. The continuum was explored in terms of the dimension of sequence (Is English learned first before other languages?), the dimension of competence (Is English our most competent language as compared to other languages, including our L1?), the dimension of culture (What culture are we most affiliated with?), the dimension of identity (Who do we prefer to be recognized as under different circumstances? For example, at job interviews, in language classrooms, and among colleagues), the dimension of environment (Did we grow up

---

[1] For example, Ms. DK came to the United States at the age of 10 as a fifth grader, Mr. K at the age of 9 as a fourth grader, and Ms. I at the age of 6 as a first grader.
[2] For example, Mr. C received formal English education since kindergarten, and Ms. T started speaking English before she spoke Tagalog .

bilingually or trilingually?), and the dimension of politics (Why should we label NNSs and NSs in a dichotomy instead of viewing it on a continuum?).

The participants assumed that *ESL professional* referred to one who has received professional training to teach English to speakers of other languages. Such a professional could be seen along the continuum of being a NNS of English at one end and being a NS of English at the other. Generally speaking, those who learned English in addition to their first language(s) could be referred to as non-native speakers of English, but the reality is far more complex than that. Scholars have begun to consider such multidimensions as language precedence, competency, social identity, cultural affiliation, language environment, and politics. Because each participant's case is unique, as illustrated in this study, a rigid definition of NNS versus NS was problematic to the participants. Rather, they preferred to view each individual in relation to the NNS-NS continuum based on the different dimensions listed and stayed away from categorizing individuals according to a strict NNS or NS dichotomy. According to the participants, such a categorization would not adequately represent the true nature of being a speaker of a language and would often diminish the experiences and language skills of ESL professionals. The participants also expressed difficulty in affiliating firmly with either the NS or the NNS category.

The Participants' Affiliation With the Continuum

Among the 7 participants in the study, 3 (Mr. C, Mr. D, and Mr. F) felt comfortable affiliating themselves with the NNS label, although their individual cases were different. Mr. C, who learned English from British teachers since kindergarten and continued to learn English as the medium of instruction in both junior and high school in the United States, considered himself a NNS of English because his parents and his friends spoke Cantonese with him at home and in the neighborhood. Because he grew up in a Cantonese environment, he classified himself in the NNS category, despite the fact that his English is near-native-like, as stated by many of his colleagues and students.

Both Mr. D and Mr. F learned English as a foreign language in their own countries when they were teenagers. They considered themselves as NNS professionals for several reasons. First, the languages they were brought up in were other than English, Dutch for Mr. D and French for Mr. F. Secondly, English is not an official language in their countries (Surinam for Mr. D, and the former Zaire for Mr. F) but is taught in school as a foreign language. Third, they made their living by teaching

English. Finally, throughout their career, their students had studied English as a foreign language in communities where English is not spoken.

None of the remaining four felt comfortable in labeling themselves as NNS professionals. Ms. DK, due to a dual-identity perspective, viewed herself as a native speaker of both Danish, her first language, which she used exclusively until the age of 10 when she moved to the United States, and English, in which she was more competent because of twenty years of exposure to it in the United States Mr. K, who moved to the United States at the age of 9, viewed himself as a Korean-American and a native speaker of English with a Korean heritage. Ms. I who arrived in the United States at the age of 6 and received her formal education from elementary school in English, felt that she was a native speaker of English, although her perceptions of being a native speaker had gradually broadened as she learned other languages and cultures. Ms. T, who spoke English before her native language Tagalog in an ESL setting in the Philippines, considered Tagalog her native language as it represents her cultural identity. She felt extremely uncomfortable in affiliating herself with the NNS label. Instead, she preferred to view herself as a bilingual professional even though her formal education as well as her written communication have predominantly been in English.

Part Two: Emerging Perspectives and Their Impact on ESL Learners

Because there is no simple definition for the term *NNS professionals in ESL*, affiliating oneself with the label is problematic. Additionally, how teachers perceive themselves is sometimes not necessarily in accord with their students' perceptions of them, based on the teachers' introspections (see Table 11.2 below).

Table 11.2 illustrates four different cases among the 7 participants. Case 1 illustrates the situation where both the teachers (Mr. C, Mr. D, and Mr. F) and the students perceived the teachers as NNS professionals in ESL. Case 2 illustrates the situation in which both the teachers (Ms. DK and Ms. I) and their students identified the teachers as NS professionals in ESL, despite the fact that both teachers learned English as a second language. In Case 3, the instructor, Mr. K, who viewed himself as a NS, was often perceived by his students as a NNS. In Case 4, the instructor, Ms. T, who was raised in a bilingual environment and who preferred to label herself as bilingual professional, was a puzzle to her students: she looked like a NNS of English but spoke like a NS.

Table 11.2 Student/Teacher Perceptions

Case	Participants	Students' perceptions of the teacher	Teacher's self-perception	Perceptional Discrepancy
1	Mr. C	NNS	NNS	No
	Mr. D	NNS	NNS	No
	Mr. F	NNS	NNS	No
2	Ms. DK	NS	NS/NNS	Some
	Ms. I	NS	NS/NNS	Some
3	Mr. K	NNS/NS	NS	Yes
4	Ms. T	NNS	Bilingual	Yes

Case Studies

Case 1

Although Mr. C, Mr. D, and Mr. F considered themselves NNSs of English, their individual cases were different. Mr. C grew up in an environment where English was the medium of school instruction. His fluent English often surprised his ESL students:

> Oftentimes, they'd like to know where I'm from and whether English is or is not my first language. And after I tell them my "story," they're usually impressed. Some may even begin to ask me questions like, "How can I improve my pronunciation?"

However, Mr. C's remarkable English has generated mixed feelings among his ESL students. Although graduate students in his class often expressed their respect and admiration of Mr. C, undergraduates felt rather intimidated by his English, simply because Mr. C was perceived both by himself and by his students as a NNS of English:

> Sometimes I'm under the impression (and I've had students who've said that to my face) that students, the undergrads especially, don't like me as well as the grads do. They think that because I'm from Hong Kong and I belong to the culture which emphasizes "HARD WORK is not enough; no matter how good you are, you can still do BETTER," and more importantly,

because I have "made it to the top," therefore I must demand the same degree of excellence in their performance, I can't sympathize with them as much as the native teachers do. That's why they think I'm a tough grader, tougher than the American teachers.

Interestingly, Mr. C's reflection reveals the high expectations of students who share the same Asian culture as Mr. C. Many undergraduate students in ESL programs come from Asia and some have been in the United States for quite a long time. Others are immigrants and have attended junior or senior high schools in the United States Due to their relatively longer length of stay in the United States, they are more acclimatized to the U.S. culture in many ways than most Asian students at the graduate level. As a result, some undergraduate students appeared to trust their abilities more than their effort, a model coined by Stevenson and Stigler (Liu, 1996). Their attitude toward Mr. C suggests that they were unsure whether they should make the extra effort endorsed in Asian culture and illustrated by Mr. C. As Mr. C continues,

> Some of them don't like to be in my class not because they think I'm not good enough, but because I'm too good for them ("good" in the sense that they think I'm expecting "perfection" from them). I guess, what I can try, and maybe that's the only way, is to avoid being judgmental. I can show them my poor drafts so that they can see the process of writing. That I don't expect them to be perfect because I'm not perfect either. Indeed, I've got something I can offer them. I know where they come from and I've been there and I can share with them my struggles.

Mr. C felt a sense of pride in being a NNS professional in ESL. His pride came from the fact that he had been properly trained and had the experience of learning English as a second language. He did not hesitate to show the unique ways in which he as a NNS professional could help ESL students:

> In general, to motivate my students, I seek to help them locate their unique problems and show them there's a variety of ways to tackle their problems. Even when they don't know what their problems are, I show them I know and I can offer some suggestions to solve their problems. I think most of my students have learned that what has happened to me in second language development can also happen to them.

Mr. D, who had no problem identifying himself as a NNS professional, did not seem to be bothered whether his students thought of him as a NS or NNS. To him,

> If the students have an opinion with regards to this issue, which I am sure they do, they have never bothered to share it with me and frankly I never did ask them to do so. To be honest, on the whole, I am more interested in their perception of me as an ESL instructor proper rather than their perception of me as a "non-native" ESL instructor. . . . For all I know, they might have even seen it as a blessing in disguise.

It is interesting that, after Mr. D came up with this reflection, he invited his students' comments and asked them whether they would have preferred a native speaker ESL teacher to a non-native ESL teacher. Here is what he found:

> One student replied saying that it really did not matter to her since there are advantages as well as disadvantages in having a NS of English as her teacher or a NNS. The advantage for her . . . was that in terms of knowledge of grammar, non-native teachers seem to be better than native speaker teachers. The fact that non-native ESL teachers do not have the proper pronunciation as compared to their native speaking counterparts to her was a disadvantage.

Although Mr. D accepted his non-nativeness, he did not have the sense of pride that Mr. C had. His explanation carries a unique perspective:

> I guess that as both a foreigner and a person of color living in this country, one is constantly reminded of who one is as well as what one's position in this society is, and being perceived as a non-native speaker by one's students would simply be one more reminder.

However, he was proud of the fact that he was teaching English in the United States as a NNS of English:

> I hope that my tutelage has contributed to make my students better users of English. In addition, I hope that those who were skeptical about a non-native's ability to teach English in an English speaking country will have come to see that a non-native can be just as capable of teaching a language that is not his/her native language as are his/her native speaking counterparts.

Mr. D believed that his main strength in teaching ESL was his ability to present learning material in a manner that not only appealed to the students but also resulted in their retaining the material much longer.

Likewise, Mr. F, whose self-perception as a NNS professional in ESL was confirmed by his students, believed that his students considered him a qualified ESL teacher regardless of his accent. However, some students had expressed concern about his handling of the class. But this, according to Mr. F, was due more to reasons such as poor preparation or exhaustion than to his non-nativeness. Mr. F embraced the consistency between how he saw himself and how he was viewed by his students:

> My students knew from day one that I was not a NS. But they did not show any kind of resentment. On the contrary, I had the feeling that they considered me as one of them, but with both knowledge and training in the specific field of ELT. I think this is an asset. Students got the sense that they also can become good English writers without being NS.

According to Mr. F, ESL students' knowledge that their teacher is a NNS was an advantage because they could look up to someone with a similar experience in learning English as a second language. Meanwhile, as a NNS professional, he or she could convince his or her students that high competency in English is possible.

Case 2

Both Ms. DK and Ms. I spoke fluent English and were usually perceived as NSs of English because of their English language skills and their European appearance. No one doubted them as NSs unless they reminded people that their first languages were Danish and Italian, respectively. Therefore, there was no confusion as to their ESL students' perception of them as NSs, except for their names, which carried some identity of their native cultures. However, it is their revelation that they learned English as a second language that brought surprise and respect from their students.

According to Ms. DK,

> I am usually perceived as a native speaker of English and even though I sometimes get questions about my unusual non-American name, students usually do not think I am not a native

speaker unless I tell them so directly. I always battle whether I should tell them or not—on the one hand, if I do tell them, I can show that I am empathetic with their language learning and that I too faced a difficult time learning English. On the other hand, I worry that telling them will make them feel discouraged—i.e., my English is good and they may feel discouraged that they will never speak English that well. That's why if I do tell them I am not a native speaker, I always explain that I began learning English at age 10, and have been practicing for 20 years, and that my Danish is no longer completely perfect. I just don't want them to compare their own English skills to mine and feel discouraged, because our language learning experiences are completely different.

As can be seen, Ms. DK thought twice before she revealed her Danish origin to her students. She also had the same concern that Mr. C has experienced: students could be intimidated by the high level of fluency of a NNS. Nevertheless, she believed that her longer exposure to English (20 years as opposed to only 10 years of Danish) would not intimidate her students as all her students came to the United States for advanced studies as adults. (We should note that Ms. DK's case is different from Mr. C's in that Mr. C's students feel threatened because he and most of his undergraduate ESL students shared the same Asian culture.) Viewing it as an asset to encourage her students, Ms. DK thought that there were more reasons to reveal her NNS status to her students:

> I think that since most of my students perceive me as a NS, even after I disclose I am a NNS, I can model the correct usage of the English language, and American pronunciation, while being empathetic to their needs and experiences. I sometimes share my own language learning experiences with them, not just English but also Japanese and German. I guess the strengths of me being a NNS is that I can relate to my students and that I can look at the language a bit more objectively, i.e., in comparing it to my native language and other languages I've learnt.

Ms. I, who considered herself a NS of English, has changed her perception of herself since she started teaching ESL in the United States Like Ms. DK, she was usually regarded as a NS of English:

> I think my students' perceptions of me when they first meet me is of a native speaker. Even though my name may sound foreign to them my accent is clearly American without any clues of being

> foreign. I generally explain on the first day of class that I was born in Italy and that I came to the United States when I was six.

She purposely told her students on the first day of class that as a child, English was not her first language. The purpose of the revelation was to motivate her ESL students to work on their English and to convince them that near native fluency and pronunciation were possible.

> I also briefly mention my experience learning English so that they realize that I went through the same process that they are going through now. I want them to feel that I have also experienced learning English as a second language.

Although Ms. I believed that her personal experiences of learning additional languages could be an encouraging example for her ESL students, she thought that her impact on a NNS was of a practical nature:

> What I mean by this is that I have had experience first hand of studying English and other foreign languages—Spanish, Italian, and French—to relate to my students. As an ESL educator, professional, and doctoral student in Foreign Language Education it is important not only having had experience teaching languages but more importantly having been a student of a second/foreign language. This creates and establishes trust and rapport with the students at their level of experience.

Case 3

Mr. K, who was born in Korea and came to the United States at the age of 9 viewed himself as a NS of English. But due to his nonEuropean appearance, he has not been perceived as a NS of English regardless of his U.S. accent. This is how he felt:

> I think initially, most students regard me with a mixture of surprise, skepticism, and disappointment, because I do not "fit" most students' perception of what a native teacher is supposed to look like. After a while, though, most of them (again, I think) consider me to be a competent teacher. The students did not overtly express their views, but, over time, as we got to know each other better and could be more open with each other, several students "confessed" how they initially felt about having me as a teacher and how their feeling changed over time.

It should be pointed out that the confessions came from a small sample of students, those who had become friends with Mr. K. There probably were other students who maintained their original perceptions and consequently did not express their feelings.

Although seeing himself as a NS of English, Mr. K did not intend to overshadow his Korean background, which he felt could help Asian students in general and Korean students in particular to build up their confidence in learning English. Overall, Mr. K felt that he has had a positive influence on his Korean students:

> Though many of them told me later that they were embarrassed, even ashamed, of being such poor speakers of English in front of another Korean (again, the students see me as being not quite one or the other: Korean or American), students have told me that my being a Korean-American (as opposed to being an American) helped them in the sense that they thought I could understand their position (problems, etc.) better than an American teacher could. For them, it also helped a lot that, whenever they had problems, they had the option of speaking in Korean with me. To a lesser extent, I seem to have a similar rapport with Asian students in general, and to a still lesser extent, with all my students (because of my "non-native-like appearance").

It appears that a non-native-like appearance together with a native-like English can bring the teacher and the students closer and can set a high and yet achievable goal for students to aim for. To a certain extent, it suggests that there are multidimensions on the continuum in characterizing one as a native or non-native speaker.

Case 4

As we recall, Ms. T considered herself a bilingual ESL professional or a NNS professional in ESL when forced to make a choice between NNS and NS. This was simply because English is the second language in the Philippines where she was born, although she started speaking English prior to Tagalog, her native language. Like Mr. K, Ms. T's native-like English with her non-native-like Asian appearance made labeling difficult:

> Most of my students do not seem to know how to take me. They seem surprised when I tell them that I have lived here in the United States for less than 6 years. My reaction to this perception

is an appreciation for whatever combination of events and training I've had in life which has somehow made it easier for me to communicate with my students.

Ms. T pointed out that she saw the benefit of sharing her learning experience with her students but almost never did so at the beginning of a course. More likely, the sharing came toward the end of the course because she was unsure how it would be interpreted. She preferred to let her teaching speak for her. She usually pointed out her background during a tutorial whenever it became relevant or at the end of the course when she gave her farewell pep talk.

In fact, seeing Ms. T as a NNS while listening to her as a NS has worked out well for her students. They usually felt appreciative and grateful to Ms. T who worked so patiently with them. Ms. T continued:

> I don't remember experiencing even a hint of negative perception in any class I've taught. In fact, I've had students express orally how comfortable they were with me as teacher and that they can understand "my English" better than their other teachers' . . .

Discussion

Although NNS professionals in ESL could be acceptable to ESL learners, to what extent can a NNS professional encourage or discourage ESL students? In a similar vein, what impact can a NS professional have on ESL students when their English learning experiences are fundamentally different?

Several implications can be inferred from the four cases discussed. First, when the self-perception of a teacher is the same as how students perceive the teacher (as in the cases of Mr. C, Mr. D, and Mr. F), there usually exists a rapport between the teacher and the students. Instead of being affected by a discrepancy in perception, students tend to appreciate and respect their NNS professionals for their competence and remarkable achievement in learning English. Secondly, when a teacher's self-perception is different from that of the students' perception of the teacher, there is usually surprise on the part of the students. On the positive side, when Ms. DK revealed her Danish origin, students took it as a pleasant surprise, admiring her English and working harder to improve their own language skills. On the negative side, when Mr. K revealed that he was a native speaker of English, his students seem to be puzzled (because he is Asian in appearance) and returned his disclosure with "a mixture of surprise, skepticism, and disappointment." Third, regardless of whether teachers preferred to be labeled as NNSs (Mr. C, Ms. S and Mr. F), NSs (Ms. I and Mr. K), or bilinguals (Ms. T and Ms. DK), there was no indication of who was the best ESL teacher. In this regard, it is the teacher's professional training, linguistic and sociolinguistic competence, understanding of the students' needs, continuous encouragement of students' efforts, and the realistic expectation of students' progress that ultimately constitutes a good ESL professional. This observation is confirmed by Samimy and Brutt-Griffler's study (Chap. 9, this volume).

That a good ESL professional should not be judged upon his or her NS or NNS status reminds us of a fundamental question: Who does the defining of a NNS or a NS? What is the purpose of the NS/NNS dichotomy? If it identifies a NNS as less competent than a NS, then the definition and the dichotomy would be political. If it is for employment purposes, then an appropriate language test could be used to determine if the person has the language competence required for the job. Nevertheless, competence would be on a continuum and not a NS/NNS dichotomy. In fact, the NS/NNS dichotomy embodies linguistic imperialism. In the case of Mr. C, he could be labeled as a NNS despite the fact that his English competence is native-like. The reason could be that Mr. C comes from a country other than the United States, Canada, Britain, Australia, or New Zealand.

Furthermore, one's ethnicity as displayed by skin color and appearance might also affect how one is judged, which in turn affects one's categorization by others as either a NNS or NS. For example, Ms. DK, as a White, might be taken for a native speaker while Mr. K, an Asian, might not, even though he came to the United States at an earlier age than Ms. DK. Whereas Ms. DK is associated with Europe/America and thus the English language, Mr. K is associated with Asia, where English is considered a second or foreign language.

Indeed, there is an invisible power relationship in using the NNS/NS dichotomy (for a detailed account, see Oda, Chap. 8, this volume). We need to keep the following questions in mind: Who labels people as NNSs and NSs and why? What purpose does this dichotomy serve? As Ms. T observes, the NNS/NS label creates a "perceptive difference," which is highly political. She sees the NNS/NS labels as passé, because the boundaries of English have gone beyond geography. People now learn ESL in their home countries without ever living in the United States or the United Kingdom. A continuum is a more objective and realistic configuration than a sharp NNS/NS dichotomy because it also implies a process in moving toward one side or the other (although the movement will probably be toward more native-like proficiency). Besides, there also appears to be a perceptive difference among speakers regarding the quality of language ability implied in the dichotomy—NSs are better at the language and better at teaching it than NNSs. For Ms. T, this issue was created and reinforced by the labeling.

Another interesting issue is: Does a person labeled a NS of one language automatically become a NNS of another language(s)? According to Mr. F, using labels to classify a person as a native speaker of one language deprives the person of the right to be a native speaker of another language(s). Although he speaks more than five languages (Kimbala, Kikingo, French, English, and Lingala), Mr. F only considers himself a native speaker of one language. He acknowledges that he is a native speaker of French as he received his early education in French, regardless of the fact that he learned Kimbala from his parents, that Kikongo was the *lingua franca* of the environment in which he grew up, that he learned English as a school subject, and that he learned Lingala in his early 20s due to a geographical relocation.

Obviously, what was defined by monolingual linguists has now been challenged by "bilingual first language acquisition" researchers (Koppe & Meisel, 1995); we too have to accept that a person such as Ms. DK can be a native speaker of more than one language. The examples of the participants of this study are self-evident: it is possible for a child who grows up bilingually (for example, Ms. T), or trilingually (Mr. F), to have dual or multiple native languages. If we can accept that one can have dual or multiple native languages, then the NNS/NS dichotomy becomes less meaningful. What we need is the NNS-NS continuum with multidimensions and multilayers.

If we accept the NNS-NS continuum, ESL students as well as ESL administrators are likely to regard us individually as ESL professionals. Our skin color, our birth place, and the sequences of our language learning will become less meaningful. The importance attached to one's nativeness or non-nativeness will give way to one's communicative competence as demonstrated in one's daily teaching, and to one's professional vitality in motivating learners to be risk takers, and in promoting learner autonomy through various kinds of activities. Undoubtedly, ESL learners' language development can be shaped by their ESL teachers. However, the teachers' impact on their ESL learners is determined not only by who they are, but also by what they do. If we perceive all ESL professionals on a NS-NNS continuum, then it is their competence and professional growth that will define their professionalism.

References

Kachru, B. B. (1992). *The other tongue.* Urbana: University of Illinois Press.

Koppe, R., & Meisel, J. (1995). Code switching in bilingual first language acquisition. In L. Milroy & P. Muysken (Eds.), *One speaker, two languages: Cross-disciplinary perspectives on code switching* (pp. 276–301). New York: Cambridge University Press.

Kresovich, B. M. (1988). *Error gravity: Perceptions of native-speaking and non-native speaking faculty in EFL.* (ERIC Document Reproduction Service No. ED 311 732).

Liu, J. (1996). *Perceptions of international graduate students towards oral classroom participation in their content courses in a U.S. university.* Unpublished doctoral dissertation, The Ohio State University, Columbus.

McNeill, A. (1994). *Some characteristics of native and non-native speaker teachers of English.* (ERIC Document Reproduction Service No. ED 386 067).

Medgyes, P. (1992). Native or non-native: Who's worth more? *ELT Journal, 46,* 340–349.

Medgyes, P. (1994). *The non-native teacher.* London: Macmillan.

Phillipson, R. (1992). ELT: The native speaker's burden? *ELT Journal, 46,* 12–18.

Phillipson, R. (1992). *Linguistic imperialism.* Oxford, England: Oxford University Press.

Rampton, M. B. H. (1990). Displacing the "native speaker": Expertise, affiliation, and inheritance. *ELT Journal, 44,* 97–101.

Soter, A. (1985). *Writing: A third "language" for second language learners becoming members of new "rhetorical communities."* (ERIC Document Reproduction Service No. ED 273 945).

CHAPTER 12

Language Training:
A Neglected Area in Teacher Education[*]

Péter Medgyes
Centre for English Teacher Training
Eötvös Loránd University, Budapest

The ELT profession may be divided into two camps: native English-speaking teachers and non-native English-speaking teachers (Medgyes, 1992). However, not everyone would agree with this statement. Today there is a growing number of researchers (Edge, 1988; Ferguson, 1982; Kachru, 1985; Paikeday, 1985; Rampton 1990) who claim that there is no such creature as the native or non-native speaker. Their main argument is that all attempts to define native-speaker competence have so far been unsuccessful (Crystal, 1985; Davies, 1991; Richards, Platt, & Weber, 1985; Stern, 1983).

But linguistic pleas apart, they also reject the native/non-native distinction on the grounds that it is suggestive of separation and conflict; in Kachru's (1992) words, it stresses the "us and them" dichotomy rather than "We-ness." A charge of a more practical nature is that birth is often set as a condition in hiring policies, which puts NNS English teachers at a disadvantage (Illés, 1991).

While acknowledging the validity of all these arguments, I am one of a dwindling minority who wishes to retain the dichotomy, if only for the sake of convenience. In agreement with Halliday, I contend that although the native/non-native distinction is an elusive concept, it is "useful precisely because it isn't too closely defined" (quoted in Paikeday, 1985). Indeed, no one would fail to discover the glaring differences between, say, Robert Kaplan's knowledge of English and mine. His superior command is not only conspicuous but also all pervasive, extending to all four skills, plus pronunciation, grammar, and

---

[*] This is a much revised version of a plenary address delivered at the 30th International Association of Teachers of English as a Foreign Language (IATEFL) Conference in 1996.

vocabulary—or by whatever yardstick linguistic competence is measured. In short, Kaplan is a native speaker of English and I am not. I may be a near-native speaker, a speaker with native-like proficiency, a pseudo-native speaker or an honorary native speaker, but I am still short of the competence any genuine native speaker is endowed with.

Does it follow that a NS English teacher by definition is a better teacher than a NNS English teacher? Seidlhofer warned against automatically extrapolating "from competent *speaker* to competent *teacher* based on linguistic grounds alone, without taking into consideration the criteria of cultural, social and pedagogic appropriacy" (1996, p. 69). As I discussed elsewhere (Medgyes, 1994), the bright side of being a NNS English teacher should also be reckoned with. Namely, NNS English teachers can

- provide a good learner model for imitation,
- teach language learning strategies more effectively,
- supply learners with more information about the English language,
- anticipate and prevent language difficulties better,
- be more empathetic to the needs and problems of learners, and
- make use of the learners' mother tongue.

For lack of space, I will not touch upon any of these items. All I wish to point out is that NNS English teachers' linguistic handicap—paradoxically—proves to be their most valuable asset, one which is capable of making up for the odds of limited proficiency. It is precisely this deficit that helps NNS English teachers develop capacities that NS English teachers would never be able to acquire.

It is not surprising that NS and NNS English teachers have been found to exhibit essential differences in their teaching behavior: no NS English teacher can be mistaken for a NNS English teacher, and vice versa. However, this implies no value judgment: neither species is better as such. If a search for the "ideal teacher" were launched, there would be equally good candidates in both camps, even though natives and non-natives would be ideal on their own terms.

What makes one an ideal teacher? Apart from such general qualities as aptitude, experience, personal traits, motivation, and love of students, teacher education is considered to play a crucial role. Hardly any teacher educator would query that the length, quality, and relevance of teacher education impinges upon the future success of the teacher, be it a NS or NNS English teacher.

In this chapter, I focus on the relevance issue, stressing that for NNS English teachers to be effective, self-confident, and satisfied professionals, first, we have to be near-native speakers of English. After all, throughout our career, this is the subject and language of most of our professional endeavors. Obviously, our bond with English does not stop at the classroom door—our personal life, too, is intricately enmeshed with the English language. It is in this sense that I contend that, secondly, we are not only the teachers but also the ambassadors of the English language. This being the case, a third point is that language training in preservice education should be a matter of paramount importance. But it is not, as a rule, and it is certainly a neglected area in my own context, the Centre for English Teacher Training (CETT) in Budapest.

A Vocabulary Course

The experience that triggered my thoughts happened to me 2 years ago when I was teaching a group of CETT students in the last year of their studies (Medgyes, 1996). The course was an elective called "Advanced Vocabulary Building." The trainees had read the course description, so they knew that they were signing up for a course that would focus on analyzing authentic texts such as articles from *Newsweek, The Economist,* and other magazines.

I soon found that my students' command of English left a lot to be desired, considering the fact that they were training to become EFL teachers. Most of them were reluctant to initiate conversation, and when they *did* speak, their utterances were often clumsy and repetitive. They overused certain words and underused others and would quickly run out of vocabulary on almost any topic. Their stock of idiomatic phrases was limited, and they would not use colloquial phrases, let alone slang. They had difficulty expressing their anger, happiness, or surprise in English. In terms of their reading skills, they would read English literature in Hungarian translation and few were in the habit of browsing English-language newspapers or journals. The level of their academic essays was well below their intellectual capacity.

Let me reiterate that they were fairly proficient users of English for ordinary language learners, but not for future EFL teachers. Therefore, as I was planning the course, I assumed that they would go to any lengths to make improvements. I made it clear to them that we would not have enough class time to create several contexts for every new lexical item, so they would be expected to do quite a bit of independent dictionary work and rote learning.

After a short spell of enthusiasm, my students began to complain that there were just too many words to learn between lessons, many of them being low-frequency items. They kept grumbling like this until one day *ungular* cropped up in a *Newsweek* article. When I asked them to learn ungular like any other word, they complained that it was rare and therefore unimportant. My reasoning and insistence was like adding fuel to the fire. In the end, they said that in my classes the Grammar-Translation Method was rising from its ashes, and I was the antithesis of communicative language teaching.

After this upsetting experience, I tottered home and checked the guilty word in the revised edition of the *Collins Cobuild Dictionary* (Sinclair, 1995). It was not there. Yet, on what grounds do the students say that this or any other lexical item is rare? Where does rarity begin? Which frequency band in *Cobuild* is the demarcation line? Or is any item acceptable as long as it is included in *Cobuild?* What is the distinguishing feature of rarity?

Of course, there is no such feature. Words are not rare in an absolute sense, but are more or less frequent in relation to other words. Thus *hoofed animal* is more frequent than *ungular*. It is on the basis of relative frequency that words are grouped in *Cobuild,* admittedly only as a matter of convenience.

It is similarly absurd to talk about important and unimportant words. Lexical items gain or lose importance according to the context in which they occur, and it is often the case that a low-frequency item is more important than the word *the,* which happens to be the most frequent word in the English lexicon. Let me illustrate my point with a story.

On the very first day of my first visit to Los Angeles, I rented a car. I was in the middle of the freeway somewhere in the downtown area, when I discovered that I had a puncture. I pulled into a lay-by, stopped, and opened the boot. There was nothing inside. In desperation, I walked to the nearest emergency phone and called for help. The man at the other end asked whether I had looked for the *ratchet.* When I said I did not understand the meaning of ratchet, he said: "You know, the thing in the trunk." Trunk? What's that? He began to explain, but then gave up and said he would be with me in half an hour. When he arrived, he opened the boot, lifted the cover and said: "But here's the ratchet, man!" After changing the wheels, he asked: "D'you have an AAA card?" "A what?" Realizing that he was talking to someone with brain damage, he just shrugged and said: "Fifty bucks . . . OK, fifty dollars."

This story may be analyzed at several levels, but for the time being all I wish to claim is that the linguistic arguments my students put forward were tenuous. Any word may be important in a given context— even ratchet. But linguistics apart, my pedagogical aim was to help my students reach a near-native level of competence in a specific area, that of vocabulary. At the beginning of the course they seemed to agree, but when push came to shove, they rebelled.

In the Classroom

Although the classroom is a far more natural habitat for NNS English teachers than the Los Angeles freeway, it is no less dangerous. By means of careful planning, however, they can defuse most of the booby-traps. This involves large amounts of language work, such as checking dictionaries, grammar books, and teaching manuals for items that they do not know or do not know how to get across. Diligent preparation enables NNS English teachers to keep the class under control, a precondition for students to feel secure and satisfied.

But despite our most painstaking efforts, we are bound to be confronted with scores of unwelcome questions. Staying within the bounds of lexis, our teenage students may ask for the English equivalent of *stamen, center of gravity, battalion, Tropic of Capricorn, valency, extraction of root, treble clef,* or *legs apart.* It turns out at every step that our repertoire of English words is quite small. All we can say is that we did not attend an English-medium school, hence our deficiencies—a rather poor excuse for students who would like to look up to their teachers for the vast knowledge of their subject matter. Should they meet a lot of teachers like us, they will lose their trust in NNS English teachers completely and long for a NS teacher, who at least "knows" English. Frustration with NNS English teachers is an all too common experience in Hungary. It is no wonder that the best private language schools strive to employ NS English teachers at all costs.

How can we hide our ignorance? At the beginning of my career, I was genuinely honest.

> One day a student named Jason asked me the English word for *kacsacsoru emlos.* I admitted I did not know the word, and promised to look it up for next time. As fate would have it, I forgot. Jason came back the next day, and I promised again. The day after, before I had a chance to apologize, he said: "Don't worry, I've looked it up. It's *platypus.*" A few weeks passed by and Jason returned with a vengeance: "Excuse me, sir, do you

know the Hungarian for platypus, by any chance?" I did not, so he supplied the Hungarian word this time. And so it went on for several weeks: he put the question alternately in English and in Hungarian until I learned platypus both ways.

Now I am old enough to have a few tricks under my belt. For example, when cornered I can say, "Never mind the word, try to put it another way." Or I may ask casually, "Anybody know?" desperately hoping that a student will come to my rescue. Or I may launch a counteroffensive: "You don't know such a simple word? Shame on you! Everybody look it up for next time."

However, my tricks pale beside the cunning of two Hungarian colleagues at my university.

Year after year, the same well-rehearsed scene is repeated. As Adam is holding a class with a group of freshmen, there is a tentative knock on the door. Putting his head round the door, Frank says: "I'm so sorry, Adam, but I just can't remember the English for *kolbászmérgezés.*" "Botulism," is the blasé response. "Wow! This guy knows everything," the students whisper in awe.

Needless to say, methodology books repudiate such ruses: "Do not ever lie to your students!" Although I condone their plea, I cannot help remembering the psychoanalyst Stengal's (1939, p. 473–474) warning: "the learner's narcissism is deeply hurt by the necessity for exposing a serious deficiency in a function which serves as an important source of narcissistic gratification" (quoted in Schumann, 1975, p. 211). The same applies to teachers, I suspect.

Beyond the Classroom

An EFL teacher's job, however, is not done when the lesson is over. Students like to use us as all-round language consultants—and not only about the material we dealt with during the lesson. In the classroom, the odds of being caught unawares are relatively small because we have time to plan our lessons at home. Outside-the-class encounters, on the other hand, are unpredictable, so they really put our language competence to the test. Here is an example:

The lesson is over. On my way out, a student steps up to me: "Sir, I simply can't understand." With some trepidation, I put the Walkman on and listen in. An unintelligible jumble. I give it another try and yet another. After the fifth try, I give up. I read resentment in the boy's eyes.

But it is not only students who take advantage of our knowledge of English—or, rather, the lack of it:

> I am back in the staff room. No sooner do I sink into my chair than a colleague zooms in with a medicine bottle and asks me to translate the instructions. Two key words are totally unfamiliar and one does not fit the context. "I'll look them up for tomorrow," I say apologetically. "Don't worry," she says. "I'll ask someone else."

> At home, the telephone rings. It is a friend who asks me to check the language of a paper he is giving in Zurich next week. "By all means," I say though I dread the thought of perusing a text in physics.

> As I am leaving home next morning, a neighbor blocks my way: "Mr. Medgyes, what is *Vihar* in English? Susy's got to write a paper on Shakespeare, you see." "Tempest," I say with relief. "*The* Tempest or Tempest, without an article?"

I am relentlessly bombarded with such questions and requests. They are often of the most atrocious kind, which render me naked and defenseless. My gut reaction is to run screaming in the opposite direction whenever I see someone approaching me with a resolute smile on his or her face. "Who do you take me for?" I would like to say. "An encyclopedia, a walking dictionary or what? I'm an English teacher. No frills attached!"

But then I remember the plight of linguists, alias language teachers, in 19th century China, a country which pursued a rigidly closed-door policy at that time:

> Nowadays those familiar with barbarian affairs are called "linguists." These men are generally frivolous rascals and loafers in the cities and are despised in their villages and communities . . . Their nature is boorish, their knowledge is shallow, and furthermore, their moral principles are mean. They know nothing except sensual pleasures and material profit. Moreover, their ability consists of nothing more than a slight knowledge of the barbarian language and occasional recognition of barbarian characters, which is limited to names of commodities, numerical

figures, some slang expressions and a little simple grammar (quoted in Teng & Fairbanks, 1954, p. 51).

To be sure, the only way we NNS English teachers can command more respect than our Chinese ancestors is through the mastery of the English language. For us, a near-native command of English, which stretches far beyond the narrow confines of the school curriculum, is an indispensable, albeit insufficient, tool. An EFL teacher whose knowledge ends with *Headway Advanced* (Soars & Soars, 1989) is like a history teacher who knows no more about the Incas than James Fenimore Cooper, or a geography teacher who looks for a river in Asia at the mention of Brazzaville. By the same token, an EFL teacher with faulty English may be compared to a music teacher who can play no musical instrument and sings out of tune, or a gym teacher who is grossly overweight and too clumsy to catch a ball.

An EFL teacher's availability should be restricted by neither space nor time. He or she is a professional in and outside the classroom; his or her working hours are flexible, that is, he or she is on duty round the clock. In this sense, a good EFL teacher is not simply a teacher but the ambassador of the English language.

Now the question is: the ambassador of (a) which English language and, by implication, (b) which English culture? Let me discuss these two issues separately.

Which English Language?

Today, English is the unchallenged lingua franca of the world, and the number of people who speak it either as a first, second or foreign language is growing exponentially. According to some estimates, there are close to one billion English speakers in the world today (Crystal, 1995a). Thus English is no longer the prerogative of native speakers; it has become a universal commodity, the official or semiofficial language in more than 60 countries over six continents.

The struggle for the emancipation of non-native varieties has definitely intensified over the past two decades. "No norm should be imposed on the users of English," runs the argument. "Native and non-native speakers should be allowed to mould it in equal measure." According to Povey (1977), when an African student was criticized by a NS teacher for using a nonstandard form, he burst out: "It's our language now and we can do what we like with it!" (p. 28).

English is traditionally spoken as a second language in a number of countries, such as India or Nigeria, but Swedish English and Dutch

English are also on their way to becoming "norm-providing varieties," to use Kachru's (1985) oft-quoted term. In 1983, a teacher from Yugoslavia (Ridjanovi, 1983) said that the time had come for Yugoslav English, too, to be admitted to the exclusive club of standard varieties; with the benefit of hindsight, this sounds rather a tragicomical claim.

Some language educators, on the other hand, perceive the spread of native and non-native varieties of English as a threat. The proliferation of English, they argue, hinders mutual intelligibility across countries and continents. To stave off this danger, they advocate the use of *International English*, which, in Campbell's definition, is "that English in all its linguistic and sociolinguistic aspects which is used as a vehicle for communication between non-native speakers only, as well as between any combination of native and non-native speakers" (1983, p. 35). Campbell also stated that "native speakers of English need training in the use of their own language in international settings" (p. 35).

If International English has become a linguistic reality, one would expect to find *The Grammar of International English* in the library. After all, such linguistic descriptions have been produced for languages and language varieties with a much smaller circulation than that of International English. However, until such a grammar book has seen the light of day, I propose that International English be regarded merely as an idealization, an amalgam of beliefs and assumptions about rules and norms to which certain people adhere with varying degrees of success. Otherwise, I have to agree with Lewis's (1995) sarcastic remark that International English is a mere euphemism for, or a politically correct equivalent of, Intermediate English. Lewis set up two categories of countries within the European Union, Britain and the others. The British are native speakers of English, and the others are intermediate speakers. Some of them, like the Swedes, are upper intermediate; others, like the Italians, are lower intermediate. This being the case, Hungary as a non-European Union country probably belongs to the category of preintermediate speakers or, worse still, to that of false beginners.

So long as International English is a nonlinguistic entity, it is unteachable, too. What is teachable is a large stock of native and non-native varieties of English. But at this point we are confronted with a dilemma: which variety shall we teach? For NS English teachers, this is not a problem: they will probably teach the native variety they were born into. NNS English teachers, on the other hand, are advised to choose a widely spoken variety. And it is not simply a matter of numbers. Few NNS teachers would teach Indian English simply on the grounds that perhaps there are more Indian English speakers today than British English speakers (Crystal, 1995b). For most of us, the obvious choice is between British and U.S. English, which does not rule out familiarity with other native and non-native varieties and tolerance toward nonstandard norms.

Which English Culture?

Language is a cultural phenomenon, determined by culture with a capital *c* as well as a small *c*. Culture with a capital *c* implies information exchange: the provision of (a) statistical data, such as facts about civilization; (b) highbrow information, such as classics of literature; and (c) lowbrow information, such as the folklore of everyday life. (So when my neighbor inquired about Shakespeare's *The Tempest*, she was seeking highbrow information.)

Culture with a capital *c* has always been the subject of language teaching. In the heyday of the Grammar-Translation Method, the principal aim of language teaching was to convey factual and highbrow information about the British Isles. By contrast, contemporary course books are brimming with tidbits of lowbrow information, keeping us up-to-date about what goes on in the English-speaking world.

Culture with a small *c*, on the other hand, is more opaque because it does not crystallize into disparate bits of information. It implies what members of a language community do, feel, talk, think, and dream about, within the framework of their system of values, attitudes, and mind-sets. Culture with a small *c* is hard to disentangle from language; as Kramsch said with reference to Halliday, culture is anchored in "the very grammar we use, the very vocabulary we choose, the very metaphors we live by" (1993, p. 8). It enables us to understand and produce language and, conversely, language use deepens our cultural awareness.

To illustrate the strong bond between language and culture, let me refer back to my mishap on the Los Angeles freeway. It may look as if the breakdown of communication was essentially caused by my language defects, that is, not knowing the words *ratchet, trunk,* and *buck,* but there was more to it than that.

> To begin with, a few minutes before I hit the freeway, I had rolled onto the iron prongs in a parking lot the wrong way up, not knowing that they would cause serious damage to the tires. When I discovered the puncture, I stopped, got out of the car and, to my horror, I found nothing in the boot, no spare wheel, no jack, no spanner, because I had been accustomed to Eastern European cars, which were not equipped with a lower layer. It

was also due to an Eastern European reflex that I began to wave for cars to stop and help—a hopeless attempt on a LA freeway. When the man on the phone asked me about AAA (the American Automobile Association, pronounced as triple A), I had no idea why he kept repeating Tripoli, the Libyan town. And what confused him was that I spoke fairly fluently (with a touch of "English" accent though) and yet was unable to communicate. As he handed me the check for fifty dollars, I saw guilt on his face: "Poor chap, he sure needs medical rather than mechanical care."

Obviously, my predicament was not occasioned by the lexical gaps but rather by a total lack of cultural knowledge about the United States, including Los Angeles, freeway rules, and U.S. cars. My ignorance led to panic and, after I had undergone a number of frustrating experiences in the first few weeks of my stay, to a protracted period of culture shock.

I have to admit, however, that mutual intelligibility is hindered by similar deficiencies even among native speakers, as demonstrated by the following incident.

A few years ago I went to a dinner party in England. All the guests were British except for an American woman and myself. As I had entered into a chat with her over an aperitif, I talked about the linguistic and cultural deficits of non-native speakers. She said she would also occasionally feel excluded in the company of Britons even though she had been living in England for several years. A few minutes later the conversation took a sudden turn around the dinner table. I was rapidly losing my bearings. Catching my eye, the American woman whispered to me across the table: "This is it. I don't have the faintest idea what they're talking about, either!" (Medgyes, 1994).

With respect to the link between language and culture, now that English is no longer the sole property of native speakers, every user is entitled to contribute to it through their own regional identity. As Kachru said, "As this transmuting alchemy of English takes effect, the language becomes less and less *culture-specific*" (1985, p. 20, emphasis added).

This assumption lends itself to two different interpretations. One is that the culture of the English-speaking world is falling into disparate pieces, a process that renders the English language itself culture-free. This relativist view is manifest in a number of contemporary course books in which nondescript characters blather on about nondescript topics in nondescript international surroundings. According to the other interpretation, languages can never lose their cultural profile, for every real-life utterance is embedded in a culturally determined context. The more contexts, the richer the language. In this sense, English, which is used in the most diverse milieus the world over, is arguably the most culture-rich language of our time.

From the individual's perspective, this is a give-and-take process. As people engage in L2 communication, they add to the cultural charge of the language being used and, simultaneously, gain from the interaction in terms of their ever-broadening cultural horizon.

Non-native speakers constitute a special class of language users. They arrive with a native command of L1, which is couched in their indigenous culture (C1). As they come into contact with L2, they become imbued with the target culture (C2) in all its manifestations. At this interface, a new cultural identity is born (C3), which incorporates certain elements of all constituent cultures, yet is characteristically different from any of them. A non-native speaker is like a child who takes after all his or her forbears and still has pronounced features of his or her own. The better he or she speaks a foreign language, the more distinct his or her new cultural individuality becomes.

As far as speakers with near-native competence are concerned, they are generally held in high esteem. This respect is due not only to the practical value of their advanced language proficiency but also to their potential to better understand the way their mother tongue works and greater sensitivity to their home culture. Although it may look a bit far-fetched to claim that bilinguals are better citizens than monolinguals (Jenkins, 1996), they are certainly the best ambassadors between peoples and cultures or, to borrow Edelhoff's (1994) phrase, the most successful "intercultural interpreters."

Near-Native or Adequate?

But let us return to the issue of the NNS English teacher's language competence. The importance of near-native proficiency is hardly ever questioned in the literature. Murdoch (1994) called language proficiency the bedrock of the NNS English teacher's professional confidence and Lange (1990) rated it as the most essential characteristic of a good language teacher. Britten (1985a, 1985b) claimed that an excellent command of English is a major selection criteria and a good predictor of NNS English teacher success—a make-or-break requirement. If this is true, language training should play a central role in teacher education programs. But does it?

Let me address this problem within the framework of my own university. We offer two basic types of preservice education: the traditional 5-year program and the innovative 3-year program, which is run at the Centre for Teacher Training. In the 5-year program, the focus is on literature and linguistics; EFL methodology and school practice play second fiddle. The 3-year program reverses the order: it gives precedence to the development of teaching skills over philology. The two programs have but one thing in common: language improvement is not a top priority in either of them. "We're not a language school!" teachers in both camps asseverate.

With regard to CETT, the curriculum document is rather ambivalent about the trainees' language competence, using the terms *near-native* and *adequate* proficiency alternately, as though they were synonyms (Griffiths & Ryan, 1994). Although CETT sets an elaborate proficiency examination with a fairly high attrition rate (Dávid, Major, & Moya, 1996)[1], hardly any students drop out of the program because of their insufficient command of English. A high level of language proficiency is not even listed among the major criteria of assessing the trainees' school practice (Bodóczky & Malderez, 1996).

It may also be interesting to dissect the following sentence: *"Whether desirable or not,* the single most important factor that gives professional credibility to language teachers in Hungary is the level of their English" (Dávid et al., 1996, p. 114, emphasis added). The oblique remark, "Whether desirable or not" is another indication of the dominance of those in the staff who play down the importance of language development. A more extreme version of this view was expressed by a senior staff member, who boldly claimed that NNS English teachers with an excellent command of English tend to be worse teachers than their linguistically less competent colleagues, partly because they are less empathetic to their students' difficulties. In view of this statement, it is no wonder that two years ago, when four teaching posts had to be given up owing to massive economic cuts, it was decided that the number of language improvement courses be drastically curtailed while the rest of the curriculum remained untouched.

The low prestige of direct language teaching, however, was just one reason why the axe fell on language development. Another one had to do with the brevity of the CETT program (Rádai & Shanklin, 1996): the

---

[1] This article, along with a few others referred to later, was published in an anthology dedicated to the Centre for English Teacher Training in Budapest (Medgyes & Malderez, 1996). To my knowledge, this is the first book ever to give a thorough account of an innovative programme being run in Central and Eastern Europe.

majority of the staff thought time was too precious to waste on an area of study that could be learnt with a little tutorial assistance.

The last point, which may have carried more weight than all the other considerations put together, brings me back to the NS English teacher/NNS English teacher division.

The Two Camps

Before the collapse of communist rule, the few NS English teachers who lived and worked in Hungary were highly respected and often regarded as the ultimate source of knowledge and expertise. This deference occasionally reached a point of adulation and their judgments, even beyond language matters, were often taken for granted (Enyedi & Medgyes, 1998).

In the post-communist era, the number of NS English teachers has multiplied. In addition to persevering expatriates, new cohorts have appeared on the ELT scene: mercurial contractees, jet-in/jet-out consultants, and pestilential backpackers. They act as bridgeheads, backed by a wealthy ELT industry and an adroit moderator called The British Council. Although they are ubiquitous, the myth of NS superiority remains unchallenged and their influence pervasive. This lopsided relationship between NS English teachers and NNS English teachers is being sustained by mutually false images and expectations.

For better or for worse, NS English teachers have left an indelible print on the philosophy and practice of ELT in Hungary. Encouraged by a handful of staunch NNS English teacher disciples, they promulgate a fairly homogeneous ideology, which is not always in key with the educational traditions of Hungary and is often ill-suited for local needs. It seems to me that most communication breakdowns between NS and NNS English teachers occur along ideological faultlines.

It is largely due to NS teachers' intervention, for example, that the CETT curriculum is permeated with catch phrases underlying new-fangled educational concepts. It is replete with adjectives like *process-oriented, student-centered, task-based, collaborative, communicative, reflective, heuristic, holistic, and humanistic* (Holliday, 1994). Old terms such as *language practice, teaching practice,* and *trainees* have been replaced by *language improvement, teaching experience* and *student-teachers,* respectively. *Foster, facilitate, enhance,* and *empower* substitute for *teach, train, impart,* and *instruct. Knowledge* and *skills* are out, *attitudes* and *awareness* are in. *Teacher training* is passé—hurray for *teacher education!*

If something falls outside the NS English teachers' frame of reference, it stands little chance of success these days. For one thing, NS

English teachers usually fail to recognize the urgency of NNS English teachers' need to improve their command of English. I remember running in-service courses together with NS trainers. They never seemed to understand (a) why the participants solicited more language practice on the course; (b) what exactly they wanted in the way of language improvement; and (c) how these demands could be satisfied. Thus it would fall to me, the NNS English teacher, to work on the language skills of fellow NNS English teachers, while my native partners would deal with methodology. Language development at CETT has fared badly for similar reasons.

Even though I do not accept Phillipson's (1992) theory of imperialistic conspiracy (perhaps because in communist Hungary *imperialism* had become an utterly discredited term), I concede that the influence of NS English teachers on present-day ELT in Hungary is not always beneficial, and progress cannot be envisaged unless steps to remedy the situation are taken on both sides simultaneously. Thus NS English teachers should not only learn about local educational traditions and culture, but "they also need to examine the preconceptions behind their own educational beliefs, so often taken for granted" (Hyde, 1994, p. 13). This process should be reinforced by a growth in NNS English teachers' self-confidence, a more cautious attitude toward "imported products" and a willingness to assume full responsibility for their own affairs.

Conclusion

Let me reiterate: language improvement is not the cutting edge of the CETT program and, as a result, trainees will not bend over backwards to make linguistic progress. The majority are content to behave like ordinary learners, sitting in ordinary classrooms, learning from ordinary ELT materials. They reject being *taught, trained, imparted,* and *instructed*— and expect to be *fostered, facilitated, enhanced,* and *empowered.* They echo the words of some of their tutors: "In an innovative teacher-education program, only the most up-to-date methodological views should be allowed." To adopt a noncommunicative attitude for language improvement classes and a communicative one for ELT methodology classes, so runs the argument, is sheer hypocrisy and implants a wrong teaching model.

My logic runs along a different path. I believe that the needs of a future EFL teacher are far more urgent than those of an ordinary language learner. If all learners were placed on an imaginary continuum according to the degree of their language needs, teacher trainees would be close to the *most urgent* end, right next to international spies (Coulmas, 1981); ordinary learners would necessarily be miles behind them.

If their needs are so divergent, why should the learning routes be the same for the two types of learners, the professional versus the amateur? For one thing, trainees can afford to spend far more time and energy on learning English than a learner with limited goals. More important, their level of motivation should be much higher and its source should be of a different kind: intrinsic and thus self-generating. For a professional language learner, learning is not a chore but a gratifying activity that refreshes the mind and almost yields sensual pleasure. For an EFL professional, trained or in training, uttering an English word, as Wittgenstein (1958, p. 4) noted, should be "like striking a note on the keyboard of the imagination" (quoted in Kramsch, 1995, p. 22). The trouble with my rebellious students was not that they had gaps in their English vocabulary but that they thought it was no use trying to acquire every lexical item that came their way. Their attitude was that of an amateur; this, and not their limited knowledge, is what I found inexcusable.

Not long ago, I read a feedback sheet written by a CETT trainee. She expressed the following concern:

> Although we had ten language improvement classes a week during our first year, a great proportion of these classes was devoted to games and activities which required a language level far lower than that of the group. And though they may have enriched our store of activities as would-be teachers, they could and should have been tailored to our language level and needs as language learners . . . All in all, I feel that CETT offers students a very effective and up-to-date training in terms of methodology, but fails to cater for their needs as language learners.

She wrote this letter and postponed her studies for one year in order to learn English in a private language school. What a pity! If I had had her in my vocabulary class, her arguments might well have received more credibility with her peers than my tirades.

Several months after my vocabulary course, a fellow tutor at CETT stopped me in the corridor and said: "As we were exploiting a text in class, one of my students exclaimed, 'Ah, I know it! It's a Medgyes word!' What did she mean?" my colleague asked. "I don't know," I said, because I thought any answer would sound presumptuous. But for days afterwards, I was walking on cloud nine.

Acknowledgment

I would like to thank James Leavey for reading my manuscript and providing useful comments on my linguistic idiosyncrasies.

References

Bodóczky, C., & Malderez, A. (1996). Out into schools. In P. Medgyes & A. Malderez (Eds.), *Changing perspectives in teacher education* (pp. 58–74). Oxford, England: Heinemann.

Britten, D. (1985a). Teacher training in ELT (Part I). *Language Teaching, 18,* 112–128.

Britten, D. (1985b). Teacher training in ELT (Part II). *Language Teaching, 18,* 220–238.

Campbell, D. (1983). English in international settings: Problems and their causes. In L. E. Smith (Ed.), *Readings in English as an international language* (pp. 35–47). Oxford, England: Pergamon.

Coulmas, F. (1981). Spies and native speakers. In F. Coulmas (Ed.), *A Festschrift for native speaker* (pp. 355–467). The Hague, The Netherlands: Mouton.

Crystal, D. (1985). *A dictionary of linguistics and phonetics.* Oxford, England: Basil Blackwell.

Crystal, D. (1995a). *The Cambridge encyclopedia of the English language.* Cambridge, England: Cambridge University Press.

Crystal, D. (1995b, April). *English conversation: 1000 years on.* Plenary address at the annual conference of the International Association of Teachers of English as a Foreign Language, York, U.K.

Dávid, G., Major, É., & Moya, S. (1996). Testing people. In P. Medgyes & A. Malderez (Eds.), *Changing perspectives in teacher education* (pp. 87–96). Oxford, England: Heinemann.

Davies, A. (1991). *The native speaker in applied linguistics.* Edinburgh, England: University of Edinburgh.

Edelhoff, C. (1994, September). *Intercultural learning in foreign languages.* Plenary address at Networking English Language Learning in Europe Conference, Innsbruck, Austria.

Edge, J. (1988). Natives, speakers, and models. *JALT Journal, 9,* 153–157.

Enyedi, Á., & Medgyes, P. (1998). ELT in Central and Eastern Europe. *Language Teaching, 31(1),* 1–12.

Ferguson, C. A. (1982). Foreword. In B. B. Kachru (Ed.), *The other tongue: English across cultures* (pp. vii–xi). Oxford, England: Pergamon.

Griffiths, J., & Ryan, C. (Eds.). (1994). *Curriculum for the three-year TEFL programme* (2nd ed.). Budapest, Hungary: Centre for English Teacher Training.

Holliday, A. (1994). *Appropriate methodology and social context.* Cambridge, England: Cambridge University Press.

Hyde, B. (1994). Albanian babies and the bathwater. *The Teacher Trainer, 8(1)*, 10–13.

Illés, É. (1991). Correspondence. *ELT Journal, 45*, 87.

Jenkins, J. (1996). Native speaker, non-native speaker and English as a foreign language: Time for a change. *IATEFL Newsletter, 131*, 10–11.

Kachru, B. B. (1985). Standards, codification and sociolinguistic realism: The English language in the outer circle. In R. Quirk & H. G. Widdowson (Eds.), *English in the world—Teaching and learning the language and literatures* (pp. 11–30). Cambridge, England: Cambridge University Press.

Kachru, B. B. (1992). World Englishes: Approaches, issues and resources. *Language Teaching, 25*, 1–14.

Kramsch, C. (1993). *Context and culture in language teaching.* Oxford, England: Oxford University Press.

Kramsch, C. (1995, March). *The privilege of the non-native speaker.* Plenary address at the Annual Convention of Teachers of English to Speakers of Other Languages, Long Beach, CA.

Lange, D. L. (1990). A blueprint for a teacher development program. In J. C. Richards & D. Nunan (Eds.), *Second language teacher education* (pp. 245–268). Cambridge, England: Cambridge University Press.

Lewis, M. (1995). *The lexical approach.* Plenary address at the Annual Conference of the International Association of Teachers of English as a Foreign Language, Szombathely, Hungary.

Medgyes, P. (1992). Native or non-native: Who's worth more? *ELT Journal, 46*, 340–349.

Medgyes, P. (1994). *The non-native teacher.* London: Macmillan.

Medgyes, P. (1996). Teachers turned ambassadors. *Novelty, 3(1)*, 7–27.

Medgyes, P. & Malderez, A. (Eds.) *Changing perspectives in teacher education.* Oxford, England: Heinemann.

Murdoch, G. (1994). Language development in teacher training curricula. *ELT Journal, 48*, 253–259.

Paikeday, T. M. (1985). *The native speaker is dead!* Toronto, Canada: Paikeday Publishing, Inc.

Phillipson, R. (1992). *Linguistic imperialism.* Oxford, England: Oxford University Press.

Povey, J. (1977). The role of English in Africa. *English Teaching Forum, 15(3)*, 27–29.

Rádai, P., & Shanklin, T. (1996). Language matters. In P. Medgyes & A. Malderez (Eds.), *Changing perspectives in teacher education* (pp. 25–35). Oxford, England: Heinemann.

Rampton, M. B. H. (1990). Displacing the 'native speaker': Expertise, affiliation, and inheritance. *ELT Journal, 44*, 97–101.

Richards, J. C., Platt, J., & Weber, H. (1985). *Longman dictionary of applied linguistics.* London: Longman.

Ridjanovi, M. (1983). How to learn a language, say English, in a couple of months. *English Teaching Forum, 21(1)*, 8–13.

Schumann, J. H. (1975). Affective factors and the problem of age in second language acquisition. *Language Learning, 25,* 209–235.

Seidlhofer, B. (1996). 'It is an undulating feeling . . .' The importance of being a non-native teacher of English. *Views, 5(1–2),* 63–80.

Sinclair, J. (Ed.) (1995). *Collins cobuild English language dictionary* (2nd ed.). London: HarperCollins.

Soars, J., & Soars, L. (1989). *Headway advanced.* Oxford, England: Oxford University Press.

Stengal, E. (1939). On learning a new language. *International Journal of Psychoanalysis, 20,* 471–479.

Stern, H. H. (1983). *Fundamental concepts of language teaching.* Oxford, England: Oxford University Press.

Teng, S., & Fairbanks, J. K. (1954). *Research guide for China's response to the West: A documentary survey, 1839–1923.* Cambridge, MA: Harvard University Press.

Wittgenstein, L. (1958). *Philosophical investigations* (3rd ed.). New York: Macmillan.

CHAPTER 13

Training Non-Native TESOL Students: Challenges for TESOL Teacher Education in the West[*]

Dilin Liu
Oklahoma City University

An obvious but seldom-noticed fact in the TESOL field is that the majority of the world's ESOL teachers are NNSs. More important, their number is still on the rise as the role of the English language as the lingua franca expands rapidly in an ever more globalized economy. Although many of these NNS teachers have received their training in their home country, a large number have acquired or are acquiring their education in North America, Britain, and Australia (hereafter referred to as NABA). In fact, of the students enrolled in the NABA TESL/TESOL teacher education programs, close to 40% are NNSs.[1] Most of these students will in due course return to their home countries to teach.

In spite of their different backgrounds and needs, these students are usually given the same training as their native speaker peers. This often results in a gap between what they learn while abroad and what they face in their teaching back home (see Burnaby & Sun, 1989; Canagarajah, 1993; Pennycook, 1989); many find themselves less than adequately

---

[*] This chapter is an expanded version of the article "Ethnocentrism in TESOL: Teacher education and the neglected needs of international TESOL students" which appeared in *The ELT Journal*, 52 (1998), 3-10. Permission to reproduce the material from the article has been granted by the Oxford University Press.

[1] The information is based on the numbers found in the TESOL's *Directory of Professional Preparation Programs in TESOL in the U.S. and Canada* (1995); 173 out of 279 programs listed in the directory reported breakdown figures of their graduates for the 1993-1994 academic year. Of the graduates, 1,998 were NSs and 1,112, that is, 37%, were NNSs. Also, in 43 of the 173 programs (one fourth), the number of NNS graduates was either equal to or larger than that of native speakers.

prepared. Therefore, how to meet the special needs of NNS TESOL students[2] has posed a great challenge to the NABA TESOL teacher educators. Unfortunately, many of us are unaware of the challenges. This chapter attempts to highlight the issue by demonstrating why and how the needs of NNS students are not met and to offer, where appropriate, some preliminary suggestions on how to resolve this matter.

That NABA TESOL teacher education has overlooked the needs of NNS TESOL students is not difficult to detect, for I have found no direct discussion about the issue in the literature. What makes this neglect more striking is that, in contrast to a virtual absence of discussion on NNS TESOL students, one finds in current literature many studies on international teaching assistants (see Halleck & Moder, 1995; Tyler, 1992; to mention just two). TESOL even has an interest section devoted to them. Although international teaching assistants clearly merit our attention, NNS TESOL students deserve equal, if not greater, concern because they are our would-be colleagues whose work will, in turn, affect hundreds of thousands of ESOL students around the world.

The discrepancy in the treatment of these two groups is no accident. Although the reasons for the overwhelming attention to international teaching assistants may be many, the primary one could be the concern that NABA college students' education could suffer because these teaching assistants often have language problems in English. In addition, influenced by their native teaching conventions, they may use methods not practiced in the West. I have no objection to training these assistants to become successful teaching staff in NABA colleges. I appreciate such efforts and I especially applaud the recognition of differences in teaching between NABA and other countries.[3] Unfortunately, such recognition appears to be missing from the training given to NNS TESOL students.

---

[2] NNS TESOL students are treated as one group here simply for the convenience of discussion in this chapter. These students are by no means a monolithic group because of the vast differences in their ethnic, linguistic, and economic backgrounds. Although they differ as a group from NABA students, their needs vary among themselves from country to country.

[3] NABA are juxtaposed here with other countries simply for the purpose of discussion in this chapter. The juxtaposition does not mean that each group is monolithic nor does it suggest that the two groups never overlap in their teaching or other practice.

Ethnocentric Ideologies:
Barriers in TESOL Teacher Education

This double standard with regard to international teaching assistants and NNS TESOL students suggests an ethnocentrism on the part of NABA TESOL educators. First, it implies that NABA TESOL teacher educators give little attention to the millions of ESOL students that NNS TESOL students teach after they graduate. Although many of us may not be conscious of such discrimination, our practice undeniably reflects it. Second, our failure in training NNS TESOL students to distinguish between teaching practice in NABA and other countries indicates a disregard for differences in socioeconomic conditions, educational ideologies and systems, and other factors that help define teaching conventions. At best, this neglect may have stemmed from an urge to make NNS TESOL students learn and practice back home the new teaching methodologies developed in NABA. Although such an agenda might be well intentioned, its effects can be harmful, because it ignores cultural differences and encourages students to adopt ideas and practices that are valued in NABA but may not be very useful in their home environment.

This ethnocentrism is clearly evident in current NABA TESOL teacher education, a field presently dominated by a "methodological dogmatism" (Reid, 1995/1996, p. 3) that fervently promotes NABA's new methodologies, particularly those entitled communicative, while condemning tried and tested traditional methods still popular in many other parts of the world. In my view, it is this dogmatism, and the Western ethnocentric ideologies behind it, that blind us to the needs of international TESOL students. One of the Western ideological forces that deserve our special concern is what Phillipson (1988, 1992) called "linguistic imperialism"—an effort to spread Western values and maintain existing powers through language education. Obviously, few Western TESOL educators nurture such an agenda, yet its presence in various forms and in different subareas has been well documented (Judd, 1983; Phillipson & Skutnabb-Kangas, 1995; Skutnabb-Kangas & Phillipson, 1994; Tollefson, 1988, 1991, 1995). I would like to argue that TESOL teacher education is no exception. Linguistic imperialism in this field manifests itself in the maintenance of a one-way flow of information, that is, exporting Western theories and methodologies to non-NABA countries. This one-way traffic has helped to sustain the imbalance of power in TESOL teacher education where the West has dominated the rest of the world by controlling the source and production of knowledge and by dictating the direction of the profession. It is, therefore, no exaggeration to say that the field mirrors "the global power structure which maintains the Periphery [non-Western countries] in a state of dependence on the Center [the West]" (Phillipson, 1988, p. 348). To stop this imbalance of power and to better serve NNS students, TESOL teacher educators should constantly guard against Western ethnocentric ideologies.

Areas of Challenges:
L2 Acquisition Theories and TESOL Methodologies

The first and the most important area in which NABA TESOL teacher preparation has failed NNS TESOL students (and also those NABA native speaker TESOL students who plan to teach in Periphery countries) is its core program—the courses on second language acquisition theories and teaching methodologies. The dominant acquisition theories and teaching methodologies currently taught are, as Kachru (1994) and Sridhar (1994) correctly pointed out, based largely on second language acquisition models found primarily in NABA. Most of the data used in developing these models was from immigrants and international students studying in NABA, and "few attempts have been made to gather evidence from stable contexts of bi/multilingualism in Africa, Asia, Europe, and Latin America" (Kachru, 1994, p. 796). As a result, the dominant L2 acquisition paradigm "leaves out vast millions of L2 users who learn and use second languages in their own countries, from their own (non-native) teachers, for use primarily with other non-native speakers, and who many never come across a native speaker face to face" (Sridhar, 1994, p. 801). In other words, without significant adaptation, many of the L2 acquisition theories that make sense in the West may be irrelevant. Further, as Burnaby and Sun (1989), Holliday (1994a, 1994b), and Prabhu (1987) showed, many of the teaching methodologies may be impractical or ineffective in non-NABA countries because of significant socioeconomic and cultural differences. It is therefore urgent for us to develop theories and methodologies that are in Sridhar's (1994) words, "functionally oriented and culturally authentic" (p. 803).

To illustrate why some of the theories and methods are irrelevant and nonfunctional in non-NABA countries, let us look at Asia, with China as a primary example in many instances. As in most non-NABA countries, English language education in China is primarily "state-run"—English being taught in state-run elementary, secondary, and tertiary schools. Besides, English is treated as a required academic subject rather than as a tool for survival in business and education, as is mostly the case with ESL in NABA. Being part of the state education program, English education in Asia is influenced and determined by national governments' rigid and often mandatory top-down educational policies/standards and by teaching practices sanctioned by tradition. Despite the fact that some changes have taken place—the extent of changes varies from country to country—English is still treated mostly as an academic subject in school rather than as "skills" (Holliday, 1994a, p. 80–81). In most Asian countries, teaching English means basically teaching grammar, reading, and translation, and this kind of teaching has been reinforced and perpetuated by state-run examinations, especially the national college entrance examination found in most Asian countries, which measure primarily grammatical competence (Berns, 1990; Burnaby & Son, 1989; Campbell & Zhao, 1993).

Situated in cultures where unconditional obedience to authority has been a long tradition and where a teacher is not seen as a facilitator but as an authority in learning, as "a fount of knowledge, which is delivered without any concession to students and which students must struggle to attain" (Holliday, 1994a, p. 59), English teaching in Asia is still dominantly didactic: product oriented or knowledge driven in nature and teacher centered in style (see also Burnaby & Sun, 1989; Campbell & Zhao, 1993; Canagarajah, 1993; Prabhu, 1987). The pervasiveness of such teaching practice has also resulted, especially in developing countries, from the limited educational resources available. Lack of funds and lack of teachers have led to crowded classrooms with little or no audiovisual teaching equipment such as TVs, VCRs, and computers which are taken for granted in language teaching in NABA. The number of students per class sometimes runs as high as 70 (Hodson, 1994/1995). Of course, the reason for large classes in Asia is not merely economic; in Taiwan, now a very wealthy place, the average class size in public schools is still 40 to 50. The large class size has remained unchanged there because it works well with its predominantly lecture-style teaching. Finally, the class time per week for English is also very limited, about 2 to 4 hours, in contrast to the many hours (as high as 20 and more) in some intensive ESL programs in NABA. Understandably, such limited class time is probably enough only to help students understand how the language works, not give them practice in using it. These factors, among many others, have made English education in these countries a very different matter from that in NABA and have rendered unsuitable some of NABA's highly valued teaching methodologies.

These methods and teaching styles are not useful without adaptation because they were developed in settings and for objectives that are entirely different. In NABA, teaching is process- or discovery-oriented. Interaction, group work, and student-centeredness are the order of the class whose normal size is less than 20 students. Furthermore, as stated earlier, ESL is taught mostly as an instrument and much of the ESL education is run "commercially" (Holliday, 1994a, p. 13). There are also far more resources than in most Asian countries. Developed in such different cultural and economic milieus, NABA's teaching methods, materials, and programs often face resistance or even rejection in Asia, and for good reasons. Burnaby and Sun (1989), Campbell and Zhao (1993), Canagarajah (1993), and Pennycook (1989) documented ample evidence of such resistance and the reasons behind it. By the same token, because of the methodological dogmatism and the failure to appreciate the differences mentioned in TESOL teacher education, many trained NABA native speaker teachers who go to teach in Asia find themselves insufficiently prepared for the job they have been sent to do. They are often overwhelmed by the sharp differences between the theories and teaching methods they have learned and the actual practices they now face. Some even return home without fulfilling their contract because they feel they have been forced into "a compromised pedagogical integrity in such situations" (Cahill, 1996, p. 5).

It is important to point out, however, that Asian teachers and students do not blindly resist or reject everything from NABA. On the contrary, they wholeheartedly welcome help from the outside world. As Dong (1995) wrote from the perspective of Chinese teachers of English, "We need more help. Readers and learners in China need more help" (p. 56). But before NABA English educators can really render any assistance, we should remember that the exchange cannot be one way; otherwise, we will never escape the ethnocentric mentality. We should respect what they do and engage in "constructive dialogue and mutual learning" (Holliday, 1994a, p. 6). Such practice may open our eyes to more possibilities and more diverse viewpoints. As Burnaby and Sun (1989) suggested, "English-speaking countries might look to the Chinese foreign language teaching model, which is undoubtedly successful in its own terms, for ideas to use domestically" (p. 236). Only through dialogues can we really find out what NNS students need and offer them productive assistance.

Unfortunately we have, by and large, failed in fulfilling that. Hodson's (1994/1995) reflections on the teacher training course she offered in Thailand were especially illuminating: "The course focuses on ESL because the resources and the practicum offered are in an ESL situation, not an EFL situation. Many of the students intended to use their teaching skills in an EFL situation but the differences required by the EFL situation are largely left to the students to investigate" (p. 21). Without significant changes, NABA TESOL teacher education is doing a great disservice to NNS students. As Burnaby and Sun (1989), Canagarajah (1993), and Pennycook (1989) indicated, NABA trained NNS ESOL teachers have to face, on their return, not only the problem of modifying the methods and techniques but also the conflict between their newly acquired ideas and those still firmly held by locals teachers and administrators. Therefore, NABA TESOL teacher educators should abandon ideological and methodological dogmatism and work with NNS students in adapting and developing methods, techniques, or anything else that will work for them in their home environment. Berns (1990), Holliday (1994a, 1994b), and Prabhu (1987) made sensible suggestions on how to modify the NABA communicative teaching models to accommodate some non-NABA situations. For example, Holliday (1994a, 1994b) argued and demonstrated that communicative language learning can take place with individual work and does not have to involve group or pair activities, which are often difficult to implement and control in large classes. Much more is needed in this area of work, especially when we consider the diversity of teaching milieus NNS TESOL students will be working in.

At the same time, we should also work closely with NNS TESOL students to identify elements in TESOL programs that may not be relevant to them. The issue of teaching Limited English Proficiency (LEP) students, which has been an important topic for many TESOL programs in North America, for example, may be such an element. Although helping LEP students is a major concern to TESOL educators here, it is not an issue in other countries because the problems LEP students have are very different from those confronting students learning English as a foreign language. Their reasons for learning English are different and the language environment varies significantly. Moreover, whereas LEP students often do not have literacy in their mother tongue, EFL students usually have developed a reasonable literacy level in their native language by the time they begin studying English. This native language literacy plays a very significant role in second language development because literacy in the native language will often be transferred into the target language (Cummins, 1979, 1980). Hence, approaches that are effective for teaching LEP students in NABA may not work for EFL students. How to capitalize on EFL students' L1 literacy in English learning should be a focus in the TESOL teacher education curriculum.

NNS TESOL students themselves seem to be aware of some of the problems discussed, as can be shown in a survey I conducted with 59 NNS students in the TESOL program at my university (20 in 1994, 23 in 1995, and 16 in 1996: 28 Mandarin-speaking Taiwanese, 2 mainland Chinese, 12 Koreans, 11 Japanese, 2 Malaysians, 2 Indonesians, 1 Jordanian, and 1 Hispanic). Concerning the question whether there was a significant difference between Teaching English as a foreign language (TEFL) and Teaching English as a second language (TESL), 38 (64%) answered "yes," 8 (14%) "not sure," and 13 (22%) "no." Regarding whether they thought the acquisition theories and teaching methodologies they had learned were very useful, only 20 (34%) replied "yes," 22 (37%) "not sure," and 17 (29%) "no."

Language Improvement

Language Proficiency

Another area where NNS TESOL students' needs have been overlooked is their lack of the English proficiency required for success in their future teaching. Although most of these students possess a commendable *knowledge* of English, particularly of grammar, not many of them have a good grasp of the use of the language. Such a command is extremely important for quality ESOL teaching. Hence, scholars such as Allen and Valette (1994) pointed out that one of the most important characteristics of outstanding foreign language teachers is having "an excellent command of the target language" (p. 6). Others (Cullen, 1994; Murdoch, 1994; Medgyes, Chap. 12, this volume) highlighted the need to incorporate language development in ESOL teacher training programs in non-English speaking countries. Murdoch (1994) contended that "high level of English language proficiency" is "the most valued aspect of a non-native English teacher's competence" (p. 253). In a survey, his trainees ranked language improvement as the most important component (out of 10 teacher training components), higher even than methodology and linguistics (pp. 262–265). Although these scholars are discussing English teacher training outside English-speaking countries, the call for helping non-native speaker teachers improve their English proficiency also applies to the NNS TESOL students in NABA, although the methods used to help them may differ.

An excellent command of English here does not mean native-like pronunciation or intonation, which few ESOL students ever achieve and which is often not necessary in most TEFL situations; it means fluent and idiomatic use of the English language. Many NNS TESOL students do not possess this and still speak and write in a way that may be grammatically correct but difficult to understand because of the interference from their native language structure and usage. By this, I am not referring to regionally institutionalized varieties of English, such as Indian or Hong Kong English, which, although differing from U.S. or British English in many ways, do not violate the major morphological or syntactical features of the English language and which are authentic and functional in their own terms.[4] With regard to institutionalized varieties of English, we should not only respect them but also include a study of them in our linguistic and grammar courses so TESOL students can have a better understanding of such Englishes to help their instruction back home.[5] The kind of English (or problems of English) that NNS students need to overcome is nonfunctional English, one that is intelligible to neither native nor NNSs. Many NNS TESOL students are keenly aware of their language problems. Asked if they believed they had the English proficiency to be a truly qualified teacher, only 8 (14%) of the NNS students in my survey said "yes," 29 (49%) "not sure," and 22 (37%) "no."

NNS TESOL students thus need help or training to improve their English. Few TESOL programs, to my knowledge, have addressed this unique need. Based on the information in the *Directory of Professional Preparation Programs in TESOL* (1995), most (about 90%) TESOL programs contain in their core curriculum a required English grammar course dealing with the phonological, morphological, and syntactical systems of the language. But this course, which in most cases focuses on enhancing students' explicit knowledge of how the language operates rather than their ability to use the language, usually does not meet non-native speaker students' needs. Most of these students enter the programs with a Bachelor's degree in English from their home country and have learned English largely by studying its grammar. What they need is not an explicit study of English grammar but training in English usage. Yet the general practice is to put these NNSs together with NSs into a grammar course, one very helpful for the latter group because many of them may have had little formal study of grammar before. To the question if they would choose between a course on explicit grammar

---

[4] Jiang (1995) offers a good discussion between these two types of English in his discussion of "Chinglish" versus "China English."

[5] Currently, most linguistics and grammar books used in TESOL cover only the varieties of English spoken in NABA, such as Black or Latino English.

and one on usage, 47 (80%) NNSs in my survey chose "usage," 9 (15%) "not sure," and 3 (5%) "grammar."

Furthermore, when asked if the program should incorporate a language improvement component in all its courses, 55 (93%) replied "yes," 4 (7%) "not sure," and none replied "no." Based on our experience, a language component could be incorporated into the program without diluting the quality of the program and without creating much work for the instructors involved. For example, in Phonetics/Phonology, a required course, we have students record their articulations of speech sounds, reading, and free speech and turn in the recording for the instructor and the class to critique; this practice has proved to be successful and is highly appreciated by the students. For the research project in the linguistics and grammar courses, we encourage NNS students to work on idioms, word collocations (phrasal verbs), registers, and other areas in which NNSs are generally weak. We urge them, in doing their research, to collect data not just from books but also from people and the media. We want them to fully capitalize on the English-speaking environment to improve their English. One objective of our Introduction to Graduate Studies course is to help NNS students improve their writing skills in English. In addition to many in-class writing activities, the instructor also works closely with the school's Writing Center to offer help for those who need individual assistance. Our students' evaluations indicate that NNS students think highly of the course.

Classroom Language Resources

Developing classroom language resources is another language-improvement-related area where NNS TESOL students need special training. Being able to speak the language fluently does not guarantee effective delivery of instruction. For NS teachers, effective instruction is often more an issue of delivery skills than an issue of command of the language. But for NNSs, it usually relates to both because many of them have rather limited classroom language resources. Johnson's (1990) argument for providing classroom language training for NNS teachers in Hong Kong has made the point clear. In his discussion, Johnson also presented a rather successful "Classroom Language" program that includes the use of a language laboratory where students learn and practice various instructional language modes such as "operative," "interactive," and "informative."

Although we do not have a classroom language program per se in our curriculum, we have tried to incorporate classroom language training in some courses such as Methods of TESOL and the Practicum in which students learn to appreciate and practice appropriate instructional language by paying special attention to it in their teaching observations. They also have to demonstrate their grasp of the different modes of classroom language in their lesson plans and their practice teaching.

Cultural Understanding

It is well known that cultural understanding is an indispensable part of second or foreign language acquisition (McKay & Hornberger, 1994). Cultural study, especially the study of cultures of English-speaking countries, is therefore a subject that many NNS students want and should do more of. This is because no language, either spoken or written, can be devoid of cultural influences. Most of the reading materials used in EFL today are either directly from or adapted from publications from NABA. For those whose students need to interact with NSs, cultural understanding is even more important. Although the cultural knowledge the teachers need will depend on the specific context, without the necessary cultural background knowledge, EFL teachers will find it difficult to understand, not to mention teach, the instructional material they face. Yet many EFL teachers do not possess a good knowledge of the cultures of the English-speaking countries. For instance, according to Burnaby and Sun (1989), who conducted an extensive survey in Chinese colleges, and Campbell and Zhao (1993), most Chinese college teachers of English sensed a major deficiency in this area and admitted a lack of confidence because of it.

Before I discuss how to help NNS students learn more about cultures of English-speaking countries, it should be made clear that studying another culture does not mean embracing it or following its sociocultural customs, nor does it mean losing one's own culture. In fact, learning another culture can in fact help one appreciate and understand one's own culture more and develop what Adler (1977) called a constructive "multicultural identity," an identity crucial to one's success in today's global community (p. 30). The purpose of cultural study in TESOL teacher education should be to make future TESOL professionals competent teachers who, in turn, empower their students to be competent English users in their own context and terms. Thomas (1983) is enlightening on this issue:

> It is not the responsibility of the language teacher qua linguist to enforce Anglo-Saxon standards of behavior, linguistic or otherwise. Rather, it is the teacher's job to equip the student to

express her/himself in exactly the way s/he chooses to do so—
rudely, tactfully, or in an elaborately polite manner. What we
want to prevent is her/his being *unintentionally* rude or
subservient. (p. 96)

The best way to understand a culture is to be immersed in that
culture. But merely being in the target language country for one or two
years will not suffice for a thorough grasp of its culture, because, among
other things, NNS students' exposure is often confined to campus
culture. Hence, while in an English-speaking country, these students
should engage in a systematic study of its culture, carried out in the form
of a course or research projects. Yet, according to a recent survey, "only
about one third of the [TESOL] programs even offered a course in
culture" (Reid, 1995/1996, p. 3). For programs that do offer such a
course, making it more effective for NNS students remains an issue of
concern. Merely knowing the surface speech differences is often not
adequate (Liu, 1995). To acquire sociocultural competence, one needs to
understand the deep sociocultural beliefs and values that underlie the
surface speech behavior. In our sociolinguistics course, we ask NNS
students to team up with U.S. students to investigate, using real life data,
and by means of surveys and observations, the differences between the
United States and their native cultures. Many of them feel that they have
gained much insight this way.

Conclusion

Non-native speaker TESOL students are a large and very important force
of future TESOL professionals. Differing from their native speaker peers
in various ways, they call for special attention and training. Yet so far,
TESOL teacher educators, burdened by ethnocentrism and dogmatism,
have, by and large, failed to accommodate their needs, specifically their
demand for more appropriate L2 acquisition theories and methodologies,
language improvement, and cultural understanding. Of course, these are
certainly not all the areas where non-native speaker TESOL students
require special consideration. More studies and discussions should be
conducted to determine accurately and comprehensively what the
various ethnic/linguistic groups of NNS TESOL students demand from
TESOL education in order to become successful teachers in their native
countries, and how we can better serve these would-be TESOL
professionals whose work will influence millions of ESOL students to
come. I have no doubt that with increased cultural sensitivity and

devoted effort, NABA teacher educators will and can, in close cooperation with NNS students and teachers alike, successfully meet all these and other challenges ahead.

References

Adler, P. S. (1977). Beyond cultural identity: Reflections upon cultural and multicultural man. In R. W. Brislin (Ed.), *Culture Learning* (pp. 24–41). Honolulu, Hawaii: East-West Center.

Allen, E. D., & Valette, R. M. (1994). *Classroom techniques: Foreign languages and English as a second language.* Prospect Heights, IL: Waveland Press.

Berns, M. (1990). *Contexts of competence: Social and cultural considerations in communicative language teaching.* New York: Plenum Press.

Burnaby, B., & Sun, Y. (1989). Chinese teachers' views of Western language teaching: Context informs paradigms. *TESOL Quarterly, 23,* 219–238.

Cahill, L. (1996, Spring). Forgoing the "other-culture" experience: English language teaching in the U.S. *Newsletter: English as a Foreign Language* (TESOL EFL Interest Section), *16,* 1–2, 5.

Campbell, K. P., & Zhao, Y. (1993). The dilemma of English language instruction in the People's Republic of China. *TESOL Journal, 2(4),* 4–6.

Canagarajah, A. S. (1993). Critical ethnography of a Sri Lankan classroom: Ambiguities in student opposition to reproduction through ESOL. *TESOL Quarterly, 27,* 601–626.

Cullen, R. (1994). Incorporating a language improvement in teacher training programs. *ELT Journal, 48,* 162–172.

Cummins, J. (1979). Linguistic interdependence and the educational development of bilingual children. *Review of Educational Research, 49,* 222–251.

Cummins, J. (1980). The cross-lingual dimensions of language proficiency: Implications for bilingual education and the optimal age issue. *TESOL Quarterly, 14,* 175–187.

Directory of professional preparation programs in TESOL in the United States and Canada, 1995-1997. (1995). Alexandria, VA: Teachers of English to Speakers of Other Languages.

Dong, L. (1995). English in China. *English Today, 11,* 53–56.

Halleck, G. B., & Moder, C. L. (1995). Testing language and teaching skills of international teaching assistants: The limits of compensatory strategies. *TESOL Quarterly, 29,* 733–758.

Hodson, E. (1994, December/1995, January). TESOL methodology and the constraints of context. *TESOL Matters, 4(6),* 21.

Holliday, A. (1994a). *Appropriate methodology and social context.* Cambridge, England: Cambridge University Press.

Holliday, A. (1994b). The House of TESEP and the communicative approach: The special needs of state English language education. *ELT Journal, 48,* 3–11.

Jiang, Y. (1995). Chinglish and China English. *English Today, 11,* 51–53.

Johnson, R. K. (1990). Developing teachers' language resources. In J. K. Richards & D. Nunan (Eds.), *Second language teacher education* (pp. 269–281). Cambridge, England: Cambridge University Press.

Judd, E. L. (1983). TESOL as a political act: A moral question. In J. Handscombe, R. A. Orem, & B. P. Taylor (Eds.), *On TESOL '83* (pp. 265–273). Washington, DC: Teachers of English to Speakers of Other Languages.

Kachru, Y. (1994). Monolingual bias in SLA research. *TESOL Quarterly, 28,* 795–800.

Liu, D. (1995). Sociocultural transfer and its effect on second-language speakers' communication. *International Journal of Intercultural Relations, 19,* 253–265.

McKay, S. L., & Hornberger, N. H. (1994). *Sociolinguistics and language teaching.* Cambridge, England: Cambridge University Press.

Murdoch, G. (1994). Language development provision in teacher training curricula. *ELT Journal, 48,* 253–265.

Pennycook, A. (1989). The concept of method, interested knowledge, and politics of language teaching. *TESOL Quarterly, 23,* 589–618.

Phillipson, R. (1988). Linguicism: Structures and ideologies in linguistic imperialism. In J. Cummins & T. Skutnabb-Kangas (Eds.), *Minority education: From shame to struggle* (pp. 339–368). Clevedon, England: Multilingual Matters.

Phillipson, R. (1992). *Linguistic imperialism.* Oxford, England: Oxford University Press.

Phillipson, R., & Skutnabb-Kangas, T. (1995). Linguistic rights and wrongs. *Applied Linguistics, 16,* 483–504.

Prabhu, N. S. (1987). *Second language pedagogy.* Oxford, England: Oxford University Press.

Reid, J. M. (1995, December/1996, January). President's message: Let's put the "T" back in TESL/TEFL programs." *TESOL Matters, 5* (6), 3.

Skutnabb-Kangas, T., & Phillipson, R. (1994). *Linguistic human rights: Overcoming linguistic discrimination.* Berlin, Germany: Mouton De Gruyter.

Sridhar, S. N. (1994). A reality check for SLA theories. *TESOL Quarterly, 28,* 800–805.

Thomas, J. (1983). Cross-cultural pragmatic failure. *Applied Linguistics, 4,* 91–112.

Tollefson, J. W. (1988). Covert policy in the United States refugee program in Southeast Asia. *Language Problems and Language Planning, 12,* 30–42.

Tollefson, J. W. (1991). *Planning language, planning inequality: Language policy in the community.* Harlow, England: Longman.

Tollefson, J. W. (Ed.). (1995). *Power and inequality in language education.* Cambridge, England: Cambridge University Press.

Tyler, A. (1992). Discourse structure and the perception of incoherence in international teaching assistants spoken discourse. *TESOL Quarterly, 26,* 713–730.

Contributor Biostatements

Nuzhat Amin was born and raised in Pakistan; her first language is Urdu. She is a Ph.D. candidate in the Department of Curriculum, Teaching, and Learning at the Ontario Institute for Studies in Education, University of Toronto. Her doctoral work is on the connections among race, gender, language, and power. She has taught English/ESL/EFL in Canada, Pakistan and Poland. Her articles have appeared in *Canadian Woman Studies, Resources for Feminist Research, TESOL Quarterly* and *trans/forms.* She is one of the editors of *Feminism and Education: A Canadian Perspective, Vol. 2.*

George Braine was born and raised in Sri Lanka, and his first language is Sinhala. He is an associate professor of English at The Chinese University of Hong Kong. He has also taught in Sri Lanka, Oman, and the United States. His major publications are *Academic Writing in a Second Language* (coedited with Diane Belcher) and *Writing From Sources* (coauthored with Claire May). He has been a member of the TOEFL Test of Written English (TWE) Committee and is a founding editor of *Texas Papers in Foreign Language Education* and coeditor of the *Asian Journal of English Language Teaching*.

Janina Brutt-Griffler was born and raised in Poland; her first language is Polish. She is completing her doctorate at Ohio State University, where she teaches academic writing for international undergraduate and graduate students. Her work has appeared in *World Englishes*, and she is working on *The Development of English as an International Language: Historical, Sociocultural and Linguistic Dimensions* with Multilingual Matters. Her research interests include sociolinguistics, syntax, theory of second language acquisition, language pedagogy, and computer-assisted language learning.

A. Suresh Canagarajah was born in Jaffna, Sri Lanka, and speaks Tamil as his first language. He taught English language and literature in the University of Jaffna for about 10 years after obtaining his first degree in Sri Lanka. He is presently an Assistant Professor in English at the City University of New York (Baruch College) where he teaches ESL, academic writing, and postcolonial literature. His studies have appeared in *TESOL Quarterly, Language in Society, Written Communication, College Composition and Communication, World Englishes,* and *Multilingua* among others. His book, *Resistance in ELT: Ethnographies From the Periphery,* is forthcoming from Oxford University Press.

Ulla Niemelä Connor was born in Finland, and her first language is Finnish. She is Professor of English at Indiana University at Indianapolis, where she directs the ESL Program and the Indiana Center for Intercultural Communication. Her publications include *Writing Across Languages: Analysis of L2 Text* (coedited with Robert B. Kaplan), *Coherence in Writing* (coedited with Ann M. Johns), and *Contrastive Rhetoric: Cross-Cultural Aspects of Second-Language Writing*. Her articles have appeared in *TESOL Quarterly, Applied Linguistics, Research in the Teaching of English, Journal of Second Language Writing,* and *Text.* She has served as chair of TESOL's Research Interest Section and taught at five TESOL Summer Institutes in the early 1990s.

Lía D. Kamhi-Stein was born and raised in Argentina. Her first language is Spanish. She is assistant professor in the TESOL MA program at California State University, Los Angeles, where she teaches courses in English for academic purposes; ESL/EFL, curriculum design; and methodology. She was an EFL teacher in Argentina and an EFL teacher educator in Argentina and other Latin American countries. She has authored or coauthored chapters in edited books, and her articles have appeared in *Text, TESOL Journal, Advances in Physiology Education, CAELL Journal, College ESL,* and other publications. She has forthcoming articles in *The Journal of Adolescent and Adult Literacy, Lectura y Vida,* and *The Journal of Intensive English Studies.*

Claire Kramsch was born, raised and educated in France; her first language is French. She learned German as a foreign language in high school and did her graduate studies in Germanistik at the Sorbonne in Paris. She moved to the United States at age 28. She is now Professor of German and Foreign Language Acquisition at the University of California at Berkeley and Director of the Berkeley Language Center. She is the author of many books and articles on the teaching of language and culture, in particular *Context and Culture in Language Teaching* (Oxford University Press, 1993), *Redefining the Boundaries of Language Study* (Heinle, 1995), and *Language and Culture* (Oxford University Press, 1998).

Wan Shun Eva Lam was born and raised in a Cantonese-speaking Chinese family in Hong Kong. She started learning English in elementary school and received her formal education primarily through English. She is a Ph.D. student in the Language, Literacy and Culture program in the School of Education at the University of California, Berkeley. One of her papers will be published in a volume entitled *Tokens of Exchange: The Problem of Translation in Global Circulations* by Duke University Press.

Xiao-ming Li was born and raised in the People's Republic of China, and her first language is Chinese. She is an associate professor of English at Long Island University, Brooklyn Campus, where she teaches ESL writing, Rhetoric and Composition Theory, Asian and Asian American Literature. Her major publication is *"Good Writing" in Cross-Cultural Context*, based on her doctoral dissertation and published by State University of New York Press in 1996.

Dilin Liu was born in China and speaks Chinese as his first language. He did his undergraduate work in English and taught college English in China. He came to the United States in 1985 and received a Ph.D. in English literature from Oklahoma State University where he taught composition and critical writing. He is an Associate Professor and Director of MATESOL at Oklahoma State University. His academic interests include language usage, sociolinguistics, TESOL pedagogy/teacher education, and English/American literature. He has published in *ELT Journal, English Today, International Journal of Intercultural Relations, Midland Review, Short Story,* and *TESOL Quarterly.*

Jun Liu, born in Changshu, China, speaks Chinese as his first language. He is Assistant Professor in the English Department at The University of Arizona, Tucson. He has taught English for more than 14 years in both China and the United States. He has published in *TESOL Quarterly*, *TESOL Journal*, *Modern Language Journal*, and *Educational Research Quarterly*. His major research interests include second language acquisition, classroom-oriented research, syllabus design and curriculum development, sociocultural and affective aspects of language learning and teaching, and ESL composition.

Péter Medgyes was born and, apart from a few years, has spent all his life in Hungary; his native language is Hungarian. He is the founding director of the Centre for English Teacher Training at Eötvös Loránd University, Budapest. Previously, he was a teacher trainer at a high school for more than a decade. Professor Medgyes has written several ELT textbooks and articles, which have appeared both in his home country and abroad. One of his recent publications, *The Non-Native Teacher*, was the winner of the 1995 Duke of Edinburgh English Language Book Competition. At present, Professor Medgyes is Deputy State Secretary at the Hungarian Ministry of Culture and Education.

Masaki Oda was born in Kanagawa, Japan, and his first language is Japanese. He is an associate professor of EFL and Applied Linguistics at Tamagawa University in Tokyo, Japan. He has taught ESL/EFL in Japan and the United States, and Japanese as a second language in the United States. He has published several EFL textbooks locally and translated Azar's *Understanding and Using English Grammar* into Japanese. He has been an active member of JALT since 1987 and served as its National Public Relations Chair between 1992 and 1994.

Keiko K. Samimy was born in Japan, and her first language is Japanese. She is associate professor in foreign and second language education at Ohio State University. She has taught English in Japan. Her main research interests include non-native speaker professionals and affective variables in SLA. She has published in *Language Learning, Modern Language Journal,* and *TESOL Journal.*

Jacinta Thomas was born in Singapore and raised in Singapore, Canada, the United States, and India. Her first language is Indian/Singapore English. She is a professor of English and Coordinator of the Intensive English Program at the College of Lake County in Grayslake, IL. She has also taught English at the American Language Institute at Indiana University of Pennsylvania, Indiana, Pennsylvania and at Fatima College, India. Her publications include a chapter in *Teaching Composition Around the Pacific Rim* and an article in the *TESOL Journal*. She is engaged in a longitudinal case study of an at-risk African American student.

Author Index

A

Abagi, J., 85, *92*
Adler, P. S., 207, 209
Alford, R., 73, *75*
Allen, E. D., 204, 209
Almarza, G. G., 153, 157
Altbach, P., 24, *27*
Amin, N., 8, *12*, 94, 96, 97, 103, 146, 152, 157
Appadurai, A., 70, *72*
Arnaud, J., *92*
Auerbach, E., 80, 90, *92, 150*, 154, 157

B

Bailey, K. M., 148, 157
Barahona, B., *92*
Bergthold, B., 157
Berkenkotter, C., 30, *38*
Berns, M., 200, 202, 209
Blanc, M. H. A., 78, *92*
Bodóczky, C., 189, 193
Boyle, J., 73, *75*
Braine, G., 156, 157
Braunstein, B., 157
Brinton, D. M., 147, 157
Britten, D., 80, *92*, 189, 193
Broyard, A., 9, *12*
Bunyi, G., 85, *92*
Burnaby, B., 197, 200, 201, 202, 206, 209

C

Cage, J., 54, 55, *55*

Cahill, L., 202, 209
Campbell, D., 185, 193
Campbell, K. P., 200, 201, 206, 209
Canagarajah, A. S., 7, 8, *12*, 21, 24, 26, *27*, 197, 201, 202, 209
Carson, J. G., 147, 158
Cherland, M. R., 69, *72*
Cheshire, J., 100, 103
Chiellino, G., 61, 64, *72*
Chomsky, N., xv, *xix*
Cleghorn, A., 85, *92*
Connor, U., 32, 34, 35, 36, *38*
Coulmas, F., 192, 193
Crawford, J., 152, 157
Crystal, D., 177, 184, 186, 193
Cullen, R., 204, 209
Cummins, J., 93, 103, 203, 209

D

Das Gupta, T., 96, 103
Dávid, G., 189, 193
Davidson, D., *55*
Davies, A., xiv, xvii, *xix*, 127, 128, 129, 143, 177, 193
Dean, T., 11, *12*
Dissanayake, W., 70, *72*
Dong, L., 202, 209

E

Edelhoff, C., 188, 193
Edge, J., 12, *12*, 138, 143, 177, 193
Edwards, J. R., 97, 100, 103
Enyedi, Á., 190, 193

Subject Index

A

Accent, see also Pronunciation
    American, 26, 89, 171
    Australian, 26
    British, 26, 89, 98, 187
    Canadian, 98
    Indian, 98
    in writing, 51
    Japanese, 11
    Pakistani, 97
    Trinidadian, 98
    White, 97–101
Anti-immigrant movement, 11
Asian Journal of English Language Teaching (AJELT), 24

B

Balanced bilinguals, 78–79

C

Canadian
    ESL teachers, 93–97
    Minorities, 101–105
Center
    academic institutions, 83, 84, 85
    communities, 83, 87, 89, 90
    Englishes, 82, 83, 92
    professionals, 15, 85, 86, 89
    speakers of English, 79, 81, 83, 84
    teachers, 82–83, 86, 88, 90–91

Center for English Teacher Training (CETT), 179, 189–195
Comic books,
    American, 67–69
    Japanese, 65–68
Communicative competence, 131–134, 141, 175
Communicative teaching, 180, 202
Cultural Revolution, 44, 49, 52

D

Discrimination, against non-native teachers
    as graduate students, 9
    as professionals, 150
    effects, 9–11
    from colleagues, 10, 22–23
    from students, 8, 23, 44, 150
    in hiring, 6–7, 22–23
    in publications, 7–8, 21, 24–25
    relating to accent, 5
    relating to race, 5
    within professional organizations, 7–8

E

ELT journals, scarcity of, 17
English
    Canadian, 94
    international, 185
    standard, 82
Essay, 47–48